FALL OF MR WHYMPER.

MOUNTAIN ADVENTURES

IN

VARIOUS PARTS OF THE WORLD.

SELECTED FROM THE NARRATIVES OF CELEBRATED TRAVELLERS.

WITH AN

INTRODUCTION AND ADDITIONS,

BY J. T. HEADLEY,

AUTHOR OF "NAPOLEON AND HIS MARSHALS," "WASHINGTON AND HIS GENERALS," "SACRED SCENES AND SACRED MOUNTAINS," ETC., ETC.

With Forty-one Illustrations.

NEW YORK:
CHARLES SCRIBNER AND COMPANY,
1872.

CONTENTS.

LIST OF ILLUSTRATIONS.

MOUNTAIN ADVENTURES.

MOUNTAINS AND MOUNTAIN CLIMBING.

BY HON. J. T. HEADLEY.

MOUNTAINS rising from the earth, and drawing their gigantic outlines along the sky, form the most striking features of our planet. Heaved up by the action of internal fires, they reveal in their broken, twisted strata the omnipotent power that piled them so high into the heavens. The mountain system, so to speak, that characterizes the earth is not the result of the lawless action of blind forces ; but of infinite wisdom. The great Ural chain, with its lateral branches—those mighty masses of Central Asia, crowned by the Himalaya, rising nearly 30,000 feet into the heavens—the splintered snow-capped pinnacles of the Alps—the vast extended chains of the Rocky Mountains and the Andes, lining the Pacific coast, with their smoking tops, with numberless minor ridges, seem to form a net-work of granite bands to hold the globe together.

Doubtless, a similar system to that which marks the visible surface of the earth, characterizes the bed of the ocean—both the development of some all-wise plan, the full purpose of which we may not know.

Independent of the laws that created them, or the purpose for which they were formed, they have a fascination for man like the nightly heavens.

Great landmarks to the eye, many of them furnish great landmarks in human history, and stand also as monuments of God's interviews with man. The rainbow bending over the ark on Mount Ararat, and the law given in thunder and flame on Mount Sinai, have consecrated these mountains forever. Aaron's death on Mount Hor, and Moses on Pisgah, and Elijah gazing on God passing by on Mount Horeb, have surrounded these mountains with a mystery they will retain to the end of time. The same is true of lesser mountains.

To stand where such scenes have occurred, awakes no common emotions. Indeed one cannot stand on any lofty mountain summit without experiencing feelings that move the heart to its profoundest depths. It is true that the desire to make new scientific experiments, to correct old theories, or establish new ones, has often induced men to make difficult and dangerous ascents. Much light has thus been thrown on meteorology—the barometer has become a simple instrument with which to measure heights—while the difference of temperature as we ascend, and the rarity of the atmosphere, indeed, all atmospheric changes of the upper regions, have become pretty well known to us. Many adventures have been undertaken and dangers encountered in the cause of science, still the mere *love of adventure* has prompted most of the perilous ascents that have been made. The Alps, standing in the centre of Europe, with their bases easy of access, have been the great theatre for the exploits of mountain tourists, while their precipitous crevasses, avalanches and crags have presented difficulties great enough to satisfy the most daring.

Saussure, the first to ascend Mont Blanc, in 1787, was lauded for his bravery in facing, in the cause of science, the appalling obstacles that met him ; but it is doubtful if anything but the love of adventure, and the desire to accomplish what others had failed to perform, had much to do with it. He had for twenty years and more been pursuing his investigations in the Alps, and made thirty different ascents during that time, but from each turned away dissatisfied, because the white, smooth, snow-summit of Mont Blanc, mocked his endeavors. It is not probable that the comparatively slight difference between its elevation and that of others which he had ascended, would give any materially different results from those already obtained ; hence it must have been the mere love of adventure, and the wish to plant his feet where a human foot had never trod, that prompted him to make the attempt. In fact, he confesses as much, for he says, "It became a mania with me. My eyes never rested upon this Colossus without producing a painful impression."

He had hoped from repeated observations to get some light on the mysterious laws that govern that mighty electrical current, that unceasingly rolls its unseen flood around the earth, and yet does not correspond with its axis. The magnetic needle that reveals the existence of this everflowing current, at a certain latitude ceases to turn to the north pole, showing that it has passed out of its influence. But even this strong desire yielded to the stronger one of simple achievement. So Humboldt added largely to scientific knowledge by his observations from lofty elevations in the Cordilleras, yet when he stood on the brink of an impassable chasm near the summit of Chimborazo, with the blood oozing from his gums and lips, and strained his eye upward willing to suffer and dare more, it was not for the sake of science that he felt so sorely disappointed.

The ascent of Mont Blanc, the "monarch of mountains," is to-day almost as much an object of ambition as fifty years ago. The frequent death of adventurers does not deter others from making the attempt. Even women have dared the glaciers, avalanches and crevasses of this mountain. Only last year, an English lady lost her life on its slope. But the most tragical event of recent date, indeed, of any period, was the destruction last year of an entire party of eleven persons, when near the summit. Three gentlemen, two of them Americans, the other a Scottish clergyman, and eight guides set out in the latter part of August, and having safely reached the summit at half-past two, had commenced the descent, when they were suddenly wrapped in a whirlwind of snow. When last seen by those watching them through their glasses in Chamouni, they were huddling close together, as if to hold on to each other for mutual support, and then the driving snow hid them from sight, and they were never seen alive again. It was two days before any party could attempt to go to their relief, and they, after battling for two hours and a half with the storm, were compelled to give it up, and it was ten days before the spot where they were last seen could be reached. During all this time the cold, unfeeling mountain was constantly swept by glasses whenever a rift in the storm clouds would give a glimpse of the summit. At length some black spots could be detected on the white surface, and fifty men set out toward them. They proved to be five bodies of the unhappy party. One of these was Dr. Bean of Baltimore, who was found sitting up in the snow with his head fallen forward on his hands. For two days he had sat there nearly three miles in the heavens, listening to the roaring of the storm that shut out the world below to him. During these two dreadful days, he traced with his stiffening fingers a few lines in a diary which was found upon him. The first entry was made in the morning after they had been overtaken by the storm. He says, "We reached the summit at half-past two o'clock. Immediately after having quitted it, I found myself enveloped in a whirlwind of snow, at 15,000 feet, English height. We have passed the night in a grotto dug in the snow—an uncomfortable asylum, and I have been ill all night."

"*September 7th, morning.*—Cold very intense. Much snow. It falls without cessation; the guides are uneasy.

"*September 7th, evening.*—We have been on Mont Blanc two days in a terrible snow storm. We are lost, and I have no hope of descending. Perhaps some one will find this book and send it to you."

Then, after leaving a message for his wife and directions in regard to his son, he continues: "We have no provisions. My feet are already frozen, and I am already exhausted; I have only strength to write these words. I die believing in Jesus Christ, with the sweet thought of my family, my friendship and all. I hope we shall meet in heaven. Yours always." This is all that is known of the ill-fated party.

The last effort of departing life was put forth to give his dying testimony for Christ, and express the love he bore his friends and family to the last.

When the bodies were brought back to Chamouni, the little Swiss hamlet became a scene of sorrow and mourning. A part of the lost party lay far up Mont Blanc, wrapped in their winding sheet of snow, to be disturbed no more till the sea gives up its dead. Whether swept by the force of the storm into some deep abyss, or whether in the last effort of despair they attempted to descend to the Grands Mulets, till blinded and lost they perished, one after another, will never be known.

But thrilling, and often painfully interesting, as some of the accounts are, of ascents of the Alps by small parties, they sink into insignificance beside the struggles of armies over these snow covered heights. The ascent of the Pragel by Suwarrow with 24,000 men, and their passage over the mountains into the Grisons, has few parallels in history. He had forced the St. Gothard, only to find his way blocked by Marshals Mortier and Massena with their victorious troops.

His only possible way of escape was over the Kinzig Culm, into the Muotta Thal. This desperate feat he accomplished, fighting his way along the dizzy cliffs. But when he reached the Muotta valley a sight met his gaze fearful enough to appall the stoutest heart. Molitor and his battalions looked down on him from the surrounding heights; Mortier and Massena blocked the only road out; while Lecourbe hung like a storm-cloud on his rear. The Russian bear was apparently denned, and the fate of the army sealed.

Pragel lifting its rugged peak into the heavens, crossed by a mere bridle path, was the only avenue left unguarded, as though it was a sufficient barrier of itself to an army of 24,000 men. To attempt to cross it was a desperate chance; but this the iron-hearted old chieftain, scorning to surrender, determined on, and the order, "forward," was given. The rear guard held back the enemy, while the head of the column slowly wound its way upward. For ten awful days he struggled along these heights, the thunder of cannon below answered by the roar of descending avalanches above, mowing down men and beasts of burden together.

On the eleventh day the weary, bleeding army

found itself in the Naefels, on the other side. But here, too, the enemy blocked its way out of the valley; and Suwarrow took the desperate resolution of leading his army over the Grisons, that lifted their snow-covered peaks 7,600 feet into the heavens. Up this a narrow zigzag path went winding over glaciers, and along precipices till lost in the snow fields on the distant summit. It was a frightful undertaking to lead 24,000 men over this mountain by such a path; but the stern order was given, and the thin, weary, bleeding column moved up the ascent. As if to insure its destruction, a snow storm commenced to rage on the heights, that soon covered them two feet deep, and blotted out all traces of the path. Slowly, wearily, in single file, the mighty host wound its way upward. Only half the ascent was made the first day; and without a fire to cheer the solitude, the army lay down in the snow, and, cold and hungry, passed the night. The next day the head of the column reached the summit, and lo, what a spectacle met its gaze! Mountains enfolding mountains, with untrodden abysses between, filled all the field of vision. No smoke arose to cheer the savage solitude; no sound came out of the mysterious depths but the sullen roar of the avalanche; and no path was visible to guide the feet in the downward march. This was more perilous than the ascent, for a freezing wind had hardened the snow into a crust, that frequently bore the soldiers, who had to thrust their bayonets into it to keep from sliding over the precipices. Hundreds, exhausted and despairing, lay down to die, while whole companies, slipping together, would strike those in front, and all go in one black mass into abysses from which even the cry for help could not be heard. Beasts of burden, too, with their loads, would come sliding against the line, carrying the poor soldiers with them over the precipices.

The army was five days struggling over these heights, leaving nearly 8000 men scattered along the precipices and snow fields, or piled together in the abysses below. For months after, vultures hovered incessantly along the line of this terrible march, gorging themselves with the dead bodies.

The passage of the Splugen by McDonald, with fifteen thousand men, in the winter, was a similar achievement, though he had no enemy but the elements to encounter.

The sketches in this volume embrace every variety of scenery, of almost every zone of the earth. The beautiful and entrancing succeed the grand and awful in rapid alternation, carrying the reader from one mountain top to another with an interest that never flags.

The adventurous spirit of man has enabled him to overcome apparently insuperable obstacles, and reach the top of almost every high mountain on the globe; yet there are some that his feet will never profane. Humboldt and others have cast their longing looks in vain on the round, smooth peak of Chimborazo, while that most beautiful of all the colossal summits of the Andes, Cotopaxi, is declared inaccessible.

A perfectly smooth, pure, and spotless cone, it

rises nearly 19,000 feet in the surpassingly clear atmosphere of that region—a thing of wondrous beauty. A huge volcano blazes from its snowy top, sending its tongue of flame far up into the serene heavens, once reaching the extraordinary height of nearly three thousand feet. Its roarings are terrific, so that Humboldt, on standing on the shore of the ocean, nearly two hundred miles distant, could distinctly hear them. In the eruption of 1744 its tremendous explosions were heard six hundred miles.

Nothing is more interesting than a tour among mountains; and the toil and the danger are forgotten in the varied emotions they awaken.

I.

MONT BLANC.

ASCENT IN 1787 BY DE SAUSSURE.

ON my way to Chamounix, in the beginning of July, I met at Sallenche the courageous Jacques Balmat, who was coming to Geneva to inform me of his recent success: he had ascended to the summit of the mountain with two other guides. Rain was falling when I arrived at Chamounix; and the bad weather lasted four weeks. But I was determined to wait until the end of the season rather than miss a favorable opportunity.

It came at last,—that moment so much desired,—and I set off on the 1st of August, 1787, accompanied by a servant, and by eighteen guides, who carried the scientific instruments, and all the baggage that I required. My son had an ardent desire to go with me; but I feared that he was not as yet either robust enough, or sufficiently inured to such violent and prolonged exertion, and therefore insisted on his renouncing the project. He remained at the Priory, where he most carefully took observations corresponding to those which I made on the summit.

In order to be perfectly free in the choice of the places where we should pass the nights, we carried with us a tent under which I reposed the first evening on the top of the Montagne de la Côte. This day was free from hardships and dangers; we walked up either on turf or over rocks, and did it easily in five or six hours. But from thence to the summit we marched on over ice and snow.

The second day's work was not the easiest. We had first to cross the glacier de la Côte in order to gain the foot of a little chain of rocks which are embosomed in the snows of Mont Blanc. This glacier is difficult and dangerous. It is cut up into wide, deep, and irregular crevasses, which sometimes can only be crossed by means of bridges of snow, which are occasionally very thin, and suspended over deep abysses. One of my guides had a narrow escape. He had gone in the evening with two others to examine the passage; and happily they had taken the precaution of tying themselves to each other with cords; for the snow gave way under him in the midst of a large and deep crevasse; and he remained suspended between his two companions. We passed close to the opening which had formed under him, and I trembled at the sight of the danger which he had run. The passage of this glacier is so difficult and so tortuous that it took me three hours to go from the top of La Côte to the first rocks of the isolated chain, although the distance is not more than three-quarters of a mile in a straight line.

After having reached these rocks we set out from them again in order to ascend, in a serpentine manner, into a little valley filled with snow which stretches from north to south, to the very foot of the highest point. These snows are divided at intervals by enormous and superb crevasses, the clean and sharp cuttings of which show the snows disposed into horizontal beds, each of which beds corresponds to a year. And whatever might be the width of these crevasses we could nowhere discover their depth.

My guides wished to spend the night in the neighborhood of one of the rocks which we passed on this route; but as the highest of them is from 600 to 700 fathoms below the summit, I wished to ascend higher. For that purpose it was necessary to encamp in the midst of the snows, and to this I had the greatest difficulty in getting my companions to consent. They imagined that during the night there reigns in these high snows a cold absolutely insupportable; and they seriously feared that they should perish through it. I told them at last that as for myself I was determined to go on with those of them of whom I was sure; that we should dig deeply in the snow, cover the excavation with the tent-cloth, then shut ourselves closely up in it, and that thus we should not suffer at all from the cold, however rigorous it might be. This arrangement reassured them, and we went forward. At four o'clock in the evening we reached the second of the three great plateaux of snow which we had to cross; and there we encamped, at 1455 fathoms above the Priory, and at 1995 above the sea, being 90 fathoms higher than the summit of the Peak of Teneriffe. We did not go on to the last plateau, because it is exposed to avalanches. The first one over which we had just passed, is not exempt from them. We had crossed two of these avalanches which had fallen since Balmat's last journey, and the ruins of which covered the valley in all its extent.

My guides set themselves first to excavate the spot in which we had to pass the night; but they quickly felt the effect of the rarity of the atmosphere (the barometer being at 16.3 inches). These robust men, for whom seven or eight hours' march was absolutely nothing, had not raised more than five or six shovelfuls of snow when they felt the impossibility of going on. They were obliged to rest every minute. One of them, who had turned back to get a barrel of some water which we had seen in a crevasse, became ill on his way, came back without the water, and passed the evening in the greatest pain. Even I, who am so accustomed to the air of mountains, and always feel better in it than in that of the plain, was utterly exhausted by the exertion of just preparing my meteorological instruments. This affection produced in us an unquenchable thirst; and we could only procure water by melting snow, for the water which we had seen in ascending proved to be frozen when we returned for it; and the little charcoal chafing dish served twenty thirsty persons but slowly.

In the middle of this plateau, enclosed between the last peaks of Mont Blanc on the south, its high steps on the east, and the Dôme du Goûté on the west, one sees hardly anything but snow, of a pure and dazzling whiteness; and on the highest peaks this forms the most singular contrast with the almost black sky of these high regions. You see there no living being, no appearance of vegetation; it is the abode of cold and silence. When I pictured to myself Doctor Paccard and Jacques Balmat arriving here just as the sun was declining, without shelter, without assistance, without even the certainty that men can live in the places which they aspired to reach, and notwithstanding, intrepidly pursuing their way, I was filled with admiration at their energy of mind and their courage.

My guides, constantly haunted by fear of the cold, closed all the edges of the tents with such exactness that I suffered much from the heat and from the closeness of the air. Indeed I was obliged to go out in the night to breathe. The moon was shining with the greatest splendor in the midst of a sky black as ebony. Jupiter also appeared particularly radiant from behind the highest point on the east of Mont Blanc: and the light reflected by all this basin of snow was so dazzling that one could only distinguish stars of the first and second magnitude. We were just falling asleep when we were aroused by the noise of an avalanche which covered part of the slope which we intended to climb on the morrow. At break of day the thermometer was three degrees below freezing.

We set out late, because it was necessary to melt the snow for breakfast and for the journey. It was drank as soon as melted; and these fellows who most religiously abstained from the wine which they had to carry, robbed me continually of the water which I had put in reserve.

We began by ascending to the third and last plateau; then we turned to the left in order to reach the highest rock on the east of the summmit. The declivity is very steep, about 36 degrees in some places; everywhere it abounds in precipices, and the surface of the snow was so hard that those who went first could only make sure of their footing by chopping steps with a hatchet. We took two hours to ascend this slope, which is about 250 fathoms in height. Arrived at the last rock, we turned towards the right, to the west, in order to climb the last slope, of which the perpendicular height is about 150 fathoms. This slope only inclines from 28 to 29 degrees, and presents no danger; but the air there is so rare that our strength was quickly exhausted; near the top I could not go more than fifteen or sixteen steps without taking breath. I felt even from time to time such a failure of strength that I was forced to sit down; but as soon as respiration returned my strength returned with it; and then it seemed to me that I should be able at one effort to reach the top of the mountain. All my guides, in proportion to their strength, were in the same state. We took two hours from the last rock to the summit; and it was eleven o'clock when we arrived there.

My eyes were first turned towards Chamounix, where I knew that my wife and sister were following my course through the telescope, with an anxiety unnecessarily great, no doubt, but none the less cruel; and I experienced a very sweet and consoling feeling when I saw floating in the air the flag which they had promised to hoist the moment when they espied me on the highest point, and when their fears would be at least relieved for the time.

I could then enjoy, without regret, the grand spectacle which lay beneath my eyes. A light vapor suspended in the lower regions of the air robbed me of the sight of the lower and more distant objects, such as the plains of France and Lombardy; but I did not much mind this loss. What I saw, and saw with the greatest clearness, was the whole collection, the whole group of these high peaks of which I had so long desired to know the organization. I could not believe my eyes; it seemed to me that it must be a dream when I beheld beneath my feet those majestic peaks, those veritable needles, Le Midi, l'Argentière, and Le Géant, whose bases even I had so long found difficult and dangerous of access. I seized on their bearing one to another, their connection, their structure; and one glance removed all those doubts which years of labor had not been able to clear up.

During this time our guides set up the tent and placed in it the little table on which I was to make my experiments. But when I came to fix my instruments, I found myself every instant obliged to interrupt my work in order to get breath. And if we consider that the barometer stood there only at 15.1 inches, and that thus the air was of hardly more than half its usual density, we shall understand that it is necessary to supplement the density by the frequency of inspiration. Then this frequency accelerates the motion of the blood, and the more so as the arteries were no longer counter-balanced on the outside by a pressure equal to that which they usually felt. So we were all feverish.

When I remained perfectly quiet, I only felt a little uneasiness and a slight disposition to sickness. But, when I took any trouble or fixed my attention for a few moments together, and above all, when by stooping down I had contracted my chest, I was obliged to rest, and take breath for two or three minutes. My guides experienced similar sensations; they had no appetites; and, in truth, our provisions, which had become frozen by the way, were not calculated to excite them. They cared for neither wine nor brandy. In fact, they had discovered that strong liquors augment these uncomfortable sensations, no doubt by increasing the quickness of the circulation. Nothing but fresh water was found agreeable; and both time and trouble in lighting a fire were necessary in order to obtain that.

I remained on the summit until half-past three; and although I did not lose a single moment, yet I could not in these four hours and a half make all the experiments which I had frequently finished in less than three hours by the sea-side. I took great care, however, with those which were most essential.

Quitting this magnificent belvedere I came, in three-quarters of an hour, to the rocks which formed the shoulder on the east of the summit. The descent of this declivity of which the ascent had been so painful, was easy and agreeable; the snow was neither too hard nor too soft; and, as the movements of our bodies in coming down did not com-

The Col du Géant.

press the diaphragm, it did not try the breathing; and so we did not suffer from the rarity of the air. Besides, as this descent is broad, and free from precipices, there was nothing to alarm us or to retard the march. But it was not thus with the descent which, from the top of the shoulder, conducts to the plateau on which we had slept. The great rapidity of this slope, the unbearable brightness of the sun reflected by the snow, which showed to us the precipices under our feet, and made them appear more terrible than they were, rendered it extremely painful. Besides, as the hardness of the snow had made our march difficult in the morning, so now its softness, produced by the heat of the sun, incommoded us in the evening, because under this softened surface we found it hard and slippery.

As we had all doubted of this descent some of the guides had sought for another while I was occupied in making my observations; but their search having been in vain, we were constrained to return by the same way that we had gone up. However, thanks to the care of my guides, we did it without accident, and that in less than an hour and a quarter. We passed near the place where we had, if not slept, at least rested, on the preceding night; and we pushed on a league further, as far as the rock, near which we had stopped in ascending. I determined to sleep there, and made them fix the tent against the southern extremity of this rock in a truly singular situation. It was on the snow, on the edge of a declivity exceedingly rapid, which descends from the valley commanded by the Dôme du Goûté with its crown of *séracs*,* and which is terminated on

* In the Alps they give the name of "sérac" to a species of white, close cheese which they obtain from whey, and which they press into rectangular cases, in which they take the form of cubes, or rather of rectangular parallelopipeds. The snows, at a great height, frequently take this form when they freeze, after having been drenched by rain. They become then extremely compact, and in this state, if a thick bed of hardened snow gets on to a declivity, so that it slides in a mass, and that, in sliding, some

the south by the peak of Mont Blanc. At the bottom of this declivity there was a large and deep crevasse which separated us from the valley, and which engulfed everything that we let fall from anywhere near our tent.

We had chosen this position to avoid the danger of avalanches, and in order that the guides finding shelter in the clefts of the rock we should not be crowded into the tent, as we had been on the previous night.

I contemplated the mass of clouds which floated under my feet above the valleys and mountains which were less elevated than we were. These clouds, instead of presenting flat or smooth surfaces, such as one sees when looking up from below at them, displayed forms that were extremely odd,—towers, castles, giants,—and appeared to be moved by vertical winds, which came from different points of the countries situated under them. Above all these clouds I saw the horizon bounded by a band composed of two lines, the lower one of a blackish red, and the upper one lighter and resembling a flame of a beautiful yellow color, varying, transparent, and shaded.

We supped merrily and with good appetites, after which I passed an excellent night on my mattress. It was then only that I enjoyed the pleasure of having accomplished the design formed twenty-

---

portions of the mass do not go straight, their weight forces them to break into fragments nearly rectangular, of which some are perhaps fifty feet every way, and which, on account of their homogeneity, are as regular as if they had been cut with scissors.

seven years before, in my first journey to Chamounix, in 1760; a project which I had so often abandoned and taken up again, and which had been to my family a continual subject of anxiety and disquiet. This prepossession of mind had the character of a sort of malady; my eyes had never met Mont Blanc, which could be seen from many places in our neighborhood, without my experiencing a sort of sorrowful pang. At the moment in which I reached the top, my satisfaction was not complete; it was still less so when I left it, for I only then saw what I had not been able to do. But in the silence of the night, after I had well rested from my fatigue; when I recapitulated the observations that I had made; when, above all, I retraced the magnificent picture of the mountains which I carried graven in my head; and when, lastly, I encouraged the well-founded hope of finishing on the Col du Géant what I had not been able to do, and which really will never be done on Mont Blanc,—then I felt a true and unmixed satisfaction.

On the 4th of August, the fourth day of our journey, we did not set out until six o'clock in the morning. Shortly after we arrived at the hut. We were next obliged to descend a slope of snow, the inclination of which was about forty-six degrees, and to cross a large crevasse over a bridge of snow so slight that it was not at first more than three inches thick; and one of the guides who swerved a little from the middle, got one of his legs over the side. At an hour's march beyond the hut we came to crevasses which were open; and in order to avoid them it was necessary to descend an inclined slope of fifty degrees. Coming at last to the glacier which we must recross, we found it so changed in the last four-and-twenty hours, that we could not discover the route which we had taken in ascending; for the crevasses were widened, the bridges were broken, and often, finding no way we were forced to return on our steps; while oftener still we were obliged to make use of our ladder in order to cross crevasses which it would have been impossible to pass without its assistance. Just as he had reached the other side, one of the guides lost his footing; he slid to the edge of a chink, into which he all but fell, and in which he lost one of the stakes of my tent. In this moment of fright an enormous piece of ice fell into a great crevasse, with a noise which shook the whole glacier. But at last we got safe on to the rock at half-past nine in the morning free from all further trouble or danger. We took only two hours and a half from thence to the priory at Chamounix, to which I had the satisfaction of bringing back all my guides in perfectly good health.

Our reception was at once joyful and affecting; for all the relations and friends of the guides came to embrace them and congratulate them on their return. And my wife, my sister, and my sons, who had passed together a long and anxious time at Chamounix in the expectation of this expedition, as well as several of our friends who came from Geneva to join in the welcome,—all expressed at this joyful moment the satisfaction which the fears that had preceded it, rendered only the more lively and touching according to the degree of interest which we had inspired.

I remained the next day at Chamounix in order to make some comparative observations, after which we all returned happily to Geneva, from whence I could now look on Mont Blanc with a true pleasure, and without that feeling of longing and anxiety which it had before caused me.

H. B. de Saussure, *Voyage dans les Alpes.*

II.

MONT BLANC.

ASCENT IN 1844 BY MM. CHARLES MARTINS, BRAVAIS, AND LEPILEUR.

I COME now to the scientific ascent which I made in 1844, with my friends Auguste Bravais, a naval lieutenant, and Auguste Lepileur, a medical practitioner.

With the former I had visited Spitzbergen in 1838 and 1839, during the two campaigns of "La Recherche" in the Frozen Ocean. He had wintered alone at Bossecop, in Lapland; but we had staid together on the Faulhorn, in 1841, for eighteen days, at a height of 8710 feet. He himself had met the following year with the physician, Auguste Peltier, and had staid with him twenty-three days. A comparison of the northern regions of the globe with high Alpine regions was the habitual subject of our conversations. On the Faulhorn we had made a number of observations, and proposed a certain number of problems which could only be solved by an ascent and a sojourn at a very great height. Therefore we thought of Mont Blanc.

We left Geneva on the 26th of July, and following on foot a great four-wheeled wagon which carried all that we required, we arrived at Chamounix on the 28th. The preparations occupied us several days. Our design being to stay some time as high as possible on Mont Blanc, we had brought from Paris a tent for encamping, with its supports and stakes, some paletots of goats' skin, some sheepskin sacks, some blankets, etc.

Our proposed experiments required numerous physical and meteorological instruments; food for three days was necessary; but each porter could only carry about 32 lbs. weight besides his victuals. We had altogether about 956 lbs. weight to transport to a height of 9750 feet above the Valley of Chamounix.

Our caravan numbered forty-three persons, of whom three were guides, Michel Couttet, Jean Mugnier, and Theodore Balmat; and thirty-five porters, two being young men of the valley who had asked to accompany us. On the 31st of July, at half-past seven in the morning, we set out from Chamounix.

The weather was fine, only the wind blew from the southwest, and the barometer had fallen a little; but our preparations were made. We set out therefore without feeling perfect confidence in the weather, but hoping for speedy improvement. The long file of porters extended along the right bank of the Arve, in the midst of verdant meadows. But when we were arrived in front of the hamlet of Les Pèlerins, we turned to the left.

THE AIGUILLE DU MIDI.

The last house in the village was that of Jacques Balmat, the first man whose steps were printed on the then untrodden snow on the top of Mont Blanc, and who perished miserably, in 1834, in the glaciers over the Valley of Sixt. Leaving the orchards which surround the hamlet of Les Pèlerins, we entered a forest composed of high fir-trees and old larches, on the brambles of which hung the long festoons of a grey lichen. In the preceding spring an enormous avalanche, which had descended from the Aiguille du Midi, had dug a large furrow in the forest. Trees torn up by the roots covered the ground which they had once shaded,—others were broken in the middle, their tops lying at our feet; while others, only partially injured, bent over the valley. These effects are due as much to the pressure of the air driven out by the avalanche,—to the local wind which it produces—as to the snow itself. The caravan being dispersed into the woods, each one chose his own way.

A straight path goes along the side of the precipice over which falls the cascade des Pèlerins, and leads to the moraine of the glacier of Bossons; then you mount in the midst of the heaped-up blocks which compose it, and you reach the Pierre de l'Echelle, an enormous rock under which they hide the ladder generally used to cross the crevasses of the glacier. This stone is about 7949 feet above the sea, at the same elevation as the monastery of St. Bernard. It is there that the traveller bids farewell to the earth. He quits it to pass over the glacier, and up to the summit of Mont Blanc he only finds isolated rocks which surge like islands in the midst of fields of eternal snow.

The circuit around the glacier of Bossons was, as it always is, a chaos of *séracs,* of needles, and of pyramids of ice, in the midst of which is situated the eastern wall of the Grands Mulets. The vertical strata of which these rocks are composed rise to various heights, and form steps which enable one to climb up to all the points. The rock being decomposed under the influence of atmospheric agents, the particles collect between the layers. In these collections vegetate beautiful Alpine plants, sheltered by the rock, warmed by the sun which it reflects, and moistened by the snow which, even in summer, often whitens these peaks, though it melts rapidly when the sun shines on it for two or three days. In some weeks they go through all the phases of their vegetation, and I have gathered nineteen phanerogamic plants in three ascents. M. Venance-Payot having added five species to this list, there exist twenty-four flowering plants on the Grands Mulets. To these four-and-twenty phanerogams, we must add twenty-six species of mosses, two hepaticæ, and thirty lichens, which brings the total number of plants that grow on these isolated rocks, in the midst of a sea of ice, rocks which appear to be deprived of all vegetation, up to eighty-two. Who would believe it? These plants serve for nourishment to a little gnawing animal, the campagnol of the snow, the only mammifer which is found high on the Alps, whilst almost all his brethren are inhabitants of the plain.

Bravais took on himself the task of measuring the variations of the magnetic intensity with the height. For that purpose a compass is used, in which a needle is suspended horizontally by a thread of silk not twisted. This needle is made to oscillate during a series of intervals of time perfectly equal; and from the number of these oscillations after infinite corrections and an extreme minuteness, a conclusion is arrived at as to the relative intensity of magnetic force at the place compared with that at Paris. The importance of these measures will be understood, as they will one day disclose to us the now mysterious laws of those currents which circulate around the terrestrial globe, that colossal magnet, the two poles of which do not coincide with the two extremities of the ideal axis on which the earth describes its daily revolution.

Meanwhile the sun was nearing the horizon; already he had disappeared behind the Monts Vergy, and the valleys of Sallanche and of Chamounix had been long in the shade, whilst the neighbouring granite points appeared of a white heat like hot iron coming out of the fire. Soon the peak of Varens and the rocks of the Fiz were extinguished, and the shadow gained the glaciers of Mont Blanc. The snows which had been so luminous an instant before, took the dull and livid color of a corpse; and cold and death seemed to invade these regions with the darkness and to reveal all their horrors. The point of Goûté, the Monts Maudits, successively grew dim; while the top of Mont Blanc alone remained light for a little time; then the rosy tint which had enlivened it gave place also to a livid one, as if life had abandoned it in its turn. Towards the horizon, above the sea of clouds, the heavens appeared of a light green, the result of the combination of the yellow rays of the sun with the blue of the celestial vault; and the forms of the clouds were marked out by a border of the most brilliant orange. In these high regions there is no twilight, night succeeds to day quite suddenly. We retired behind a wall made of dry stones which were built up before a cavity. Our guides were grouped on the steps of the rock around the little fires fed with the wood of the juniper, brought by them from the neighborhood of the Pierre de l'Echelle; and they sang in unison slow and monotonous songs which borrowed from the spot a melancholy charm. By little and little the songs ceased, and the fires went out. Then nothing was heard but the noise of avalanches falling from the surrounding heights. Soon the moon rose behind the Monts Maudits, and, while still herself invisible, showed up in strong relief the Dôme du Goûté, of which the snows seemed to give an extraordinary phosphorescent light. When she showed herself above the peak of the Goûté, she was surrounded by a greenish halo which stood out clearly on a sky as black as ink. The stars also sparkled brightly, but the wind had not gone down: it blew in strong gusts, followed by moments of perfect calm. Everything gave warning of bad weather on the morrow, yet no one dreamt of returning; we all preferred to try our chance to the very last, and not to go back until we found it quite impossible to continue the ascent.

Next day, whilst we were engaged in distributing anew the burdens of our porters who had changed their loads, I perceived all at once an old man, unknown to us, who was coming slowly up the slope which leads to the Petit Plateau. Bending over the snow, and assisting himself sometimes with his hands, he ascended slowly, but with that equal and measured step which indicates a practised mountaineer. This old man turned out to be Marie Couttet; he was now eighty years of age, and in his youth he had served as guide to De Saussure. He still possessed an agility which caused him to be named 'The Chamois;' and he well deserved this *sobriquet*, for no one could have been more intrepid. One day he accompanied an English traveller in a a difficult journey. The traveller preserved that phlegmatic and indifferent air which characterizes the English gentleman. The sight of the most slippery passages neither drew from him a gesture of astonishment, nor a word which betrayed the least hesitation. Irritated by this imperturbable *sang-froid*, Couttet spied out a pine *cembro* which projected horizontally over a precipice about a thousand feet in depth; he walked boldly along this trunk, and when at the extremity he lay down upon it, and lastly, suspended himself by his feet over the precipice. The Englishman looked on quietly, and when Couttet returned to him he gave him a gold piece on condition that he would not do so again. Such was, in his youth, the man who was before us on the lower slopes of the Petit Plateau. His mind had become weakened before his body; he thought that he had found a new road by which to reach the top of Mont Blànc, and offered himself as guide to every traveller who attempted the ascent. Although his offer was declined he accompanied them as a volunteer up to a certain height in order to point out to them the new road which he had discovered. Having been warned of the monomania of the old man, we had carefully hidden from him the day of our departure, but knowing that we were on the Grands Mulets, he had set off the same evening, had crossed the glacier and arrived about midnight at our bivouac, where he took his place by the fire among the guides. At dawn he set out first to show the way.

The Grand Plateau is a vast circuit of snow and ice, the foundation of which is a plane raised towards the south. But we hardly caught a glimpse of the configuration of the various objects, for before we knew where we were, the clouds had completely enveloped us, and snow whirled violently around our heads. There was no time to hesitate; we must either go down immediately or put up our tent. Two porters, Auguste Simond and Jean Cachat, offered to remain with the three guides and us. The others threw down their bundles on the snow and precipitated themselves in haste towards the Petit Plateau; they vanished like shadows in the mist which thickened more and more. Left alone, we began to remove the snow about a foot deep for a space of

MONT BLANC, FROM THE BREVENT.

about twelve feet by six; then, guided by a cord prepared beforehand, which was knotted to correspond to the stakes of the tent, we planted in the snow long and strong wooden pegs, each of which was furnished with a hook. That done, the tent was raised on the cross piece and the two supports which were to sustain it; and the rings of the cords were passed over the heads of the pegs. The tent set up, we next hastened to put under shelter, first, all our instruments, and then all our provisions. We were forced to make all possible haste, for several bottles of wine left outside could not be found; at the end of an hour the snow which fell and that which the wind had brought up had covered them. Under the tent we had improvised a floor with light planks of fir-wood placed over the snow. Our guides were at one extremity, and we at the other. The space was small, and we could not stand upright; we were forced either to sit or lie, and the cooking was performed in the middle of the tent. Our first care was to melt some snow in a jar heated by a spirit-lamp, for at these heights charcoal burns badly. Bravais hit on the happy idea of pouring this water over the stakes of the tent; the water froze, and then, instead of being driven only into the yielding snow, these stakes were fixed in masses of compact ice. Besides this, a cord fixed to the iron pin which joined the horizontal cross piece of one of the vertical supports, and attached, like the shrouds of a ship, on the side whence came the wind, was made fast to two stakes driven into the snow. These precautions taken, we had only to wait. Every observation was impossible, saving that of the barometer inside the tent, and the thermometer outside; the latter was 27° on our arrival; at two o'clock it had fallen to 25°, at five o'clock to 22°. When night came we lighted a lantern which, suspended over our heads, lighted up our littl· interior. The guides huddled together, talked in a low voice, or slept as quietly as if in their beds. The wind redoubled its force; it blew in squalls, interrupted by those moments of profound calm which had so much astonished De Saussure when he was on the Col du Géant in circumstances exactly similar. The tempest raged in the vast amphitheatre of snow on the edge of which our little tent was placed. Like an avalanche of air, the wind appeared to fall on us from the top of Mont Blanc. Then the covering of the tent puffed out like a sail filled with the breeze; the supports bent and vibrated like the cords of a violin, and the cross-beam bent. Instinctively we held up the canvas with our backs during these gusts, for our safety depended on the firmness of this protecting shelter; if we only took a few steps outside we were able to form an idea of what would become of us if we were carried away. Never before had I comprehended how travellers full of vigor and health could perish at a few paces from the place in which the tempest had surprised them; I understood it on that day. Under the tent the cold was supportable. The thermometer oscillated between 36° and 38°. Our goatskin clothes and our sheepskin sacks protected us effectually, although the hair of these things became frozen to the tent's cover. During the night the wind abated, but unfortunately the snow continued to fall, the temperature also became lower and lower, and at half-past five in the morning the thermometer pointed to 10°. The new snow was a foot and a half deep; but the tent cover was pretty free, the wind having swept it off as it fell, as it continued to drive along the sleet and snow of the Grand Plateau. The barometer remained as low as on the previous evening. In a light moment we saw the peaks of Mont Blanc, and on the Monts Maudits and Dromadaire, each terminated by a sort of tuft of snow which the south-west wind had collected on them.

To ascend to the summit was impossible, and even on the Grand Plateau we were condemned to inaction. So we settled our plans, and after having arranged our instruments in the tent, we filled up the entrance with snow; it was now seven in the morning, and the thermometer showed still thirteen degrees below freezing. The snow which had just fallen had hidden all the clefts and crevasses; but we tied ourselves together and descended rapidly to the Grands Mulets. After some moments of rest, we then crossed the glacier of Bossons. The narrow path which leads to the Pierres-Pointues, being covered with fresh snow, was become slippery and difficult. Snow had also fallen still lower, as far as the place called the Barmes Dessous, only about 2,500 feet above Chamounix. Our return reassured every one: for there had been bad weather in the valley as well as on the mountains, and the report had spread that we had all perished.

On the 25th of August fine weather set in; the barometer rose steadily; and the northwest wind blew in the upper regions of the air. We knew that our tent was still standing on the Grand Plateau; for we had seen it from the top of the Brevent; but it appeared to be buried in the snow on the south-west side; and the opposite one seemed to be quite disarranged.

Confident that we should find our instruments in good condition, we set out again on the 27th, at half-past twelve at night. The moon enlightened our march; and at half-past three we were on the Pierres-Pointues. The sky was beautifully clear, but isolated mists remained on the Col de Balme, and on the Mont Vergy. A fresh breeze descending, and the slight twinkling of the stars, were signs to us of good weather. Castor and Pollux shone with a quiet light over the peaks of Charmoz.

On arriving at the precipitous parts, we followed each other very closely, and took care that the angles formed by our zig-zags should have an opening of at least fifteen degrees. We marched knee-deep in snow, of which the temperature was always about 12° at a depth of four inches. The rarefied state of the air and the depth of the snow, from which we were obliged constantly to drag up our legs, forced us to walk slowly; every twenty steps we stopped quite out of breath, and our feet were painfully cold and ready to freeze. During our short halts we struck them with a stick, in order to warm them. This part of the ascent was very fatiguing, though a fine sun and a quiet wind favored our efforts; but, when we reached the slope which separates the Roches-Rouges from the Petits Mulets, we perceived all at once the mountains situated on the south of Mont Blanc, and beyond the plains of Italy. Nothing then sheltered us any longer; the wind from the northwest, imperceptible before, took off Mugnier's hat, and, although warmly dressed, I suddenly felt myself as if without any clothes, the wind was so cold and penetrating. Turning off to the right, we soon arrived at the Petits Mulets, which are protogine rocks, situated at less than 500 feet below the summit. We were near the end now, but we walked slowly, with heads lowered and heaving chests, like a company of invalids. The effect of the rarefaction of the air was felt in a painful manner; and every minute the column stopped. Bravais tried how long he could go on at his greatest speed, and stopped at the thirty-second step, because he could not take one more. At last, at a quarter to two, we reached the summit so much desired. It is formed of a sort of back-bone turning from the east-northeast to the south-southwest; but this ridge or backbone is not sharp, as De Saussure found it, but from 15 to 18 feet wide.

On the north side it abuts on an immense slope of snow of from 40 to 45 degrees, which terminates in the Grand Plateau. On the south side this is continued with a little flat surface parallel to the ridge, sloping about 10 degrees, and about 300 feet wide. This surface is prolonged towards the south, or else it joins another steep descent, which suddenly stops at the level of the great collection of precipitous rocks which stand over the Állée Blanche. After having taken breath, our first glance was at the immense panorama which surrounded us: I will not describe it after De Saussure.

The height of Mont Blanc does not appear to have sensibly varied since the first measurement was made, in 1775, by Shuckburgh, up to the present moment, which is surprising when we consider that the summit is formed only of ice and snow of the thickness of more than 200 feet. It appears evident that Mont Blanc is a pyramid like its neighbor, the Aiguille du Midi. The Rochers-Rouges, the Petits Mulets, and the Tourette, are all striking points of this pyramid; the rest is covered with a cap of snow, which never melts, on account of the height of the mountain, on the top of which the temperature is rarely up to freezing point, and almost always very much below it.

We may ask, then, how it is that the thickness of this cap of snow is invariable, and that the altitude of the mountain does not change in the course of seasons or even years. And, in fact, the quantity of snow which falls, the winds which sweep it, and the evaporation which diminishes the thickness, as well as the condensation of the clouds which increase it—all these do vary from year to year; so that the form of the summit is never the same. Let any one compare the description of De Saussure, of Clissold, of Markham Sherwill. of Henry de

Tilly, and of Bravais, made successively in 1787, 1822, 1827, 1834, and 1844, and he will see that each of these travellers found a different form, with the exception of the fundamental feature, a sloping ridge running from east to west. How could it be otherwise? Snows fall on Mont Blanc, which are brought there by all the winds of the compass; they have hardly fallen before they are swept, displaced, and carried away, so that the surface looks like a ploughed field. Even in fine weather, when the most perfect calm reigns in the plain, a light smoke seems to issue from the top, which is drawn off horizontally by a violent wind. 'Then,' say the Savoyards, 'Mont Blanc smokes his pipe.' And it is a sign of fine weather if the smoke goes towards the south. It comes to this, however, that all these various causes of ablation and of addition compensate one another; and the height of the peak remains the same. Nature never proceeds otherwise; nothing is absolutely stable: everything oscillates, from the smallest particle to the ocean. And this oscillation around a middle state is the condition of life; it is immobility which is a sign of death; and the general powers of nature, which regulate the inorganic as well as the organic world, never rest.

The meteorological and geodesic operations were hardly finished when the sun approached the lines of the Jura, in the direction of Geneva; it was a quarter past six; the thermometer showed for the temperature of the air, 11°; for that of the snow on the surface, zero, and 7° at the depth of 8 inches. The contact with this snow even through our boots was a real suffering. Nevertheless, we were very anxious to make signal fires, which should be visible at the same time at Geneva, Lyons, and Dijon, where the astronomers were forewarned: and these signals, seen simultaneously at the three cities, might have enabled them to determine exactly their differences of longitude; but the cold was so extreme that we saw that to remain longer would have been to risk our own lives and those of the guide. Auguste Simond was willing to remain alone to make these signals; but we refused our permission, and we did well. Since then the electric telegraph has enabled us to obtain, without stirring and without trouble, a result which would, perhaps, have been purchased by the life of the father of a family.

Our return was resolved on, and we had begun to descend, when we were stopped all at once before the most extraordinary sight that a man could behold. The shadow of Mont Blanc, forming an immense cone, extended itself over the white mountains of Piedmont: it advanced slowly towards the horizon, and rose in the air above the Becca di Nonna; but then the shadows of the other mountains came in succession to join it, in proportion as the sun sank below their peaks, and formed a cortege to the shadow of the ruler of the Alps. All, by the effect of perspective, converged towards it; and these shadows of a greenish blue at their base, were surrounded by a strong purple tint, which melted into the red of the heavens. A poet might have said that angels with flaming wings were bending round a throne on which sat an invisible God. The shadows disappeared in the sky, yet we were still nailed to the spot, immovable, though not mute, with astonishment; for our admiration broke forth in the most various exclamations. Only the aurora borealis of the north of Europe could produce a spectacle comparable in magnificence to this unexpected phenomenon, which no one before us had witnessed from the summit of Mont Blanc.

The sun set; and we were obliged to go forward. We were, first, all attached to one cord, and then we plunged downwards toward the Grand Plateau. In passing near the Petits Mulets, I picked up two stones on the snow, which I afterwards discovered to be fragments of rock broken off by the thunderbolts which so often fall on these mountain-tops. After starting from the Petits Mulets, we stopped no more, but descended like an avalanche in a straight line, without choosing our route; each one being pulled on by him who preceded him, and Mugnier, who went first, threw himself bounding over the declivity, plunging at each spring deep into the snow, which thus moderated just sufficiently the impetus of the moving chain. Arrived at the Grand Plateau, we were obliged to stop a moment for breath; then, with rapid steps, we made for our tent, which we reached at a quarter to eight. In fifty-five minutes we had descended from the peak, a distance of 2800 feet. When we entered our tent, we felt as if once again by the domestic hearth, and there we enjoyed a well-earned repose. But, notwithstanding, the meteorological observations were continued heroically every two hours during the night.

CHARLES MARTINS, *Du Spitzberg au Sahara.*

III.

THE FINSTERAARHORN.

ASCENT IN 1858 BY J. TYNDALL.

Since my arrival at the hotel, on the 30th of July, I had once or twice spoken about ascending the Finsteraarhorn; and on the 2d of August my host advised me to avail myself of the promising weather. A guide, named Bennen, was attached to the hotel, a remarkable-looking man, between thirty and forty years old, of middle stature, but very strongly built. His countenance was frank and firm, while a light of good nature at times twinkled in his eye. Altogether the man gave me the impression of physical strength, combined with decision of character. The proprietor had spoken to me many times of the strength and courage of this man, winding up his praises of him by the assurance that if I were killed in Bennen's company, there would be two lives lost; for that the guide would assuredly sacrifice himself in the effort to save his *Herr*.

He was called, and I asked him whether he would accompany me alone to the top of the Finsteraarhorn. To this he at first objected, urging the possibility of his having to render me assistance, and the great amount of labor which this might entail upon him; but this was overruled by my engaging to follow where he led, without asking him to render me any help whatever. He then agreed to make the trial, stipulating, however, that he should not have much to carry to the cave of the Faulberg, where we were to spend the night. To this I cordially agreed, and sent on blankets, provisions, wood, and hay, by two porters.

My desire, in part, was to make a series of observations at the summit of the mountain, while a similar series was made by Professor Ramsay, in the valley of the Rhône, near Viesch, with a view to ascertaining the permeability of the lower strata of the atmosphere to the radiant heat of the sun. During the forenoon of the 2nd, I occupied myself with my instruments, and made the proper arrangements with Ramsay. I tested a mountain thermometer which Mr. Casella had kindly lent me, and found the boiling point of water on the dining-room table of the hotel to be 199°.29 Fahrenheit.

At about three o'clock in the afternoon, we quitted the hotel, and proceeded leisurely with our two guides up the slope of the Eggischhorn. We once caught a sight of the topmost pinnacle of the Finsteraarhorn; beside it was the Rothhorn, and near this again the Oberaarhorn, with the Viesch glacier streaming from its shoulders. On the opposite side we could see, over an oblique buttress of the mountain on which we stood, the snowy summit of the Weisshorn; to the left of this was the ever grim and lonely Matterhorn; and farther to the left, with its numerous snow-cones, each with its attendant shadow, rose the mighty Mischabel. We descended, and crossed the stream which flows from the Mörjelen See, into which a large mass of the glacier had recently fallen, and which was now afloat as an iceberg. We passed along the margin of the lake, and at the junction of water and ice I bade Ramsay good-bye. At the commencement of our journey upon the ice, whenever we crossed a crevasse, I noticed Bennen watching me; his vigilance, however, soon diminished, whence I gathered that he finally concluded that I was able to take care of myself. Clouds hovered in the atmosphere througout the whole time of our ascent; one smoky-looking mass marred the glory of the sunset, but at some distance was another, which exhibited colors almost as rich and varied as those of the solar spectrum. I took the glorious banner thus unfurled as a sign of hope, to check the despondency which its gloomy neighbor was calculated to produce.

Two hours' walking brought us near our place of rest; the porters had already reached it, and were now returning. We deviated to the right, and having crossed some ice-ravines, reached the lateral moraine of the glacier, and picked our way between it and the adjacent mountain wall. We then reached a kind of amphitheatre, crossed it, and, climbing the opposite slope, came to a triple grotto, formed by clefts in the mountains. In one of these a pine-fire was soon blazing briskly, and casting its red light upon the surrounding objects, though but half dispelling the gloom from the deeper portions of the cell. I left the grotto, and climbed the rocks above it to look at the heavens. The sun had quitted our firmament, but still tinted the clouds with red and purple, while one peak of snow in particular glowed like fire, so vivid was its illumination. During our journey upwards, the Jungfrau never once showed her head, but, as if in ill temper, had wrapped her vapory veil around her. She now looked more good-humored, but still she did not quite remove her hood, though all the other summits, without a trace of cloud to mark their beautiful forms, pointed heavenward. The calmness was perfect; no sound of living creature, no whisper of a breeze, no gurgle of water, no rustle of *débris*, to break the deep and solemn silence. Surely if beauty be an object of worship, those glorious mountains, with rounded shoulders of the purest white snow, crested and star-gemmed, were well calculated to excite sentiments of adoration.

I returned to the grotto, where supper was prepared and waiting for me. The boiling point of water, at the level of the "kitchen floor," I found to be 196° Fahr. Nothing could be more picturesque than the aspect of the cell before we went to rest. The fire was gleaming ruddily. I sat upon a stone bench beside it, while Bennen was in front with the red light glimmering fitfully over him. My boiling water apparatus, which had just been used, was in the foreground; and telescopes, opera-glasses, haversacks, wine-keg, bottles, and mattocks, lay confusedly around. The heavens continued to grow clearer, the thin clouds, which had partially overspread the sky, melting gradually away. The grotto was comfortable, the hay sufficient materially to modify the hardness of the rock, and my position at least sheltered and warm. One possibility remained that might prevent me from sleeping—the snoring of my companion; he assured me, however, that he did not snore, and we lay down side by side. The good fellow took care that I should not be chilled; he gave me the best place, by far the best part of the clothes, and may have suffered himself in consequence; but happily for him he was soon oblivious of this. Physiologists, I believe, have discovered that it is chiefly during sleep that the muscles are repaired; and ere long the sound I dreaded announced to me at once the repair of Bennen's muscles and the doom of my own. The hollow cave resounded to the deep-drawn snore. I once or twice stirred the sleeper, breaking thereby the continuity of the phenomenon; but it instantly pieced itself together again, and went on as before. I had not the heart to wake him, for I knew that on him would devolve the chief labor of the coming day. At half-past one he rose and prepared coffee, and at two I was engaged upon the beverage. We afterwards packed our provisions and instruments; Bennen bore the former and I the latter, and at three o'clock we set out.

We first descended a steep slope to the glacier, along which we walked for a time. A spur of the Faulberg jutted out between us and the inladen valley through which we must pass; this we crossed in order to shorten our way to avoid crevasses. Loose shingle and boulders overlaid the mountain; and here and there walls of rock opposed our progress, and rendered the route far from agreeable. We then descended to the Grünhorn tributary, which joins the trunk glacier at nearly a right angle, being terminated by a saddle which stretches across from mountain to mountain, with a curvature as graceful and as perfect as if drawn by the instrument of a mathematician. The unclouded moon was shining; and the Jungfrau was before us so pure and beautiful that the thought of visiting the 'Maiden' without further preparation occurred to me. I turned to Bennen, and said: 'Shall we try the Jungfrau?' I think he liked the idea well enough, though he cautiously avoided any responsibility. 'If you desire it, I am ready,' was his reply. He had never made the ascent, and nobody knew anything of the state of the snow this year; but Lauener had examined it through a telescope on the previous day, and pronounced it dangerous. In every ascent of the mountain hitherto made, ladders had been found indispensable; but we had none. I questioned Bennen as to what he thought of the probabilities, and tried to extract some direct encouragement from him; but he said that the decision rested altogether with myself, and it was his business to endeavor to carry out that decision. 'We will attempt it, then,' I said; and for some time we actually walked towards the Jungfrau. A grey cloud drew itself across her summit, and clung there. I asked myself why I deviated from my original intention? The Finsteraarhorn was higher, and therefore better suited for the contemplated observations. I could in no wise justify the change, and finally expressed my scruples. A moment's further conversation caused us to 'right about,' and front the saddle of the Grünhorn.

The dawn advanced. The eastern sky became illuminated and warm, and high in the air across the ridge in front of us stretched a tongue of cloud like a red flame, and equally fervid in its hue. Looking across the trunk glacier, a valley which is terminated by the Lötsch saddle, was seen in a straight line with our route; and I often turned to look along this magnificent corridor. The mightiest mountains in the Oberland form its sides; still the impression which it makes is not that of vastness or sublimity, but of loveliness not to be described. The sun had not yet smitten the snows of the bounding mountains; but the saddle curved out a segment of the heavens which formed a background of unspeakable beauty. Over the rim of the saddle the sky was deep orange passing upwards through amber, yellow, and vague ethereal green to the ordinary firmamental blue. Right above the snow-curve purple clouds hung perfectly motionless, giving depth to the spaces between them. There was something saintly on the scene. Anything more exquisite I had never beheld.

We marched upward over the smooth crisp snow to the crest of the saddle, and here I turned to take a last look along that grand corridor, and at that wonderful 'daffodil sky.' The sun's rays had already smitten the snows of the Aletschhorn, the radiance seemed to infuse a principle of life and activity into the mountains and glaciers; but still that holy light shone forth, and those motionless clouds floated beyond, reminding one of that Eastern religion whose essence is the repression of all action, and the substitution for it of immortal calm. The Finsteraarhorn now fronted us; but clouds turbaned the head of the giant, and hid it from our view. The wind, however, being north, inspired us with a strong hope that they would melt as the day advanced. I have hardly seen a finer ice-field than that which now lay before us. Considering the *névé* which supplies it, it appeared to me that the Viescher glacier ought to discharge as much ice as the Aletsch; but this is an error due to the extent of *névé*, which is here at once visible; since a glance at the map of this portion of the Oberland shows at once the great superiority of the mountain treasury from which the Aletsch glacier draws support. Still, the ice-field before us was a most noble one. The surrounding mountains were of imposing magnitude, and loaded to their summits with snow. Down the sides of some of them the half-consolidated mass fell in a state of wild fracture and confusion. In some cases the riven masses were twisted and overturned, the ledges bent, and the detached blocks piled one upon another in heaps; while in other cases the smooth white mass descended from crown to base without a wrinkle. The valley now below us was gorged by the frozen material thus incessantly poured into it. We crossed it, and reached the base of the Finsteraarhorn, as-

THE FINSTERAARHORN

cended the mountain a little way, and at six o'clock passed to lighten our burdens and to refresh ourselves.

The north wind had freshened; we were in the shade, and the cold was very keen. Placing a bottle of tea and a small quantity of provisions in the knapsack, and a few figs and dried prunes in our pockets, we commenced the ascent. The Finsteraarhorn sends down a number of cliffy buttresses, separated from each other by wide couloirs filled with ice and snow. We ascended one of these buttresses for a time, treading cautiously among the spiky rocks; afterwards we went along the snow at the edge of the spine, and then fairly parted company with the rock, abandoning ourselves to the *névé* of the couloir. The latter was steep, and the snow so firm that steps had to be cut in it. Once I paused upon a little ledge, which gave me a slight footing, and took the inclination. The slope formed an angle of 45° with the horizon; and across it, at a little distance below me, a gloomy fissure opened its jaws. The sun now cleared the summits which had before cut off his rays, and burst upon us with great power, compelling us to resort to our veils and dark spectacles. Two years before, Bennen had been nearly blinded by inflammation, brought on by the glare of the snow, and he now took unusual care in protecting his eyes. The rocks looking more practicable, we again made towards them, and clambered among them till a vertical precipice, which proved impossible of ascent, fronted us. Bennen scanned the obstacle closely as we slowly approached it, and finally descended to the snow, which wound at a steep angle round its base; on this the footing appeared to me to be singularly insecure; but I marched without hesitation or anxiety in the footsteps of my guide.

We ascended the rocks once more, continued along them for some time, and then deviated to the couloir on our left. This snow-slope is much dislocated at its lower portion, and above its precipices and crevasses our route now lay. The snow was smooth, and sufficiently firm and steep to render the cutting of steps necessary. Bennen took the lead; to make each step he swung his mattock once, and his hindermost foot rose exactly at the moment the mattock descended; there was thus a kind of rhythm in his motion, the raising of the foot keeping time to the swing of the implement. In this manner we proceeded till we reached the base of the rocky pyramid which capped the mountain.

One side of the pyramid had been sliced off, thus dropping down almost a sheer precipice for some thousands of feet to the Finsteraar glacier. A wall of rock, about ten or fifteen feet high, runs along the edge of the mountain, and this sheltered us from the north wind, which surged with the sound of waves against the tremendous barrier at the other side. 'Our hardest work is now before us,' said my guide. Our way lay up the steep and splintered rocks, among which we sought out the spikes which were closely enough wedged to bear our weight. Each had to trust to himself; and I fulfilled to the letter my engagement with Bennen to ask no help. My boiling-water apparatus and telescope were on my back, much to my annoyance, as the former was heavy, and sometimes swung awkwardly round as I twisted myself among the cliffs. Bennen offered to take it: but he had his own share to carry, and I was resolved to bear mine. Sometimes the rocks alternated with spaces of ice and snow, which we were at intervals compelled to cross; sometimes when the slope was pure ice and very steep, we were compelled to retreat to the highest cliffs. The wall to which I have referred had given way in some places, and through the gaps thus formed the wind rushed with a loud, wild, wailing sound. Through these spaces I could see the entire field of Agassiz's observations; the junction of the Lauteraar and Finsteraar glaciers at the Abschwung, the medial moraine between them, on which stood the Hôtel des Neufchâtelois, and the pavilion built by M. Dollfus, in which Huxley and myself had found shelter two years before. Bennen was evidently anxious to reach the summit, and recommended all observations to be postponed until after our success had been assured. I agreed to this, and kept close at his heels. Strong as he was, he sometimes paused, laid his head upon his mattock, and panted like a chased deer. He complained of fearful thirst, and to quench it we had only my bottle of tea; this we shared loyally, my guide praising its virtues, as well he might. Still the summit loomed above us; still the angry swell of the north wind beating against the torn battlements of the mountains, made wild music. Upward, however, we strained; and at last, on gaining the crest of a rock, Bennen exclaimed, in a jubilant voice, '*Die hochste Spitze!*'—the highest point. In a moment I was at his side, and saw the summit within a few paces of us. A minute or two placed us upon the topmost pinnacle, with the blue dome of heaven above us, and a world of mountains, clouds, and glaciers beneath.

A notion is entertained by many of the guides that if you go to sleep on the summit of any of the highest mountains you will

'Sleep the sleep that knows no waking.'

Bennen did not appear to entertain this superstition, and before starting in the morning I had stipulated for ten minutes' sleep on reaching the summit, as part compensation for the loss of the night's rest. My first act, after casting a glance over the glorious scene beneath us, was to take advantage of this agreement; so I lay down and had five minutes' sleep, from which I rose refreshed and brisk. The sun at first beat down upon us with intense force; and I exposed my thermometers; but thin veils of vapor soon drew themselves before the sun, and denser mists spread over the valley of the Rhone, thus destroying all possibility of concert between Ramsay and myself. I turned, therefore, to my boiling-water apparatus, filled it with snow, melted the first charge, put more in and boiled it, ascertaining the boiling point to be 187° Fahrenheit. On a sheltered ledge, about two or three yards south of the highest point, I placed a minimum thermometer, in the hope that it would enable us in future years to record the lowest winter temperatures at the summit of the mountain.*

It is difficult to convey any just impression of the scene from the summit of the Finsteraarhorn; one might, it is true, arrange the visible mountains in a list, stating their heights and distances, and leaving the imagination to furnish them with peaks and pinnacles, to build the precipices, polish the snow, rend the glaciers, and cap the highest summits with appropriate clouds. But if imagination did its best in this way, it would hardly exceed the reality, and would certainly omit many details which contribute to the grandeur of the scene itself. The various shapes of the mountain—some grand, some beautiful—bathed in yellow sunshine, or lying black and riven under the frown of impervious cumuli; the pure white peaks, cornices, bosses, and amphitheatres; the blue ice-rifts, the stratified snow precipices, the glaciers issuing from the hollows of the eternal hills, and stretching like frozen serpents through the sinuous valleys; the lower cloud-field—itself an empire of vaporous hills—shining with dazzling whiteness, while here and there grim summits, brown by nature, and black by contrast, pierced through it like volcanic islands through a shining sea. Add to this the consciousness of one's position, which clings to one *unconsciously*, that under-current of emotion which surrounds the question of one's personal safety, at a height of more

* This thermometer was found in August 1859, and the reading of the index was —22° Cent.

than 14,000 feet above the sea, and which is increased by the weird, strange sound of the wind surging with the full deep boom of the distant sea against the precipice behind, or rising to higher cadences as it forces itself through the crannies of the weather-worn rocks—all conspire to render the scene from the Finsteraarhorn worthy of the monarch of the Bernese Alps.

My guide at length warned me that we must be moving, repeating the warning more impressively before I attended to it. We packed up, and as we stood beside each other ready to march, he asked me whether we should tie ourselves together, at the same time expressing his belief that it was unnecessary. Up to this time we had been separate, and the thought of attaching ourselves had not occurred to me till he mentioned it. I thought it, however, prudent to accept the suggestion; and so we united our destinies by a strong rope. 'Now,' said Bennen, 'have no fear; no matter how you throw yourself, I will hold you.' Afterwards, on another perilous summit, I repeated this saying of Bennen's to a strong and active guide; but his observation was that it was a hardy untruth, for that in many places Bennen could not have held me. Nevertheless, a daring word strengthens the heart, and though I felt no trace of that sentiment which Bennen exhorted me to banish, and was determined, as far as in me lay, to give him no opportunity of trying his strength in saving me, I liked the fearless utterance of the man, and sprang cheerily after him. Our descent was rapid, apparently reckless, amid loose spikes, boulders and vertical prisms of rock, where a false step would assuredly have been attended with broken bones ; but the consciousness of certainty in our movements never forsook us, and proved a source of keen enjoyment. The senses were all awake, the eye clear, the heart strong, the limbs steady, yet flexible, with power of recovery in store, and ready for instant action should the footing give way. Such is the discipline which a perilous ascent imposes.

We finally quitted the crest of rocks, and got fairly upon the snow once more. We first went downwards at a long swinging trot. The sun having melted the crust which we were compelled to cut through in the morning, the leg at each plunge sank deeply into the snow ; but this sinking was partly in the direction of the slope of the mountains, and hence assisted our progress. Sometimes the crust was hard enough to enable us to glide upon it for long distances while standing erect ; but the end of these glissades was always a plunge and a tumble in the deeper snow. Once upon a steep hard slope Bennen's footing gave way ; he fell, and went down rapidly, pulling me after him. I fell also, but turning quickly, drove the spike of my hatchet into the ice, got good anchorage, and held both fast ;—my success assuring me that I had improved as a mountaineer since my ascent of Mont Blanc. We tumbled so often in the soft snow, and our clothes and boots were so full of it, that we thought we might as well try the sitting posture in gliding down. We did so, and descended with extraordinary velocity, being checked at intervals by a bodily immersion in the softer and deeper snow. I was usually in front of Bennen, shooting down with the speed of an arrow, and feeling the check of the rope when the rapidity of my motion exceeded my guide's estimate of what was safe. Sometimes I was behind him, and darted at intervals with the swiftness of an avalanche right upon him, sometimes in the traverse line with him, with the full length of the rope between us; and here I found its check unpleasant, as it tended to make me roll over. My feet were usually in the air, and it was only necessary to turn them right or left, like the helm of a boat, to change the direction of motion and avoid a difficulty, while a vigorous dig of leg and hatchet into the snow was sufficient to check the motion and bring us to rest. Swiftly, yet cautiously, we glided into the region of crevasses, where we at last rose, quite wet, and resumed our walking, until we reached the point where we had left our wine in the morning, and where I squeezed the water from my wet clothes, and partially dried them in the sun.

We had left some things at the cave of the Faulberg; and it was Bennen's first intention to return that way and take them home with him. Finding, however, that we could traverse the Viescher glacier almost to the Eggischhorn, I made this our highway homewards. At the place where we entered it, and for an hour or two afterwards, the glacier was cut by fissures, for the most part covered with snow. We had packed up our rope; and Bennen admonished me to tread in his steps. Three or four times he half disappeared in the concealed fissures, but by clutching the snow he rescued himself and went on as swiftly as before. Once my leg sank, and the ring of icicles, some fifty feet below, told me that I was in the jaws of a crevasse: my guide turned sharply—it was the only time that I had seen concern on his countenance,—

'*Sie haben meine Tritte nicht gefolgt.*'

'*Doch!*' was my only reply, and we went on. He scarcely ever tried the snow that he crossed, as from its form and color he could in most cases judge of its condition. For a long time we kept at the left-hand side of the glacier, avoiding the fissures, which were now permanently open. We came upon the tracks of a herd of chamois, which had clambered from the glacier up the sides of the Oberaarhorn, and afterwards crossed the glacier to the right-hand side, my guide being perfect master of the ground. His eyes went in advance of his steps; and his judgment was formed before his legs moved. The glacier was deeply fissured; but there was no swerving, no retreating, no turning back to seek more practicable routes; each stride told, and every stroke of the axe was a profitable investment of labor.

We left the glacier for a time, and proceeded along the mountain side, till we came near the end of the Trift glacier, where we let ourselves down an awkward face of rock along the track of a little cascade, and came upon the glacier once more. Here again I had occasion to admire the knowledge and promptness of my guide. The glacier, as is well known, is greatly dislocated, and has once or twice proved a prison to guides and travellers; but Bennen led me through the confusion without a pause. We were sometimes in the middle of the glacier, sometimes on the moraine, and sometimes on the side of the flanking mountain. Towards the end of the day we crossed what seemed to be the consolidated remains of a great avalanche; on this my foot slipped; there was a crevasse at hand, and a sudden effort was necessary to save me from falling into it. In making this effort, the spoke of my axe turned uppermost, and the palm of my hand came down upon it, thus inflicting a very angry wound. We were soon upon the green cliff, having bidden a last farewell to the ice. Another hour's hard walking brought us to our hotel. No one seeing us crossing the Alps would have supposed that we had laid such a day's work behind us; the proximity of home gave vigor to our strides, and our progress was much more speedy than it had been on starting in the morning. I was affectionately welcomed by Ramsay, had a warm bath, dined, went to bed, where I lay locked in sleep for eight hours, and rose next morning as fresh and vigorous as if I had never scaled the Finsteraarhorn.

JOHN TYNDALL, *Glaciers of the Alps.*

IV.

THE PEAK OF MORTERATSCH.

ASCENT IN 1864 BY J. TYNDALL.

TOWARDS the end of last July, while staying at Pontresina, in Ober Engadin, I was invited by two friends to join in an expedition up the Pic Morteratsch. This I willingly did, for I wished to look at the configuration of the Alps from some commanding point in the Bernina mountains, and also to learn something of the capabilities of the Pontresina guides.

We took two of them with us—Jenni, who is the man of greatest repute among them, and Walter, who is the head of the bureau of guides. We proposed to ascend by the Roseg, and to return by the Morteratsch glacier, thus making a circuit, instead of retracing our steps.

About eight hours of pleasant, healthful exertion placed us on the Morteratsch, where we remained for an hour, and where the conviction forced on my mind on many another summit was renewed; namely, that these mountains and valleys are not, as supposed by the renowned President of the Geographical

Society, ridges and heaps tossed up by the earth's central fires, with great fissures between them, but that ice and water, acting through long ages, have been the real sculptors of the Alps.

Jenni is a heavy man, and marches rather slowly up a mountain; but he is a thoroughly competent mountaineer. We were particularly pleased with his performance in descending. He swept down the slope, and cleared the 'schrouds' which cut the upper snows with great courage and skill. We at length reached the point at which it was necessary to quit our morning's track, and immediately afterwards got upon some steep rocks, which were rendered slippery here and there by the water which trickled over them. To our right was a broad couloir, which was once filled with snow, but this had been melted and re-frozen, so as to expose a sloping wall of ice. We were all tied together at this time in the following order:—Jenni led, I came next, then my friend H., our intrepid mountaineer, then his friend L., and last of all the guide Walter. L. had had but little experience of the higher Alps, and was placed in front of Walter, so that any false step on his part might be instantly checked. After descending the rocks for a time, Jenni turned and asked me whether I thought it better to adhere to them, or to try the ice-slope to our right. I pronounced in favor of the rocks; but he seemed to misunderstand me, and turned towards the couloir. I stopped him before he reached it, and said, 'Jenni, you know where you are going, the slope is pure ice?' He replied, 'I know it, but the ice is quite bare for a few yards only. Across this exposed portion I will cut steps, and then the snow which covers the ice will give us footing.' He cut the steps, reached the snow, and descended carefully along it—all following him, apparently in good order. After a little time he stopped, turned, and looked upward at the last three men. He said something about keeping carefully to the tracks, adding that a false step might detach an avalanche. The word was scarcely uttered when I heard the sound of a fall behind me, then a rush, and in the twinkling of an eye my two friends and their guide—all apparently entangled together, whirled past me. I suddenly planted myself to resist their shock, but in an instant I was in their wake, for their impetus was irresistible. A moment afterwards Jenni was whirled away, and thus all of us found ourselves riding downwards with uncontrollable speed on the back of an avalanche which a single slip had originated.

When thrown back by the jerk of the rope, I turned promptly on my face, and drove my baton through the moving snow, seeking to anchor it in the ice underneath. I had held it firmly thus for a few seconds, when I came into collision with some obstacle, and was rudely tossed through the air, Jenni at the same time being shot down upon me. Both of us here lost our batons. We had, in fact, been carried over a crevasse, had hit its lower edge, our great velocity causing us to be pitched beyond it. I was quite bewildered for a moment, but immediately righted myself, and could see those in front of me half buried in the snow, and jolted from side to side by the ruts, among which they were

Avalanche on the peak of Morteratsch.

passing. Suddenly I saw them tumbled over by a lurch of the avalanche, and immediately afterwards found myself imitating their motion. This was caused by a second crevasse. Jenni knew of its existence, and plunged right into it—a brave and manful action, but for the time unavailing. He was over thirteen stone in weight, and he thought that by jumping into the chasm a strain might be put upon the rope sufficient to check the motion. He was, however, violently jerked out of the fissure, and almost squeezed to death by the pressure of the rope.

A long slope was before us, which led directly downwards to a brow where the glacier suddenly fell in a declivity of ice. At the base of this declivity the glacier was cut by a series of profound chasms; and towards these we were now rapidly borne. The three foremost men rode upon the forehead of the avalanche, and were at times almost wholly immersed in the snow; but the moving layer was thinner behind, and Jenni rose incessantly, and with desperate energy drove his feet into the firmer substance underneath. His voice shouting, '*Halt, Herr Jesus, halt!*' was the only one heard during the descent. A kind of condensed memory, such as that described by people who have narrowly escaped drowning, took possession of me; and I thought and reasoned with preternatural clearness as I rushed along. Our start, however, was too sudden, and the excitement too great, to permit of the development of terror. The slope at one place became less steep, the speed visibly slackened, and we thought we were coming to rest; the avalanche, however, crossed the brow which terminated this gentler slope, and regained its motion. Here H. drew his arm round his friend, all hope for the time being extinguished, while I grasped my belt and struggled for an instant to detach myself. Finding this difficult, I resumed the pull upon the rope. My share in the work was, I fear, infinitesimal; but Jenni's powerful strain made itself felt at last. Aided probably by a slight change of inclination, he brought the whole to rest within a short distance of the chasm, over which, had we preserved our speed, a few seconds would have carried us. None of us suffered serious damage. H. emerged from the snow with his forehead bleeding; but the wound was superficial. Jenni had a bit of flesh removed from his hand by collision against a stone; the pressure of the rope had left black welts on my arms; and we all experienced a tingling sensation over the hands, like that produced by incipient frost-bite, which continued for several days. I found a portion of my watch-chain hanging round my neck, another portion in my pocket, the watch itself gone.

This happened on the 30th of July. Two days afterwards I went to Italy, and remained there for ten or twelve days. On the 16th of August I was again at Pontresina, and on that day made an expedition in search of the lost watch. Both the guides and myself thought the sun's heat might melt the snow above it; and I inferred that if its back should happen to be uppermost, the slight absorbent power of gold for the solar rays would prevent the watch from sinking as a stone sinks under like circumstances. The watch would thus be brought quite to the surface, and although a small object, it might possibly be seen from a distance. I was accompanied up the Morteratsch glacier by five friends, of whose conduct I cannot speak too highly. One of them in particular, a member of the British Legislature, sixty-four years of age, exhibited a courage and collectedness in places of real difficulty, which was perfectly admirable.

Two only of the party, both competent mountaineers, accompanied me to the scene of the accident, and none of us ventured on the ice where it originated. Just before stepping on the remains of the avalanche, a stone some tons weight, detached by the sun from the snow-slope above us, came rushing down the line of our glissade. Its leaps became more and more impetuous, and on reaching the brow near which we had been brought to rest it bounded through the air, and with a single spring reached the lower glacier, raising a cloud of ice-dust in the air. Some fragments of rope found upon the snow assured us that we were upon the exact track of the avalanche, and then the search commenced. It had not continued for twenty minutes when a cheer from one of the guides—Christian Michel of Grondelwald—announced the discovery of the watch. It had been brought to the surface in the manner surmised, and on examination seemed to be dry and uninjured. I noticed, moreover, that the position of the hands indicated that it had only run down beneath the snow. I wound it up, hardly hoping, however, to find it capable of responding; but the little creature showed instant signs of animation. It had remained eighteen days in the avalanche, but the application of the key at once restored it to life, and it has gone with unvarying regularity ever since.

JOHN TYNDALL, *Letter to the Times*, 1864.

V.

THE JUNGFRAU.

ASCENT IN 1841 BY L. AGASSIZ, E. DESOR, FORBES, AND DU CHATELLIER.

A GIDDY path follows the edge of the precipice ; you walk between life and death. Two threatening peaks shut in the solitary road. Traverse noislessly this place of terror ; fear to awaken the sleeping avalanche.

The bridge which crosses the frightful abyss, no man would have dared to build. Below, without power to shake it, growls and foams the torrent.

A sombre arch seems to conduct towards the empire of the dead. But beyond appears the laughing country in which the spring marries the autumn. Ah ! if I could but escape the pains and troubles of life by taking refuge in this happy valley.

Four streams, of which the sources are all hidden, precipitate themselves into the plain. They flow towards the four quarters of the world, the west and north, the south and the east. And these boisterous waters seem scarcely to have left their mother before they have fled far off and disappeared in the vast ocean.

Above the multitudes of men, the high peaks tower into the azure sky. There float the cloudy daughters of heaven surrounded by a halo. No terrestrial witness sees their lonely rounds.

On a bright, imperishable throne, sits the queen of mountains, her forehead encircled with diamonds, a cold crown which sparkles beneath the brilliant rays of the sun. SCHILLER.

Before setting out, I will just mention an incident respecting one of our guides, which will serve to show the character of these mountaineers, and will explain at the same time the unlimited confidence that we had in them. Hans Wahren, the friend of Jacob Leuthold, and one of the most intelligent of all the guides of the hotel of the Grimsel, was in our service for more than a month. He was, in some sort, Jacob's lieutenant, and rejoiced in the idea of conducting us to the Jungfrau, because he and Jacob were the only persons who were in the secret of this expedition. But it happened that the evening before the day fixed, in going down with us to the hospice, he was taken with a violent inflammation in the knee, which the doctor considered serious. In spite of the pain which he felt, however, the poor man could not make up his mind to let us start without him. During the two days of delay which occurred, his knee was sensibly relieved, so that on the eve of our departure, he came limping to assure us that he would be able to go with us, making no doubt that he would be cured by the next day. M. Agassiz, as we think properly, refused his consent, setting before him all the dangers to which he would be exposed. The unfortunate Wahren had nothing to object to these reasons; but the bitterest chagrin was painted on his countenance; and seeing that he could not shake us, he retired into a corner of the apartment and wept, whilst his comrades were making preparations for departure. The next day, on entering the servants' room, I was much astonished at meeting there our man at breakfast, with the other guides. As I expressed my surprise, he asked whether it was not then permitted to him to take leave of us. I thanked him for his attention, and again recommended him to take care of his knee; Agassiz did the same, and we set out. We had hardly gon a quarter of a league, when all at once we saw him, against a rock, in company with the other guides. All of us cried out to him at once, asking whether he had really lost his head altogether. We tried once more to turn him from what we judged a fatal project; but in answer he only declared that he had well reflected on the danger which he ran, and that he would rather die than not be one of the party. So we insisted no further, but confined ourselves then to recommending prudence, making many reflections among ourselves on what must have passed in the mind of this man, usually so calm and submissive, before he took such a resolution.

On the 27th of August, at four o'clock in the morning, we started from the Grimsel, itself a height of 6000 feet, and directed our steps towards the upper glacier of the Aar, which is separated from the lower glacier by the mass of the Zinkenstock. We were at the little hillock which rises on the bank of the river, when the first rays of the sun touched the tops of the highest mountains, whilst their bases were still bathed in the twilight whiteness which follows the setting, and precedes the rising of the sun. Among all these summits there was one quite on the horizon, which was peculiarly lighted up; it appeared all on fire. 'What is that peak?' I asked of the guides. And they—whether they thought so, or whether they only used this stratagem in order to increase our ardor, I do not know — immediately answered, 'That is the Jungfrau!' The whole company was, as it were, electrified. We felt our courage increase, and from that moment I no longer doubted of success.

In two hours we reached the extreme point of the glacier of Oberaar; and we were astonished to see that this glacier, which in the preceding year had remained stationary, had this year participated in the progressive movement peculiar to all these glaciers of the Bernese Oberland. It had considerably pushed its moraines forward, particularly its terminal moraine, and its lateral left one; the latter in its encroachments on the side of the valley had completely raised the turf, which was cut up just as if it had been furrowed by a ploughshare.

The ascent furnished us with an opportunity of making many interesting observations on the relation of smooth and whitened rocks to the surface of the glacier. From the top, we descended on to the plateau of snow which feeds the glacier of Viesch. This is a vast circus of more than half a league in diameter, bounded on the north by the immense mass of the Finsteraarhorn, and crowned by ten great peaks, which all bear among the inhabitants of Valais the name of Viescherhörner, and of which the lowest are between 9000 and 10,000 feet high. It was in the midst of this plain that we established ourselves to get our dinner,—a dinner which, frugal though it was, we found delicious, thanks to the appetites which we brought to it.

Afterwards we descended the fields of ice which extend on the south towards the Valais. The snow was perfectly homogeneous, without any trace of fallen rocks, or of foreign bodies on its surface. The crevasses had almost entirely disappeared, or, if there were still any to be seen, it was on the sides of the valley. So we were walking in entire security, as we thought, when we perceived, at a short distance from us, several little openings. Curious to know the cause, we directed our steps in that direction; and what was our astonishment when in looking down into one of these chinks we saw that it hid an immense precipice. And in this precipice there was an azure light which surpassed in beauty, transparency, and softness, all that we had yet seen on the glaciers. Ah! if I only possessed the talent of describing in language worthy of it all the poetry that there was in this combination of snow and of light. Never had I seen any spectacle more attractive; our eyes were so fascinated by it that we did not at first perceive that the crust of snow which covered this enchanting cavern was only in this place some inches in thickness; however, I do not think that we ran a very great risk, for the snow was closely packed together, and the sun had not yet melted it. After contemplating the entrancing effect of this singular phenomenon for some time, we wished to know the cause of it, as well as its nature. It was an immense crevasse of nearly 100 feet wide, and, as we calculated, of about 330 feet deep. In the place in which we examined it, there was no other opening than the little chink of which I have spoken; but further on, it joined a large crevasse which was open on the side of the right bank, and there the light entered, while the intermediate roof tempering the reflection of the divisions of snow, gave them a sweetness and a charm quite indescribable. The divisions of these caves, like immense walls of crystal, were composed of horizontal and parallel strata from three or four inches to three feet in thickness of snow, very much hardened and pressed together, but still crystalline; for it had not yet taken that granulated form which one meets lower down. Between these strata of snow there was usually a little band of ice, but of an ice that was bulbous and not very compact, although of a deeper color than the rest of the divisions. Our guides were all agreed in affirming that each of these layers represents the snow of one year; and this explanation appeared to us the most natural. As to the thin bands of ice which separate the layers of snow, they are doubtless due to the action of the sun, which has shone every summer on the layer of the preceding winter.

In pursuing our route we found a number of other crevasses similar to the one which I have just described; we soon arrived at a certainty that the soil on which we were travelling was entirely mined; for, in looking into an open crevasse, we often saw it prolonged into the interior of the mass, far beyond its superficial limits; but others were open to the surface the whole way.

After having travelled for about an hour over fields of snow, we passed over the *névé*, in which we met with a prodigious quantity of red snow. As the little organisms which compose this red snow are usually accumulated in the greatest numbers just beneath the surface, we, of course, rendered them more apparent by disturbing the ground; so at every step we left, as it were, a trace of blood, which could be seen at a great distance.

It was on the right bank of the glacier, at about three hours' march from the village of Viesch, that we anticipated the most difficult work. It was necessary to descend over a barrier of rock almost vertical and very steep, at the foot of which fell a beautiful cascade. The road was a species of couloir, which presented here and there some slight projections on which we could place our feet. When these points of support were insufficient, we endeavored to cling on the best way we could against the sides of the couloir, helping ourselves with a stick, or making use of the assistance of one of the guides; but this latter was a method to which our *amour-propre* resigned itself as a last resource. When we were out again on the glacier, and could look at the descent which we had just made, it seemed impossible to us that this could be the road which the shepherds ordinarily take. But Jacob assured us that there was no other. We understood still less how they transported their flocks there; and Jacob did not know this himself; yet he maintained that it is this way that they would come up. We informed ourselves about it afterwards at Viesch, where they told us that this is really the only way to the upper pasturage; that they hoist the sheep by means of cords, which they attach to their horns, and in default of horns, to their necks. As for the shepherds, they do not often pass over this road; for, when once the sheep are up, they leave them to themselves until the autumn ; and it is only from time to time that a shepherd goes up to give them the salt which they require.

We had many opportunities of proving, along the glacier of Viesch, the manner in which it wears away and forms its banks. The predominant rock is here still the granite, sometimes composed of fine grains, sometimes of coarse crystals ; which, however, does not prevent it from being in many parts as smooth as polished marble. We remarked in it also, in a very distinct manner, those parallel striæ which constitute one of the distinctive characteristics of the glaze or polish produced by the action of glaciers.

It was four o'clock in the evening when we made the last halt, still on the right bank of the glacier of Viesch, in a spot from whence we could see, for the first time, the bottom of the Valais. We observed from hence several ancient moraines, which extend a long way on the left bank of the glacier, to a height of several inches above its own level. A quantity of loose blocks are scattered to higher levels still, and indeed loose blocks are found up to the summit of the mountain.

We had still two leagues to go. No one was very tired, although we had been on foot for twelve hours ; but a cry of surprise escaped us when, at the turn of the mountain, Jacob showed us the way up which we had to go. It was a very steep slope, about 1,000 feet high, by the edge of which went a little path, and apparently by no means a pleasant one. The look of despair on some faces, and the expression of resignation on others, might have furnished subjects for a capital picture, if there had been an artist among us who was not too much fatigued to draw. However, we arrived at six o'clock in the evening at the châlets of Mörjelen, where we were to pass the night and where the shepherds received us very cordially.

Next day we ascended straight on to the glacier of Aletsch. On the right where it bends we enjoyed a magnificent view in two directions, The Dent Blanche, the Matterhorn, Monte Rosa, and the Strahlhorn, formed a picture on the southwest, whilst before us, on the north, rose the grand peaks of the Jungfrau, the Eiger, and the Monch, which looked so near that they seemed to invite us to persevere.

The glacier of Aletsch is, in general, very smooth; it is of all the glaciers the one which has the slightest inclination. We walked nearly two hours on the compact ice, after which we passed into the region of crevasses, which is the division between the ice and the *névé*. This region is almost a league wide. The *névé*, which succeeds to it, is the finest in Switzerland. It begins about the height of the Faulberg. It may be known from a distance by a certain air of age about it which forms a striking contrast with the dazzling whiteness of the upper snows. It is depressed in the middle and raised at the edges, which is, in fact, an essential characteristic of all *névés*, Crevasses were very rare this year; and we only came across a few very narrow ones. On the fields of snow, which began with the ascent, we made, at half-past nine, the first halt in a place which we called the Repose, because the passage that we had just made, and the immense slopes which rise in front of it, naturally invite one to take rest there.

We found on the first plateau of snow some crevasses which occur frequently just where the slopes begin to be steep. These are, like those of the *névé* of Viesch, crevasses of embankment. We saw some here again which were nearly 100 feet wide; but as they are not very long as well as wide, we were generally able to go round them; but sometimes they were hidden; and, therefore, our guide had to use the utmost circumspection to preserve us from danger; so we got on less quickly than we desired; and, in spite of all the precautions, several of us got slips, but without sustaining any real injury.

We thus scaled several terraces, and directing our steps always to the west, we arrived at a vast opening, commanded on all sides by great peaks, of which the highest was the Jungfrau. Jacob made us halt here a second time, doubtless that he might reconnoitre. As for us, we only saw on all sides difficulties insurmountable. On the right, vertical slopes; on the left, masses of ice which threatened to crush us in their fall; and before us the *rimaye*, or great crevasse, which appeared impassable, it was so gaping. I asked Jacob in what direction we were going to ascend, but he refused to answer me, contented himself with saying that we had only to follow him in all confidence, and that he already

THE JUNGFRAU

saw the road which we must take. Afterwards I saw that he was right to elude my question; for it is very likely that we should never have arrived, if every one had been allowed to give his opinion on the difficult passages.

It was then nearly mid-day; the heat was excessive; and, in order to refresh themselves, our guides applied handfuls of snow on the nape of the neck. Several of us did the same, in spite of the remonstrances of the others, who, alarmed at what appeared imprudence, forgot that in these elevated regions, the material organization, as well as the moral nature, is much more independent of pernicious influences than in the plain. The reflection of the light from the snow was most intense and almost insupportable. In such circumstances one can hardly do without a veil; but there is, on the other side, the great inconvenience of rendering your steps less sure, and of considerably increasing the heat of the face, by hindering the fresh air from getting at it. So Agassiz preferred to expose himself to having his face scorched rather than use one.

We directed our course straight for the great *rimaye*, which we reached after having climbed up a fourth terrace. It is a gulf of an unknown depth, which opens on to the slope of the last terrace but one, and penetrates a little obliquely into the mass of snow: in another place its width is not less than 10 feet, so that there is no way of getting over it but by a ladder. Before passing over, we went to examine the ruins of a fallen mass which was lying on our left, and which appeared to have been detached a little while before; for the impression which it had left in rolling over the surface of the snow was still quite fresh. We saw with interest that the ruins of this avalanche, detached from a peak, of which the height is nearly a thousand feet, were composed of alternate layers of compact blue ice and of white ice, which had the appearance of congealed snow. These different layers were an inch or two in thickness, and alternated three or four times in a block of a cubic yard.

We had now to pass over the great crevasse. Our ladder was nearly 25 feet long, and was, consequently, more than sufficiently large. But immediately above the gulf, the slope of the ground was frightfully rapid, for a space of more than thirty feet. We reckoned the inclination at about 50 degrees. And further, the snow which, up to that point, had been very soft and almost powdery, assumed all at once an excessive hardness, so that the guides were obliged to cut steps. Our courage was ready to sink at the first trial; but Jacob and Jaun mounted first. When they were arrived at about half the distance across, they flung us the rope which they held by one end, and which, fixed by the other to the ladder, served us as a sort of banister. We thus all reached the summit of the terrace, though not without difficulty. The guides themselves, perhaps, exaggerated the dangers of this first passage a little; for they lavished their directions and their support with a liberality which we might have found superfluous, if not injurious, some hours later.

It was two o'clock when we arrived at the Col du Roththal. This defile resembles very much that of the Oberaar; and, like this latter, it is commanded by two very high peaks; the Jungfrau on the north, and the extremity of the Kranzberg on the south. It is several yards wide here. The hanging mists collected in bottom of the Roththal only allowed us some fugitive glances into this wild and rugged valley, which the country people consider to be the abode of a band of turbulent spirits, known under the name of the *Barons of Roththal.*

We calculated the height of the last peak at nearly 1000 feet above our level; and we hoped to ascend it in less than an hour, in spite of its excessive steepness. However, we soon saw that the ascent was more difficult than we had supposed. In place of snow, we only found on all sides compact ice, in which the guides were obliged to cut steps, lest we should slide down; and we had to advance very slowly. So we had ascended for an hour without the peak seeming to be sensibly nearer, when the thickest fog enveloped us; and we could hardly discern from behind those who were at the head of the column.

This was just the steepest point of the ascent. Mr. Forbes, having measured the inclination, found it to be 45°. The ice was so hard and impenetrable that for a little while we could not make more than fifteen steps in a quarter of an hour. The cold also was so intense, that there was reason to fear that we should get our feet frozen, in spite of all our care to give them as much motion as possible. Seeing then that our position began to be really critical, Agassiz asked Jacob if he hoped that we should ever arrive at the top. The latter replied to him with his habitually calm manner, that he had never doubted it, and at the cry of '*Vorwärts!*' (Forward) we again set ourselves to mount with the same ardor as at the beginning. One, however, of the guides had quitted us, not having been able longer to bear the sight of the precipices to the right of us; and truly the road which we had to follow was enough to frighten any one who was not sure of his head and his legs. This last ridge, which is in form like a vertical section of an inclined cone, commands on the east those fields of snow which we had just crossed, and on the west the *névé* of the Roththal. The inclination is, however, rather more on the west than on the east, for the fragments of ice broken off by the strokes of the hatchet always rolled into the latter valley. As we had no time to lose, we went up quite straight without making any zigzag. It was also the most rational and the surest method; for, by the laws of mechanics, one has much more strength when one bears on the toes and turns the face forwards, than when one goes up obliquely; so that if unfortunately one of us had slipped, it would not have been impossible for the others to hold him up, whilst in the other case it would have been at least very difficult. And further, Jacob made us walk on the edge of the ridge; because the ice was generally rather less hard there, which accelerated our ascent a little. The result was that we had the precipice constantly under our eyes, only being separated from it by a sloping roof of snow. Several times, in putting my stick out a little further than usual, I felt it go through this snow, which was in some places only about a foot and a half thick; and we could then, if the fog had happened to clear away for a few moments, look through these holes made by the stick on to the vast table land beneath our feet. Far from dissuading us from this exercise, the guides rather encouraged us in it, at least all who were not liable to giddiness; and I believe that truly it was a good way of giving us assurance.

But the fog still hung round the summit, and we only had a clear view of the east over the Eiger, the Mönch, and the peaks which enclose the glaciers of the Oberaar and of the Unteraar. Already we had begun to despair of enjoying the spectacle which our imagination tried to paint, when all at once the veil of clouds withdrew, and, as if touched by our perseverance, the Jungfrau showed herself to our astonished eyes in all the beauty of her mighty and majestic form. I leave you to fancy what delight we felt at the sight of this unexpected change! It was a sort of picture of life, if I mistake not. *Audaces fortuna juvat.*

After having ascended still for some time in the same direction, we turned suddenly to the left, in order to reach a place where the rock was bare, crossing thus the inclined surface of the demi-cone, of which the breadth is here still about 25 feet. During this little crossing, the summit remained hidden from us; and when we arrived at the rocky place we saw, as by magic, at some steps from us, the culminating point, which, until then, had seemed to flee from us in proportion as we rose higher. Of thirteen of us who left the chalets de Mörjelen, eight of us were about to succeed in our attempt; MM. Agassiz, Forbes, Du Châtelier, and myself, accompanied by four guides, Jacob Leuthold, Michel Baunholzer, Johannes Ablanalp, and Hans Jaun, from Meyringen. Switzerland, England, France, and Germany, were thus represented in this ascent.

Here, for the first time, we beheld the Swiss plain. We were on the western border of the section of the cone, having at our feet the mass which separates the valleys of Lauterbrunnen from those of Grindewald. From this moment the scene appeared to us entirely changed, and the mass which had seemed to shrink as we rose, looked larger now by all the height we had gained. Quite close to the rocky place the mountain forms a little elbow at ten feet below the highest point. This is at the same time the limit of the ice, which, higher up, gives place anew to the snow, or rather to a coarse-grained *névé*. We saw, with a sort of fear, that the space which separated us from the highest point was a sharp ridge of from, perhaps, two-thirds of a foot to rather over a foot in width only, for the distance of about twenty feet; while the sides, both right and left, sloped at an inclination of 60 or 70 degrees. 'There is no way of reaching it,' said Agassiz; and this was the opinion of nearly all. Jacob, on the contrary, asserted that there was no difficulty, and that we should all go up. Putting down the things which he carried, he set forward, passing his stick over the ridge, so as to have the latter under his right arm, and thus walked along the eastern slope, crushing the snow as much as possible under his feet, so as to make our road easier. He thus, in an instant, and without difficulty, reached the peak. So much courage and *sang-froid* re-animated our courage, and when he returned for us no one ventured to refuse.

The summit is a very small space, about two feet long by a foot and a half wide. It is in the form of a triangle, with the base turned towards the Swiss plain. As there was not room for more than one, each went in turn. Agassiz ascended first, supported on the arm of Jacob who preceded him. He remained about five minutes, and when he rejoined us I saw that he was very much agitated; and, in fact, he confessed to me that he had never felt such emotion. It was my turn next; I experienced no difficulty in crossing, but when I was at the summit I could, no more than Agassiz, repress the most lively emotion in presence of such a spectacle of surpassing grandeur. I also only remained a few minutes, but long enough to remove all fear that the panorama of the Jungfrau would ever be effaced from my memory.

It is not the vast field which the eyes embrace which is the charm of these mountains. Already in the preceding year, on the Col de la Strahleck, we had had experience which taught us that distant views are generally rather indistinct. Here, on the summit of the Jungfrau, the forms of the far-off mountains appeared still less defined. But had they been as clear as is the line of the Jura when seen from an eminence in the plain, I believe that our eyes would not have rested long on them, so much were they fascinated by the spectacle which our immediate neighborhood offered. Before us was extended the Swiss plain, and at our feet were stretched the anterior chains which, by their apparent uniformity, appeared to set off the great peaks which rose almost to our level. At the same time, the valleys of the Oberland, which at the moment of our arrival were enveloped in light mists, discovered themselves in several places, and permitted us to see, through the breaks in them, the world below. We distinguished on the right, the Valley of Grindelwald; on the left, in the depth, an immense crevasse, and at the bottom of the latter a light line which seemed to follow its windings. This was the Valley of Lauterbrunnen, with the Lutschine river running through it. But, above all, the Eiger and the Mönch attracted our attention. We had some difficulty in realizing that these were the same peaks which seem nearer to heaven than to the earth when one sees them from the plain. Here we contemplated them from above, and their great proximity permitted us, in some sort, to observe them in detail, for we were only separated from them by the extent of the Névé d'Aletsch. Opposite, on the western side, rose another peak less colossal, but more graceful, the sides of which being entirely clothed with snow, it has obtained the name of Silberhorn (Silver Peak). However, in the same direction we discovered several other peaks in like manner crowned with snow, of which the nearest and most pointed appeared to us to be the Gletscherhorn. These summits formed the immediate cortége of the Jungfrau, which rises like a queen in the midst of them. Beyond the Eiger and the Mönch, in the eastern direction the great masses which surround the glaciers of Finsteraar and of Lauteraar, form another group still more extensive and severe-looking than that in the midst of which we were placed. These were the Viescherhörner, the Oberaarhorn, the Schreckhörner, the Berglistock, the Wetterhörner, and, in the centre, the Finsteraarhorn, the highest mountain of Switzerland, which, alone amongst them all, rose above our level, and whose steep and rocky sides seemed to defy our ambition.

On the south the view was contracted by the clouds which had accumulated for several hours over the chain of Monte Rosa. But this inconvenience was more than compensated by a very extraordinary phenomenon which was presented to our eyes and which interested us exceedingly. Thick fogs appeared, as it were, massed together on our left, in a southwesterly direction. They rose from the base of the Roththal, and began to extend to the north, over the mass which separates this valley from that of Lauterbrunnen. We were already beginning to fear that they would a second time come over us, when their progress was suddenly stopped, no doubt from the effect of some current of the plain, which prevented them from coming further in this direction. Thanks to this circumstance, we found ourselves, all at once, before a vertical wall of fog, the height of which must have been over 12,000 feet at least, for it penetrated to the bottom of the Valley of Lauterbrunnen and rose much above our heads. As the temperature was down to freezing point, the little drops of mist were transformed into icy crystals, and reflected in the sun all the colors of the rain-bow; so that one might have said that a golden mist sparkled around us.

It was more than four o'clock when we again put ourselves *en route*. And now came the difficult part; for if the ascent had been perilous what must the descent be! I am quite sure of this,—that when we measured with our eyes the immense declivity that we had to get down, more than one of us would have been very glad to have been already at the bottom. It was too steep to think of walking in the usual way, so we had to descend backwards. I confess that the first steps caused me a little uneasiness; for, as we had not—that is, Agassiz and I—guides before us to direct our steps, we were obliged constantly to look between our legs to find the cuttings, which made the way appear more giddy than it might otherwise have done. But some moments sufficed to get used to this; and such was the regularity of the cuttings, that, after having taken some hundred of steps, we could, if necessary, have trusted to our feet, and have dispensed with looking at them at all. Yet the steepness of the descent was almost always the same, oscillating between 40 and 45 degrees, that is to say, much the same as that of the roofs of our Gothic cathedrals. There was, indeed, one place in which it must have been about 47 degrees. But in spite of this excessive steepness, we did not take more than an hour in reaching the Col de Roththal, for it was about five when we arrived there.

There remained still six leagues to make before we could regain our chalets; so that, as we had foreseen, we should have to cross that part of the glacier which was most full of crevasses by night. However, no one seemed at all uneasy about it, and the moon was not late in rising, while the clouds had almost entirely disappeared from the horizon. We marched at a quickened pace for three hours over the *névé* which succeeded the plateau of snow; and that part was accomplished without difficulty, for the *névé* here has a smooth surface, so that it is as easy to walk on it as on a highroad. And it was scarcely dark when we saw the moon right in front of us.

We were then at the height of the two passes which I have mentioned, that of Lötsch on the west, and that which conducts into the *névé* of Viesch on the east. The moon was just in the axis of the glacier, so that all this great sea of ice was uniformly illuminated, and reflected a light much softer than that of the sun, from which we had suffered so much during the day. The entrances of the two passes of Lötsch and Viesch presented a truly magical effect; for, as they are at right angles with the direction of the glacier, the mountains which bound them on the south project into them shadows of a fantastic grandeur, whilst the heavy clouds collected behind the Aletschhorn, gave to the picture all the vigor worthy of such a subject. Add to this, that there was a perfect calm in the atmosphere, and that an absolute silence reigned around us, and it will be understood that we still felt extreme pleasure in gazing on this wonderful spectacle, notwithstanding that all day we had been looking on prospects of marvellous splendor.

Very soon we entered the region of crevasses. Then we judged it prudent to have recourse to the cord again; for although the light of the moon was very lovely, it was not sufficiently strong to enable us always to discern precisely when we were on old snow and when on that which had recently fallen, especially during the first quarter of an hour. In fact, we all made summersaults by turns, the guides as well as ourselves. There was, indeed, one moment in which we began to feel really uneasy as to the issue of this crossing; for at almost every step one or another had to be drawn out of a crevasse. However, by degrees, we learnt to avoid them, and we completed this part of the journey without any serious accident.

After having made a good supper we once more put ourselves *en route* for the last stage. There remained before us about three leagues, but excepting these crevasses which we had still to leap, the way was easy, and we arrived, before we suspected that we were so near, at the Lake of Mörjelen. Here we made a last halt in order that we might thoroughly admire a magnificent spectacle. The blocks of floating ice which swam on the surface of the water glistened beautifully in the moonlight; while at the same time the edge of the glacier appeared like an immense wall of crystal, and then what added to the beauty of the scene was, that arriving just at the time when the moon was about to pass behind the mountain mass which headed the lake we saw in a quarter of an hour effects of light and contrasts the most various. It was a worthy ending to such a day.

E. Desor.

VI.

THE GALENSTOCK.

ASCENT IN 1845 BY MM. E. DESOR, DOLLFUS-AUSSET, AND DANIEL DOLLFUS.

ALL who have visited the Oberland and are possessed of the least observation, even among ordinary tourists, must have remarked, in the midst of the numerous bold and steep peaks, a mountain distinguished from the others by its rounded form, which represents a magnificent cupola of snow. This is the Galenstock (15,853 feet high), which stands right over the splendid glacier of the Rhone, at the culminating point of the chain which separates the Valais from the canton of Uri. I had several times conceived the project of going to study it on the spot, and had conversed with the most experienced guides on the subject; but they, without combating the idea, had, nevertheless, never seemed disposed to encourage it; not that they thought the mountain too high or too steep, but on account of its peculiar form.

'You must take notice,' said Jacob Leuthold to me, 'that this is a mountain by itself. It has an inclined slope of ice uninterrupted for more than

FALL OF M. DOLLFUS DOWN THE GALENSTOCK.

3000 feet, which we could only scale by cutting steps the whole way. In a case of necessity this might be done; but on a hot day we should run the risk of finding these steps melted on our return. And you know that to cut others in descending and backwards would be no easy matter. Still there is one way of doing the thing,' he added, after an instant's reflection, 'we might try it some day after a heavy snow, in August or September.'

The brave Leuthold was not, however, to have the satisfaction. He died the same year; and for a long while no one spoke of the Galenstock.

It was in 1845 that an opportunity presented itself of reviving the project of ascent which seemed to have been forgotten. One day, when we had been interrupted in the course of our observations by one of those violent tempests which sometimes break suddenly over the higher valleys,* we were obliged to beat a retreat, and it was not without difficulty that we reached the Grimsel. Hardly had we arrived at the hospice when the weather suddenly

---

* Mr. Tuckett writes to the "Alpine Journal" in 1865: "I left Geschenen at 3:30 A.M. on the 16th of July, with Christian and Peter Michel of Grindelwald, and, after a charming walk through lovely scenery and amidst magnificent specimens of glacier action, found myself, at 6:20, at the little collection of houses called the Geschenen Alp (near the Galenstock). Here the curé was taking his morning walk, and I took the opportunity of a halt for breakfast to have a little chat with him. He stated that the Alp was inhabited all the year round: that last winter had been a *remarkably* mild one, as the snow had *only* lain twenty-five feet deep, instead of covering the chapel altogether, and rising above the eaves of his house, as usual."

cleared up. To the tempestuous day succeeded a superb and perfectly calm evening. But the snow had fallen in too great a quantity to permit us immediately to resume our studies, and we met on the steps of the old hospice, and were deploring together that we were prevented from taking advantage of such fine weather, when our principal guide, he who had taken Jacob Leuthold's place, drew me aside.

'You remember what Jacob said to you two years ago? Poor Jacob, if he could have been here now!'

'What would happen then?' I asked him.

'Why, we would go to-morrow ——'

'Where?'

'To the Galenstock. Now is the time or never,' he added; 'for there must be at least some feet of snow up there; if we set out early before the thaw begins we should mount without any difficulty; and as to the descent, why we would make a grand sledge party of it. What do you think of it?'

I went at once to consult with MM. Dollfus, father and son, and, after some consideration, it was decided that we should make the attempt. The instruments which we expected to want were packed up at once, the provisions prepared, and M. Dollfus brought out a roll of stuff, of which he had always a stock, that he might cut out a flag which was to float from the top of the Galenstock.

Next day, the 18th of August, at three o'clock in the morning, we set out on the road towards the Col du Grimsel. The company was composed of eight persons, M. Dollfus-Ausset, his son Daniel, and myself, accompanied by five guides. At four o'clock we had reached the elevation of the Col, the summit of which is occupied by the Lac des Morts. The sky was without a cloud, and the chain of Monte Rosa appeared like an immense fire of red-hot coals in the brilliant morning tints, whilst the lower chains allowed us to see over their valleys that transparent halo which our celebrated landscape-painter, Calame, has so happily depicted in the splendid painting of Monte Rosa, which is so much admired in the museum of Neufchatel.

From the first plateau we descended by an easy slope, though a somewhat steep one, on to the upper part of the glacier of the Rhone, which we crossed without any difficulty, taking care, however, to attach ourselves to one another, on account of the crevasses hidden by the fresh snow. The glacier once crossed, we soon reached the mass of the Galenstock itself, directing our steps zigzag towards the lower part of the ridge. The snow was frozen, and only yielded an inch or two under our feet. Without causing any fatigue, it just gave way enough to afford secure footing. It was not ten o'clock when we reached the depression in question, which we have designated by the name of the Col de Galen. The view which one has from this point is imposing; it embraces, on one side, the great chain of the Finsteraarhorn and its deep valleys; on the other, the upper part of the valley of Realp, which is passed through in going from Andermatt to La Furka.

We took our way at eleven o'clock towards the culminating point, ascending a very gentle slope along the ridge, but keeping a certain distance from the edge; for we had observed that, in the line of the principal declivity, the snow overhung the edge of the wall of rocks in several places. Never has any ascent of a high mountain been effected more easily and merrily than this. We might have been taken for a troop of school-boys going up the Naye or the Chasseral rather than for a party of naturalists making the conquest of a virgin peak of the Alps. On reaching the top I gave way to M. Dollfus, junior, that he might have the satisfaction of planting the standard and taking possession, in some sort, in the name of Science, of a point on which the foot of man had not yet trodden.

In a picturesque point of view we had occasion to verify, once more, the truth of a remark which we had often made; for we were more than ever convinced that the charm of the views, from great elevations, consists much more in the details of the nearer points of interest than in the extent of the panorama which lies beneath the eye. That which fascinates is the sublime chaos of sharp ridges and pointed peaks in the midst of the vast fields of snow, of broken arches and detached pieces, out of which the most experienced eye seeks in vain to reconstruct the original chain. Then there are the contrasts of light and shade which set these objects off in high relief. Here was, first, that deep crevasse of the Valley of the Aar, and that other, not less sombre, in which the Rhone plays his first frolics on leaving the glacier; then, on the plateau between the two valleys, were those two rounded rocks, stretching out their polished surfaces, the witnesses of the ancient abodes of glaciers. There were, lastly, a little further on, the giants of the Alps, with their steep sides and toothed and rugged summits, seeming like old acquaintances, who recalled to us the happiest moments of our Alpine life,—amongst others, the Schreckhorn, on the top of which we still perceived the staff of the standard which I had planted there in 1842, with my friend, Escher de la Linth; and a little further on, to the right, the three twin peaks of the Wetterhorn, which we had visited together in the preceding year, and of which one, the Rosenhorn, also retained tokens of our visit. We found ourselves, further, surrounded with the same guides who had accompanied us up these different mountains, and who enjoyed not less than ourselves this grand spectacle. They found, above all, a great charm in recalling to each other, and to us, all the incidents of our different ascents, from the Jungfrau to the Galenstock, and in reviewing the difficulties encountered, and the dangers which we had run on each of these summits.

It was nearly one o'clock when we set off again. The snow was considerably softened on the declivities exposed to the sun, so much so that we sank knee-deep into it. On one side the slope was not sufficient in the direction which we had to go to permit us to slide. 'We wanted,' as the guides said, 'horses to the sledge;' an expression which they use when they take their masters by the legs and run down the side of a mountain with them.

We were now approaching the place where we had reason to believe that the snow sloped over the rocks. So we took care, for greater safety, to follow exactly our morning's track. We marched in a file, the guide Jaun being at the head of the column. I followed him at some paces back : then came M. Dollfus, junior ; after him three other guides, and at some distance behind, M. Dollfus, senior, accompanied by the fifth guide. Merry and light-hearted we chatted about our good fortune, and about the surprise which the sight of our standard would cause to the tourists and guides of the Oberland, as it floated on the summit of the inaccessible peak of the Galenstock, when, all at once, I saw a fissure in the ground open before me and split with the rapidity of lightning. I shall have ever before my mind's eye the spectacle of this gulf with its azure walls, though they only remained so for the twinkling of an eye, the time it takes for the side of a mountain to sink. The cleft, which had grazed my left foot in splitting, had passed between the legs of the guide who preceded me. Whether by instinct or by accident he had thrown himself on to the side of the mountain. Not a cry, not a sound escaped from my mouth during this scene. But when I turned to inquire of my companions I saw all faces horror-struck. They were not there in full number. At two steps behind me a stick was hanging over the abyss, but he who carried it had disappeared, borne away with the part of the mountain which had just broken off. M. Dollfus, who was at a little distance, did not immediately understand the cause of the agitation. He was going to exhort us to be prudent, when he discovered that the party was no longer complete. And certainly, in presence of such a discovery, the emotion of a father needs neither excuse nor explanation. The one who was missing was his son!

Before we had time to collect ourselves, we were enveloped in a thick cloud of snow: this was, as it were, the dust of the fallen mass, which came over us like a whirlwind. It would be difficult to say what happened to us while in these circumstances. We expected every instant while this was going on to see another portion of the side of the mountain give way and draw us, in our turn, into the gulf, and a thousand plans and recollections rushed at once into my mind. What must then have passed through the soul of him whom we regarded as already a victim!

Little by little, however, I cannot possibly say in what space of time, the thick clouds of snow began to grow lighter, so that they permitted us to discern some forms. Hope also began to rekindle in us when we saw that no new crevasses were opening. I then immediately went to the edge of the precipice and stretched myself at full length on the snow, having first fastened round my waist a girdle with which M. Dollfus was always furnished, in order that the guides might, if necessary, draw me up again, if, from the weight of my body, another piece should detach itself from the side. I cannot describe the anxiety with which M. Dollfus, the father, followed me with his eyes, or how many times he asked whether I did not see some trace of his son. At first I saw nothing except an enormous mass of moving snow at a depth of more than 3000 feet below me. This was the mass which had fallen which was precipitating itself like an avalanche into the Valley of Gorschen, above Réalp. After some instants, however, I thought that through the mist, and almost perpendicularly beneath me, just in the track of the avalanche, I could perceive a dark object. Was it he? I did not yet dare to believe it; above all, I did not dare to answer affirmatively to all the questions asked by the guides. Soon, however, I had no doubt. It was my friend's hat and part of his shoulder which I saw. Another question, not less urgent, was to know whether he were living or dead. It was M. Dollfus who asked this time. It would have been very sweet to me, as may be imagined, to perceive, at this moment, a sign of life in him on whom I kept my eyes fixed, and to be able to reply at once to the despairing father, 'Your son lives!' But how could I nourish such a hope? It appeared to me that without a miracle he must have been crushed or smothered by the snow; yet still it was a sort of miracle that instead of being drawn down by the avalanche, he had remained there, so near the surface, at about eighty feet below us. A few moments afterwards I thought that I really could perceive a movement. He was not then dead! The impression which this discovery produced may be imagined. But what will not be understood, what will scarcely be believed, is the devotion of which one of the guides at this moment gave proof. Hardly had I articulated those words, 'He lives!' than Hans Wahren, the chosen guide of M. Dollfus, precipitated himself over the edge of the crevasse. We all uttered a cry of terror when we saw him disappear. Happily he fell into the snow of the avalanche only thirty feet from the top, and as this snow was very soft, he sank so deeply that it was impossible for him to disengage himself.

In the meanwhile, young M. Dollfus had begun to recover from the stun which the fall had caused. He made an effort to look up, and when he perceived me at the top of the precipice his first thought, as may be conceived, was for his father. The news that his father was safe and sound, and that he had not been drawn down like himself, restored his courage. He tried to rise, when he perceived that he had not the use of his right arm. Was it broken or put out of joint? He could not tell yet. 'But broken or dislocated it is nothing,' he cried to us, 'since there is no one hurt but me.'

How then did it happen that he had stopped in his fall at such a comparatively small distance? The fact was that in this long and abrupt slope of the Galenstock there was one isolated point of rock, a sort of little rocky pyramid, and against this that part of the fallen mass struck on which M. Dollfus was. A portion of the snow remained there, and in it he whom it had drawn with it in its fall. If he had been in any other part of this great mass he must infallibly have been drawn with the avalanche, and would not have been long in disappearing amidst its gigantic heaps.

We had now to consider what means we should take to rescue M. Dollfus from this position. And we did not exactly see what to do. We knew, however, one thing, which was that we were not going to return without him. But our guides, generally so calm in the presence of danger, were completely at a loss now. There was no way of effecting our descent down the declivity which the avalanche had taken. It was therefore indispensable to draw M. Dollfus up again. But between him and us there was first a vertical wall of over thirty feet, the edge of the crumbled *névé*, then a very steep slope representing a height of some fifty feet.

In order to proceed with as much method as possible, we fastened a cord round one of the guides and let him down thirty feet to the place where his comrade Wahren was stuck fast; and first he assisted him to get free, after which they endeavored to descend by one of those tricks of which only the chamois-hunters have the secret, and which consists in finding the exact spots in which the snow is sufficiently firm to bear a man's weight.

They managed this by dint of address and patience, and by literally clinging to the snow, to reach M. Dollfus, whom they had in the first place almost to disinter. But when they had got him out, they discovered with dismay that he had not only an injured arm, but that his leg also was so much hurt that it could do him no service. And how then could a man in such a state be raised up an acclivity of 60 and sometimes 70 degrees. Had it been a descent the thing would have been impossible; but there are always more resources for an ascent. So our two brave men manœuvred so well that they got M. Dollfus to the top of the slope. They then fastened the cord round him, and we drew him up to us, taking care to pull the cord over our sticks which we had placed over the edge of the precipice. We employed the same means to raise the two guides, who arrived safe and sound at the top.

Several long hours had passed in this search, and these efforts to recover him whom we had thought lost. When we were all once more together again on the top of the precipice, the sun was already visibly sinking over the Finsteraarhorn. M. Dollfus was unable to walk, so one of the guides took him on his back and carried him to the Col de Galen. It was there that we meant to take some refreshment, because then only could we believe ourselves entirely out of danger.

E. Desor.

VII.

THE MATTERHORN.

A SOLITARY SCRAMBLE IN 1862.

SUNDAY, the 6th of July, was showery, and snow fell on the Matterhorn, but we started on the following morning with our three men, and pursued my route of the previous year. I was requested to direct the way, as none save myself had been on the mountain before; but I did not distinguish myself on this occasion, and led my companions nearly to the top of the small peak before the mistake was discovered. The party becoming rebellious, a little exploration was made towards our right, and we found we were upon the top of the cliff overlooking the Col du Lion. The upper part of the small peak is of a very different character to the lower part; the rocks are not so firm, and they are usually covered, or intermixed with snow, and glazed with ice: the angle too is more severe. While descending a small snow-slope, to get on to the right track, Kronig slipped on a streak of ice, and went down at a fearful pace. Fortunately he kept on his legs, and, by a great effort, succeeded in stopping just before he arrived at some rocks that jutted through

THE MATTERHORN.

the snow, which would infallibly have knocked him over. When we rejoined him a few minutes later, we found that he was incapable of standing, much less moving, with a face corpse-like in hue, and trembling violently. He remained in this condition for more than an hour, and the day was consequently far advanced before we arrived at our camping-place on the Col. Profiting by the experience of last year, we did not pitch our tent actually on the snow, but collected a quantity of débris from the neighboring ledges, and after constructing a rough platform of the larger pieces, levelled the whole with the dirt and mud.

* * * * * * * * * *

Three times I had essayed the ascent of this mountain, and on each occasion had failed ignominiously. I had not advanced a yard beyond my predecessors. Up to the height of nearly 13,000 feet there were no extraordinary difficulties; the way so far might even become "a matter of amusement." Only 1800 feet remained; but they were as yet untrodden, and might present the most formidable obstacles. No man could expect to climb them by himself. A morsel of rock only seven feet high might at any time defeat him, if it were perpendicular. Such a place might be possible to two, or a bagatelle to three men. It was evident that a party should consist of three men at least. But where could the other two men be obtained? Carrel was the only man who exhibited any enthusiasm in the matter; and he, in 1861, absolutely refused to go unless the party consisted of at least *four* persons.

Want of men made the difficulty, not the mountain. The weather became bad again, so I went to Zermatt on the chance of picking up a man, and remained there during a week of storms. Not one of the good men, however, could be induced to come, and I returned to Breil on the 17th, hoping to combine the skill of Carrel with the willingness of Meynet on a new attempt, by the same route as before; for the Hörnli ridge, which I had examined in the meantime, seemed to be entirely impracticable. Both men were inclined to go, but their ordinary occupations prevented them from starting at once.

My tent had been left rolled up at the second platform, and whilst waiting for the men it occurred to me that it might have been blown away during the late stormy weather; so I started off on the 18th to see if this were so or not. The way was by this time familiar, and I mounted rapidly, astonishing the friendly herdsmen—who nodded recognition as I flitted past them and the cows—for I was alone, because no man was available. But more deliberation was necessary when the pastures were passed, and climbing began, for it was needful to mark each step, in case of mist, or surprise by night. It is one of the few things which can be said in favor of mountaineering alone (a practice which has little besides to commend it), that it awakens a man's faculties, and makes him observe. When one has no head to guide him except his own, he must needs take note even of small things, for he cannot afford to throw away a chance; and so it came to pass, upon my solitary scramble, when above the snow-line, and beyond the ordinary limits of flowering plants, when peering about noting angles and landmarks, that my eyes fell upon the tiny straggling plants—oftentimes a single flower on a single stalk—pioneers of vegetation, atoms of life in a world of desolation, which had found their way up—who can tell how?—from far below, and were obtaining bare sustenance from the scanty soil in protected nooks; and it gave a new interest to the well-known rocks to see what a gallant fight the survivors made (for many must have perished in the attempt) to ascend the great mountain. The Gentian, as one might have expected, was there, but it was run close by Saxifrages, and by *Linaria alpina*, and was beaten by *Thlaspi rotundifolium*, which latter plant was the highest I was able to secure, although it too was overtopped by a little white flower which I knew not, and was unable to reach.

The tent was safe, although snowed up; and I turned to contemplate the view, which, when seen alone and undisturbed, had all the strength and charm of complete novelty. The highest peaks of the Pennine chain were in front—the Breithorn (13,685 feet), the Lyskamm (14,889), and Monte Rosa (15,217); then, turning to the right, the entire block of mountains which separated the Val Tournanche from the Val d'Ayas was seen at a glance, with its dominating summit the Grand Tournalin (11,155). Behind were the ranges dividing the Val d'Ayas from the Valley of Gressoney, backed by higher summits. More still to the right, the eye wandered down the entire length of the Val Tournanche, and then rested upon the Graian Alps with their innumerable peaks, and upon the isolated pyramid of Monte Viso (12,643) in the extreme distance. Next, still turning to the right, came the mountains intervening between the Val Tournanche and the Val Barthelemy: Mont Rouss (a round-topped snowy summit, which seems so important from Breil, but which is in reality only a buttress of the higher mountain, the Château des Dames), had long ago sunk, and the eye passed over it, scarcely heeding its existence, to the Becca Salle (or, as it is printed on the map, Bec de Sale),—a miniature Matterhorn—and to the other, and more important heights. Then the grand mass of the Dent d'Hérens (13,714) stopped the way; a noble mountain, encrusted on its northern slopes with enormous hanging glaciers, which broke away at mid-day in immense slices, and thundered down on to the Tiefenmatten glacier; and lastly, most splendid of all, came the Dent Blanche (14,318), soaring above the basin of the great Z'Muttgletscher. Such a view is hardly to be matched in the Alps, and *this* view is very rarely seen, as I saw it, perfectly unclouded.

Time sped away unregarded, and the little birds which had built their nests on the neighbouring cliffs had begun to chirp their evening hymn before I thought of returning. Half mechanically I turned to the tent, unrolled it, and set it up; it contained food enough for several days, and I resolved to stay over the night. I had started from Breil without provisions, or telling Favre—the innkeeper, who was accustomed to my erratic ways—where I was going. I returned to the view. The sun was setting, and its rosy rays, blending with the snowy blue, had thrown a pale, pure violet far as the eye could see; the valleys were drowned in a purple gloom, while the summits shone with unnatural brightness; and as I sat in the door of the tent, and watched the twilight change to darkness, the earth seemed to become less earthy and almost sublime; the world seemed dead, and I, its sole inhabitant. By and by, the moon as it rose brought the hills again into sight, and by a judicious repression of detail rendered the view yet more magnificent. Something in the south hung like a great glow-worm in the air; it was too large for a star, and too steady for a meteor; and it was long before I could realize the incredible fact that it was the moonlight glittering on the great snow-slope on the north side of Monte Viso, at a distance, as the crow flies, of 98 miles. Shivering, at last I entered the tent and made my coffee. The night was passed comfortably, and the next morning, tempted by the brilliancy of the weather, I proceeded yet higher up in search of another place for a platform.

The rocks of the southwest ridge are by no means difficult for some distance above the Col du Lion. This is true of the rocks up to the level of the Chimney, but they steepen when that is passed, and remaining smooth and with but few fractures, and still continuing to dip outwards, present some steps of a very uncertain kind, particularly when they are glazed with ice. At this point (just above the Chimney) the climber is obliged to follow the southern (or Breil) side of the ridge, but, in a few feet more, one must turn over to the northern (or Z'Mutt) side, where, in most years, nature kindly provides a snow-slope. When this is surmounted, one can again return to the crest of the ridge, and follow it, by easy rocks, to the foot of the Great Tower. This was the highest point attained by Mr. Hawkins in 1860, and it was also our highest on the 9th of July.

This Great Tower is one of the most striking features of the ridge. It stands out like a turret at the angle of a castle. Behind it a battlemented wall leads upwards to the citadel. Seen from the Theodule pass, it looks only an insignificant pinnacle, but as one approaches it (on the ridge) so it seems to rise, and when one is at its base, it completely conceals the upper parts of the mountain. I found here a suitable place for the tent; which, although not so well protected as the second platform, possessed the advantage of being 300 feet higher up; and fascinated by the wildness of the cliffs, and enticed by the perfection of the weather, I went on to see what was behind.

The first step was a difficult one; the ridge became diminished to the least possible width—it was hard to keep one's balance—and just where it was narrowest, a more than perpendicular mass barred the way. Nothing fairly within arm's reach could be laid hold of; it was necessary to spring up, and then to haul one's-self over the sharp edge by sheer strength. Progression directly upwards was then impossible. Enormous and appalling precipices plunged down to the Tiefenmatten glacier on the left, but round the righthand side it was just possible to go. One hindrance then succeeded another, and much time was consumed in seeking the way. I have a vivid recollection of a gully of more than usual perplexity at the side of the Great Tower, with minute ledges and steep walls; of the ledges dwindling down and at last ceasing; and of finding myself, with arms and legs divergent, fixed as if crucified, pressing against the rock, and feeling each rise and fall of my chest as I breathed; of screwing my head round to look for hold, and not seeing any, and of jumping sideways on to the other side.

* * * * * * * * * *

This long digression has been caused by an innocent gully which I feared the reader might think was dangerous. It was an untrodden vestibule which led to a scene so wild that even the most sober description of it must seem an exaggeration. There was a change in the quality of the rock, and there was a change in the appearance of the ridge. The rocks (talcose gneiss) below this spot were singularly firm; it was rarely necessary to test one's hold; the way led over the living rock, and not up rent-off fragments. But here, all was decay and ruin. The crest of the ridge was shattered and cleft, and the feet sank in the chips which had drifted down; while above, huge blocks, hacked and carved by the hand of time, nodded to the sky, looking like the grave-stones of giants. Out of curiosity I wandered to a notch in the ridge, between two tottering piles of immense masses, which seemed to need but a few pounds on one or the other side to make them fall; so nicely poised that they would literally have rocked in the wind, for they were put in motion by a touch; and based on support so frail that I wondered they did not collapse before my eyes. In the whole range of my Alpine experience I have seen nothing more striking than this desolate, ruined, and shattered ridge at the back of the Great Tower. I have seen stranger shapes,—rocks which mimic the human form, with monstrous leering faces —and isolated pinnacles, sharper and greater than any here; but I have never seen exhibited so impressively the tremendous effects which may be produced by frost, and by the long-continued action of forces whose individual effects are imperceptible.

It is needless to say that it is impossible to climb by the crest of the ridge at this part; still one is compelled to keep near to it, for there is no other way. Generally speaking, the angles on the Matterhorn are too steep to allow the formation of considerable beds of snow, but here there is a corner which permits it to accumulate, and it is turned to gratefully, for, by its assistance, one can ascend four times as rapidly as upon the rocks.

The Tower was now almost out of sight, and I looked over the central Pennine Alps to the Grand Combin, and to the chain of Mont Blanc. My neighbor, the Dent d'Hérens, still rose above me, although but slightly, and the height which had been attained could be measured by its help. So far, I had no doubts about my capacity to descend that which had been ascended; but, in a short time, on looking ahead, I saw that the cliffs steepened, and I turned back (without pushing on to them, and getting into inextricable difficulties), exulting in the thought that they would be passed when we returned together, and that I had, without assistance, got nearly to the height of the Dent d'Hérens, and considerably higher than any one had been before. My exultation was a little premature.

About 5 P. M. I left the tent again, and thought myself as good as at Breil. The friendly rope and claw had done good service, and had smoothened all the difficulties. I lowered myself through the Chimney, however, by making a fixture of the rope, which I then cut off, and left behind, as there was enough and to spare. My axe had proved a great nuisance in coming down, and I left it in the tent. It was not attached to the bâton, but was a separate affair,—an old navy boarding-axe. While cutting up the different snow-beds on the ascent, the bâton trailed behind fastened to the rope; and, when climbing, the axe was carried behind, run through the rope tied round my waist, and was sufficiently out of the way; but in descending, when coming down face outwards (as is always the best where it is possible), the head or the handle of the weapon caught frequently against the rocks, and several times nearly upset me. So, out of laziness if you will, it was left in the tent. I dearly paid for the imprudence.

The Col du Lion was passed, and fifty yards more would have placed me on the 'Great Staircase,' down which one can run. But on arriving at an angle of the cliffs of the Tête du Lion, while skirting the upper edge of the snow which abuts against them, I found that the heat of the two past days had nearly obliterated the steps which had been cut when coming up. The rocks happened to be impracticable just at this corner, so nothing could be done except make the steps afresh. The snow was too hard to beat or tread down, and at the angle it was all but ice; half-a-dozen steps only were required, and then the ledges could be followed again. So I held to the rock with my right hand, and prodded at the snow with the point of my stick until a good step was made, and then, leaning round the angle, did the same for the other side. So far well, but in attempting to pass the corner (to the present moment I cannot tell how it happened) I slipped and fell.

The slope was steep on which this took place, and was at the top of a gully that led down through two subordinate buttresses towards the Glacier du Lion —which was just seen, a thousand feet below. The gully narrowed and narrowed, until there was a mere thread of snow lying between two walls of rock, which came to an abrupt termination at the top of a precipice that intervened between it and the glacier. Imagine a funnel cut in half through its length, placed at an angle of 45 degrees, with its point below and its concave side uppermost, and you will have a fair idea of the place.

The knapsack brought my head down first, and I pitched into some rocks about a dozen feet below; they caught something and tumbled me off the edge, head over heels, into the gully; the bâton was dashed from my hands, and I whirled downwards in a series of bounds, each longer than the last; now over ice, now into rocks; striking my head four or five times, each time with increased force. The last bound sent me spinning through the air, in a leap of fifty or sixty feet, from one side of the gully to the other, and I struck the rocks, luckily, with the whole of my left side. They caught my clothes for a moment, and I fell on to the snow with motion arrested; my head fortunately came the right side up, and a few frantic catches brought me to a halt, in the neck of the gully, and on the verge of the precipice. Bâton, hat, and veil skimmed by and disappeared, and the crash of the rocks—which I had started—as they fell on the glacier, told how narrow had been the escape from utter destruction. As it was, I fell nearly 200 feet in seven or eight bounds. Ten feet more would have taken me in one gigantic leap of 800 feet on to the glacier below.

The situation was still sufficiently serious. The rocks could not be left go for a moment, and the blood was spirting out of more than twenty cuts. The most serious ones were in the head, and I vainly tried to close them with one hand, while holding on with the other. It was useless; the blood jerked out in blinding jets at every pulsation. At last, in a moment of inspiration, I kicked out a big lump of snow, and stuck it as a plaster on my head. The idea was a happy one, and the flow of blood diminished; then, scrambling up, I got, not a moment too soon, to a place of safety, and fainted away. The sun was setting when consciousness returned, and it was pitch dark before the Great Staircase was descended; but, by a combination of luck and care, the whole 4800 feet of descent to Breil was accomplished without a slip, or once missing the way. I slunk past the cabin of the cowherds, who were talking and laughing inside, utterly ashamed of the state to which I had been brought by my imbecility, and entered the inn stealthily, wishing to escape to my room unnoticed. But Favre met me in the passage, demanded 'Who is it?' screamed with fright when he got a light, and aroused the household. Two dozen heads then held solemn council over mine, with more talk than action. The natives were unanimous in recommending that hot wine (syn. vinegar,) mixed with salt, should be rubbed into the cuts. I protested, but they insisted. It was all the doctoring they received. Whether their rapid healing was to be attributed to that simple remedy, or to a good state of health, is a question; they closed up remarkably quickly, and in a few days I was able to move again.

As it seldom happens that one survives such a fall, it may be interesting to record what my sensations were during its occurrence. I was perfectly conscious of what was happening, and felt each blow; but, like a patient under chloroform, experienced no pain. Each blow was, naturally, more severe than that which preceded it, and I distinctly remember thinking 'Well, if the next is harder still, that will be the end!' Like persons who have been rescued from drowning, I remember that the recollection of a multitude of things rushed through my head, many of them trivialities or absurdities, which had been forgotten long before; and, more remarkable, this bounding through space did not feel disagreeable. But I think that in no very great distance more, consciousness as well as sensation would have been lost, and upon that I base my belief, improbable as it seems, that death by a fall from a great height is as painless an end as can be experienced.

The battering was very rough, yet no bones were broken. The most severe cuts were one of four inches long on the top of the head, and another of three inches on the right temple: this latter bled frightfully. There was a formidable-looking cut, of about the same size as the last, on the palm of the left hand, and every limb was grazed or cut, more or less seriously. The tips of the ears were taken off, and a sharp rock cut a circular bit out of the side of the left boot, sock, and ankle, at one stroke. The loss of blood, although so great, did not seem to be permanently injurious. The only serious effect has been the reduction of a naturally retentive memory to a very common-place one; and although my recollections of more distant occurrences remain unshaken, the events of that particular day would be clean gone but for the few notes which were written down before the accident.

AN ASCENT BY MR. E. WHYMPER, LORD DOUGLAS, REV. C. HUDSON, AND MR. HADOW, IN JULY 1865.

On Wednesday morning, the 12th of July, Lord Francis Douglas and myself crossed the Col Théodule, to seek guides at Zermatt. After quitting the snow on the northern side we rounded the foot of the glacier, crossing the Furgge Glacier, and left my tent, ropes, and other matters in the little chapel at the Lac Noir. We then descended to Zermatt, engaged Peter Taugwalder, and gave him permission to choose another guide. In the course of the evening the Rev. Charles Hudson came into our hotel with a friend, Mr. Hadow; and they, in answer to some inquiries, announced their intention of starting to attempt the Matterhorn on the following morning. Lord Francis Douglas agreed with me that it was undesirable that two independent parties should be on the mountain at the same time, and with the same object. Mr. Hudson was therefore invited to join us, and he accepted our proposal. Before admitting Mr. Hadow I took the precaution to inquire what he had done in the Alps; and, as well as I can remember, Mr. Hudson's reply was, 'Mr. Hadow has done the Mont Blanc in less time than most men.' He then mentioned several other excursions that were then unknown to me, and added, in answer to a further question, 'I consider he is a sufficiently good man to go with us.' This was an excellent certificate, given as it was by a first-rate mountaineer, and Mr. Hadow was admitted without any further question.

We then went into the matter of guides. Michel Croz was with Messrs. Hadow and Hudson; and the latter thought if Peter Taugwalder went as well, that there would not be occasion for any one else. The question was then referred to the men themselves, and they made no objection.

We started from Zermatt on the 13th of July, at half-past 5, on a brilliant and perfectly cloudless morning. We were eight in number—Croz, old Peter and his two sons, Lord F. Douglas, Hadow, Hudson, and I. To ensure steady motion, one tourist and one native walked together. The youngest Taugwalder fell to my share, and the lad marched well, proud to be on the expedition, and happy to show his powers. The wine-bags also fell to my lot to carry, and throughout the day, after each drink, I replenished them secretly with water, so that at the next halt they were found fuller than before! This was considered a good omen, and little short of miraculous.

On the first day we did not intend to ascend to any great height, and we mounted, accordingly, very leisurely; picked up the things which were left in the chapel at the Schwarzsee at 8:20, and proceeded thence along the ridge connecting the Hörnli with the Matterhorn. At half-past 11 we arrived at the base of the actual peak; then quitted the ridge, and clambered round some ledges, on to the eastern face. We were now fairly upon the mountain, and were astonished to find that places which from the

Riffel, or even from the Furggengletscher, looked entirely impracticable, were so easy that we could *run about.*

Before twelve o'clock we had found a good position for the tent, at a height of 11,000 feet. Croz and young Peter went on to see what was above, in order to save time on the following morning. They cut across the heads of the snow-slopes which descended towards the Furggengletscher, and disappeared round a corner; but shortly afterwards we saw them high up on the face, moving quickly. We others made a solid platform for the tent in a well-protected spot, and then watched eagerly for the return of the men. The stones which they upset told that they were very high, and we supposed that the way must be easy. At length, just before 3 P.M., we saw them coming down, evidently much excited. "What are they saying, Peter?" "Gentlemen, they say it is no good." But when they came near we heard a different story. "Nothing but what was good; not a difficulty, not a single difficulty! We could have gone to the summit and returned to-day easily!'

We passed the remaining hours of daylight—some basking in the sunshine, some sketching or collecting; and when the sun went down, giving, as it departed, a glorious promise for the morrow, we returned to the tent to arrange for the night. Hudson made tea, I coffee, and we then retired each one to his blanket-bag; the Taugwalders, Lord Francis Douglas, and myself, occupying the tent, the others remaining, by preference, outside. Long after dusk the cliffs above echoed with our laughter and with the songs of the guides, for we were happy that night in camp, and feared no evil.

We assembled together outside the tent before dawn on the morning of the 14th, and started directly it was light enough to move. Young Peter came on with us as a guide, and his brother returned to Zermatt. We followed the route which had been taken on the previous day, and in a few minutes turned the rib which had intercepted the view of the eastern face from our tent platform. The whole of this great slope was now revealed, rising for 3000 feet like a huge natural staircase. Some parts were more, and others were less, easy; but we were not once brought to a halt by any serious impediment, for when an obstruction was met in front it could always be turned to the right or to the left. For the greater part of the way there was, indeed, no occasion for the rope, and sometimes Hudson led, sometimes myself. At 6:20 we had attained a height of 12,800 feet, and halted for half-an-hour; we then continued the ascent without a break until 9:55, when we stopped for 50 minutes, at a height of 14,000 feet. Twice we struck the N.E. ridge, and followed it for some little distance,—to no advantage, for it was usually more rotten and steep, and always more difficult than the face. Still, we kept near to it, lest stones perchance might fall.

We had now arrived at the foot of that part which, from the Riffelberg or from Zermatt, seems perpendicular or overhanging, and could no longer continue upon the eastern side. For a little distance we ascended by snow upon the arête—that is, the ridge—descending towards Zermatt, and then, by common consent, turned over to the right, or to the northern side. Before doing so, we made a change in the order of ascent. Croz went first, I followed, Hudson came third; Hadow and old Peter were last. 'Now,' said Croz, as he led off, 'now for something altogether different.' The work became difficult, and required caution. In some places there was little to hold, and it was desirable that those should be in front who were least likely to slip. The general slope of the mountain at this part was *less* than 40°, and snow had accumulated in, and had filled up, the interstices of the rock-face, leaving only occasional fragments projecting here and there. These were at times covered with a thin film of ice. produced from the melting and refreezing of the snow. It was the counterpart, on a small scale, of the upper 700 feet of the Pointe des Ecrins,—only there was this material difference: the face of the Ecrins was about, or exceeded, an angle of 50°, and the Matterhorn face was less than 40°. It was a place over which any fair mountaineer might pass in safety, and Mr. Hudson ascended this part, and, as far as I know, the entire mountain, without having the slightest assistance rendered to him upon any occasion. Sometimes, after I had taken a hand from Croz, or received a pull, I turned to offer the same to Hudson; but he invariably declined, saying that it was not necessary. Mr. Hadow, however, was not accustomed to this kind of work, and required continual assistance. It is only fair to say that the difficulty which he found at this part arose simply and entirely from want of experience.

This solitary difficult part was of no great extent. We bore away over it at first, nearly horizontally, for a distance of about 400 feet; then ascended directly towards the summit for about 60 feet; and then doubled back to the ridge which descends towards Zermatt. A long stride round a rather awkward corner brought us to snow once more. The last doubt vanished! The Matterhorn was ours! Nothing but 200 feet of easy snow remained to be surmounted.

You must now carry your thoughts back to the seven Italians who started from Breil on the 11th of July. Four days had passed since their departure, and we were tormented with anxiety lest they should arrive on the top before us. All the way up we had talked of them, and many false alarms of 'men on the summit' had been raised. The higher we rose, the more intense became the excitement. What if we should be beaten at the last moment? The slope eased off, at length we could be detached, and Croz and I, dashing away, ran a neck-and-neck race, which ended in a dead heat. At 1:40 P.M. the world was at our feet, and the Matterhorn was conquered. Hurrah! Not a footstep could be seen.

It was not yet certain that we had not been beaten. The summit of the Matterhorn was formed of a rudely level ridge, about 350 feet long, and the Italians might have been at its farther extremity. I hastened to the southern end, scanning the snow right and left eagerly. Hurrah! again; it was untrodden. 'Where were the men?' I peered over the cliff, half doubting, half expectant. I saw them immediately—mere dots on the ridge, at an immense distance below. Up went my arms and my hat. 'Croz! Croz!! come here!' 'Where are they, Monsieur?' 'There, don't you see them, down there?' 'Ah! the *coquins*, they are low down.' 'Croz, we must make those fellows hear us.' We yelled until we were hoarse. The Italians seemed to regard us—we could not be certain. 'Croz, we *must* make them hear us; they *shall* hear us!' I seized a block of rock and hurled it down, and called upon my companion, in the name of friendship, to do the same. We drove our sticks in, and pryed away the crags, and soon a torrent of stones poured down the cliffs. There was no mistake about it this time. The Italians turned and fled.

The others had arrived, so we went back to the northern end of the ridge. Croz now took the tent-pole, and planted it in the highest snow. 'Yes,' we said, 'there is the flag-staff, but where is the flag?' 'Here it is,' he answered, pulling off his blouse and fixing it to the stick. It made a poor flag, and there was no wind to float it out, yet it was seen all around. They saw it at Zermatt—at the Riffel—in the Val Tournanche. At Breil, the watchers cried, 'Victory is ours!' They raised 'bravos' for Carrel, and 'vivas' for Italy, and hastened to put themselves *en fête*. On the morrow they were undeceived. 'All was changed; the explorers returned sad—cast down—disheartened—confounded—gloomy.' 'It is true,' said the men. 'We saw them ourselves—

they hurled stones at us! The old traditions *are* true,—there are spirits on the top of the Matterhorn!'

We returned to the southern end of the ridge to build a cairn, and then paid homage to the view. The day was one of those superlatively calm and clear ones which usually precede bad weather. The atmosphere was perfectly still, and free from all clouds or vapors. Mountains fifty—nay a hundred—miles off, looked sharp and near. All their details—ridge and crag, snow and glacier—stood out with faultless definition. Pleasant thoughts of happy days in bygone years came up unbidden, as we recognized the old familiar forms. All were revealed—not one of the principal peaks of the Alps was hidden. I see them clearly now—the great inner circles of giants, backed by the ranges, chains, and *massifs*. First came the Dent Blanche, hoary and grand; the Gabelhorn and pointed Rothhorn; and then the peerless Weisshorn; the towering Mischabelhörner, flanked by the Allaleinhorn, Strahlhorn, and Rimpfischhorn; then Monte Rosa—with its many Spitzes—the Lyskamm and the Breithorn. Behind were the Bernese Oberland, governed by the Finsteraarhorn; the Simplon and St. Gothard groups; the Disgrazia and the Orteler. Towards the south we looked down to Chivasso on the plain of Piedmont, and far beyond. The Viso—one hundred miles away—seemed close upon us; the Maritime Alps—one hundred and thirty miles distant—were free from haze. Then came my first love—the Pelvoux; the Ecrins and the Meije; the clusters of Graians, and lastly, in the west, gorgeous in the full sunlight, rose the monarch of all—Mont Blanc. Ten thousand feet beneath us were the green fields of Zermatt, dotted with chalets, from which blue smoke rose lazily. Eight thousand feet below, on the other side, were the pastures of Breil. There were forests black and gloomy, and meadows bright and lively; bounding waterfalls and tranquil lakes; fertile lands and savage wastes; sunny plains and frigid *plateaux*. There were the most rugged forms, and the most graceful outlines—bold, perpendicular cliffs, and gentle, undulating slopes; rocky mountains and snowy mountains, sombre and solemn, or glittering and white, with walls — turrets — pinnacles — pyramids — domes — cones—and spires! There was every combination that the world can give, and every contrast the heart could desire.

We remained on the summit for one hour—

'One crowded hour of glorious life.'

It passed away too quickly, and we began to prepare for the descent.

DESCENT OF THE MATTERHORN.

Hudson and I again consulted as to the best and safest arrangement of the party. We agreed that it would be best for Croz to go first, and Hadow second; Hudson, who was almost equal to a guide in sureness of foot, wished to be third; Lord F. Douglas was placed next, and old Peter, the strongest of the remainder, after him. I suggested to Hudson that we should attach a rope to the rocks on our arrival at the difficult bit, and hold it as we descended, as an additional protection. He approved the idea, but it was not definitely settled that it should be done. The party was being arranged in the above order whilst I was sketching the summit, and they had finished, and were waiting for me to be tied in line, when some one remembered that our names had not been left in a bottle. They requested me to write them down, and moved off while it was being done.

A few minutes afterwards I tied myself to young Peter, ran down after the others, and caught them just as they were commencing the descent of the difficult part. Great care was being taken. Only one man was moving at a time; when he was firmly planted the next advanced, and so on. They had not, however, attached the additional rope to rocks, and nothing was said about it. The suggestion was not made for my own sake, and I am not sure that it even occurred to me again. For some little distance we two followed the others, detached from them, and should have continued so had not Lord F. Douglas asked me, about 3 P.M., to tie on to old Peter, as he feared, he said, that Taugwalder would not be able to hold his ground if a slip occurred.

A few minutes later, a sharp-eyed lad ran into the Monte Rosa hotel, to Seiler, saying that he had seen an avalanche fall from the summit of the Matterhorn on to the Matterhorngletscher. The boy was reproved for telling idle stories; he was right, nevertheless, and this was what he saw.

Michel Croz had laid aside his axe, and in order to give Mr. Hadow greater security, was taking hold of his legs, and putting his feet, one by one, into their proper positions. As far as I know, no one was actually descending. I cannot speak with certainty, because the two leading men were partially hidden from my sight by an intervening mass of rock, but it is my belief, from the movements of their shoulders, that Croz, having done as I have said, was in the act of turning round to go down a step or two himself; at this moment Mr. Hadow slipped, fell against him, and knocked him over. I heard one startled exclamation from Croz, then saw him and Mr. Hadow flying downwards; in another moment Hudson was dragged from his steps, and Lord F. Douglas immediately after him. All this was the work of a moment. Immediately we heard Croz's exclamation, old Peter and I planted ourselves as firmly as the rocks would permit: the rope was taut between us, and the jerk came on us both as on one man. We held; but the rope broke midway between Taugwalder and Lord Francis Douglas. For a few seconds we saw our unfortunate companions sliding downwards on their backs, and spreading out their hands, endeavoring to save themselves. They passed from our sight uninjured, disappeared one by one, and fell from precipice to precipice on to the Matterhorngletscher below, a distance of nearly 4000 feet in height. From the moment the rope broke it was impossible to help them.

So perished our comrades! For the space of half an hour we remained on the spot without moving a single step. The two men, paralyzed by terror, cried like infants, and trembled in such a manner as to threaten us with the fate of the others. Old Peter rent the air with exclamations of 'Chamounix! Oh, what will Chamounix say?' He meant, Who

Fatal Accident on the Matterhorn.

would believe that Croz could fall? The young man did nothing but scream or sob, 'We are lost! we are lost!' Fixed between the two, I could neither move up nor down. I begged young Peter to descend, but he dared not. Unless he did, we could not advance. Old Peter became alive to the danger, and swelled the cry, 'We are lost! we are lost!'

The father's fear was natural—he trembled for his son; the young man's fear was cowardly—he thought of self alone. At last old Peter summoned up courage, and changed his position to a rock to which he could fix the rope; the young man then descended, and we all stood together. Immediately we did so, I asked for the rope which had given way, and found, to my surprise—indeed, to my horror—that it was the weakest of the three ropes. It was not brought, and should not have been employed, for the purpose for which it was used. It was old rope, and, compared with the others, was feeble. It was intended as a reserve, in case we had to leave much rope behind, attached to rocks. I saw at once that a serious question was involved, and made him give me the end. It had broken in mid-air, and it did not appear to have sustained previous injury.

For more than two hours afterwards I thought almost every moment that the next would be my last; for the Taugwalders, utterly unnerved, were not only incapable of giving assistance, but were in such a state that a slip might have been expected from them at any moment. After a time, we were able to do that which should have been done at first, and fixed rope to firm rocks, in addition to being tied together. These ropes were cut from time to time, and were left behind. Even with their assurance the men were afraid to proceed, and several times old Peter turned with ashy face and faltering limbs, and said, with terrible emphasis, '*I cannot!*'

About 6 P.M. we arrived at the snow upon the ridge descending towards Zermatt, and all peril was over. We frequently looked, but in vain, for traces of our unfortunate companions; we bent over the ridge and cried to them, but no sound returned. Convinced at last that they were neither within sight nor hearing, we ceased from our useless efforts; and, too cast down for speech, silently gathered up our things, and the little effects of those who were lost, preparatory to continuing the descent. When, lo! a mighty arch appeared, rising above the Lyskamm, high into the sky. Pale, colorless, and noiseless, but perfectly sharp and defined, except where it was lost in the clouds, this unearthly apparition seemed like a vision from another world; and, almost appalled, we watched with amazement the gradual development of two vast crosses, one on either side. If the Taugwalders had not been the first to perceive it, I should have doubted my senses. They thought it had some connection with the accident, and I, after a while, that it might bear some relation to ourselves. But our movements had no effect upon it. The spectral forms remained motionless. It was a fearful and wonderful sight; unique in my experience, and impressive beyond description, coming at such a moment.

I was ready to leave, and waiting for the others. They had recovered their appetites and the use of their tongues. They spoke in patois, which I did not understand. At length the son said in French, 'Monsieur.' 'Yes.' 'We are poor men; we have lost our Herr; we shall not get paid; we can ill afford this.' 'Stop!' I said, interrupting him, 'that is nonsense; I shall pay you, of course, just as if your Herr were here.' They talked together in their patois for a short time, and then the son spoke again. 'We don't wish you to pay us. We wish you to write in the hotel-book at Zermatt, and to your journals, that we have not been paid.' 'What nonsense are you talking? I don't understand you. What do you mean?' He proceeded—'Why, next year there will be many travellers at Zermatt, and we shall get more *voyageurs*.'

Who would answer such a proposition? I made them no reply in words, but they knew very well the indignation that I felt. They filled the cup of bitterness to overflowing, and I tore down the cliff, madly and recklessly, in a way that caused them, more than once, to inquire if I wished to kill them. Night fell; and for an hour the descent was continued in the darkness. At half-past 9 a resting-place was found, and upon a wretched slab, barely large enough to hold the three, we passed six miserable hours. At daybreak the descent was resumed, and from the Hörnli ridge we ran down to the chalets of Buhl, and on to Zermatt. Seiler met me at his door, and followed in silence to my room. 'What is the matter?' 'The Taugwalders and I have returned.' He did not need more, and burst into tears; but lost no time in useless lamentations, and set to work to arouse the village. Ere long a score of men had started to ascend the Hohlicht heights, above Kalbermatt and Z'Mutt, which commanded the plateau of the Matterhorngletscher. They returned after six hours, and reported that they had seen the bodies lying motionless on the snow. This was on Saturday; and they proposed that we should leave on Sunday evening, so as to arrive upon the plateau at daybreak on Monday. Unwilling to lose the slightest chance, the Rev. J. M'Cormick and I resolved to start on Sunday morning. The Zermatt man, threatened with excommunication by the priests if they failed to attend the early mass, were unable to accompany us. To several of them, at least, this was a severe trial, and Peter Perrn declared with tears that nothing else would have prevented him from joining in the search for his old comrades. Englishmen came to our aid. The Rev. J. Robertson and Mr. J. Phillpotts offered themselves, and their guide Franz Andermatten; another Englishman lent us Joseph Marie and Alexandre Lochmatter. Frédéric Payot and Jean Tairraz, of Chamounix, also volunteered.

We started at 2 A.M. on Sunday the 16th, and followed the route that we had taken on the previous Thursday as far as the Hörnli. From thence we went down to the right of the ridge, and mounted through the *séracs* of the Matterhorngletscher. By 8:30 we had got to the plateau at the top of the glacier, and within sight of the corner in which we knew my companions must be. As we saw one weather-beaten man after another raise the telescope, turn deadly pale, and pass it on without a word to the next, we knew that all hope was gone. We approached. They had fallen below as they had fallen above—Croz a little in advance, Hadow near him, and Hudson some distance behind; but of Lord F. Douglas we could see nothing. We left them where they fell; buried in snow at the base of the grandest cliff of the most majestic mountain of the Alps.

All those who had fallen had been tied with the Manilla, or with the second and equally strong rope, and, consequently, there had been only one link—that between old Peter and Lord F. Douglas—where the weaker rope had been used. This had a very ugly look for Taugwalder, for it was not possible to suppose that the others would have sanctioned the employment of a rope so greatly inferior in strength when there were more than 250 feet of the better qualities still remaining out of use. For the sake of the old guide (who bore a good reputation), and upon all other accounts, it was desirable that this matter should be cleared up; and after my examination before the court of inquiry which was instituted by the Government was over, I handed in a number of questions which were framed so as to afford old Peter an opportunity of exculpating himself from the grave suspicions which at once fell upon him. The questions, I was told, were put and answered; but the answers, although promised, have never reached me.

Meanwhile, the adminstration sent strict injunctions to recover the bodies, and upon the 19th of July, twenty-one men of Zermatt accomplished that sad and dangerous task. Of the body of Lord Francis Douglas they, too, saw nothing; it is probably still arrested on the rocks above. The remains of Hudson and Hadow were interred upon the north side of the Zermatt Church, in the presence of a reverent crowd of sympathizing friends The body of Michel Croz lies upon the other side, under a simpler tomb, whose inscription bears honorable testimony to his rectitude, to his courage, and to his devotion.

So the traditional inaccessibility of the Matterhorn was vanquished, and was replaced by legends of a more real character. Others will essay to scale its proud cliffs, but to none will it be the mountain that it was to its early explorers. Others may tread its summit-snows, but none will ever know the feelings of those who first gazed upon its marvellous panorama; and none, I trust, will ever be compelled to tell of joy turned into grief, and of laughter into mourning. It proved to be a stubborn foe; it resisted long, and gave many a hard blow; it was defeated at last with an ease that none could have anticipated, but, like a relentless enemy—conquered but not crushed—it took terrible vengeance. The time may come when the Matterhorn shall have passed away, and nothing, save a heap of shapeless fragments, will mark the spot where the great mountain stood; for, atom by atom, inch by inch, and yard by yard, it yields to forces which nothing can withstand. That time is far distant; and, ages hence, generations unborn will gaze upon its awful precipices, and wonder at its unique form. However exalted may be their ideas, and however exaggerated their expectations, none will come to return disappointed!

EDWARD WHYMPER, *Scrambles among the Alps*, 1869.

VIII.

RESCUE FROM A CREVASSE.

Mr. Huxley and myself had been staying for some days at Grindelwald, hoping for steady weather, and looking at times into the wild and noble region which the Shreckhorn, the Wetterhorn, the Viescherhörner, and the Eiger feed with eternal snows. We had scanned the buttresses of the Jungfrau with a view to forcing a passage between the Jungfrau and the Monk from the Wengern Alp to the Aletsch glacier. The weather for a time kept hopes and fears alternately afloat, but finally it declared against us; so we moved with the unelastic tread of beaten soldiers over the Great Sheideck, and up the Vale of Hasli to the Grimsel. We crossed the pass whose planed and polished rocks had long ago attracted the attention of Sir John Leslie, though the solution which he then offered ignored the ancient glacier which we now know to have been the planing tool employed. On rounding an angle of the Mayenwand, two travellers suddenly appeared in front ot us; they were Mr. (now Sir John) Lubbock and his guide. He had been waiting at the new hotel erected by M. Seiler at the foot of the Mayenwand, expecting our arrival; and finally, despairing of this, he had resolved to abandon the mountains, and was now bound for Brientz. In fact, the lakes of Switzerland, and the ancient men who once bivouacked along their borders, were to him the principal objects of interest; and we caught him in the act of declaring a preference for the lowlands which we could not by any means share.

We reversed his course, carried him with us down the mountain, and soon made ourselves at home in M. Seiler's hotel. Here we had three days' training on the glacier and the adjacent heights, and on one of the days Lubbock and myself made an attempt upon the Galenstock. By the flank of the mountain, with the Rhone glacier on our right, we reached the heights over the ice cascade and crossed the glacier above the fall. The sky was clear and the air pleasant as we ascended; but in the earth's atmosphere the sun works his swiftest necromancy, the lightness of air rendering it in a peculiar degree capable of change. Clouds suddenly generated came drifting up the valley of the Rhone, covering the glacier and swathing the mountain-tops, but leaving clear for a time the upper *névé* of the Rhone. Grandeur is conceded while beauty is sometimes denied to the Alps. But the higher snow-fields of the great glaciers are altogether beautiful—not throned in repellent grandeur, but endowed with a grace so tender as to suggest the loveliness of woman.

The day was one long succession of surprises wrought by the cloud-filled and wind-rent air. We reached the top, and found there a gloom which might be felt. It was almost thick enough to cut each of us away from the vision of his fellows. But suddenly, in the air above us, the darkness would melt away, and the deep blue heaven would reveal itself spanning the dazzling snows. Beyond the glacier rose the black and craggy summit of the Finsteraarhorn, and other summits and other crags emerged in succession as the battle-clouds rolled away. But the smoke would again whirl in upon us, and we looked once more into infinite haze from the cornice which lists the mountain-ridge. Again the clouds are torn asunder, and again they close. And thus, in upper air, did the sun play a wild accompaniment to the mystic music of the world below.

From the Rhone glacier we proceeded down the Rhone valley to Viesch, whence, in the cool twilight, all three of us ascended to the Hotel Jungfrau, on the Æggischhorn. This we made our head-quarters for some days, and here Lubbock and I decided to ascend the Jungfrau. The proprietor of the hotel keeps guides for this excursion, but his charges are so high as to be almost prohibitory. I, however, needed no guide in addition to my faithful Bennen; but simply a porter of sufficient strength and skill to follow where he led. In the village of Laax, Bennen found such a porter—a young man named Bielander, who had the reputation of being both courageous and strong. He was the only son of his mother, and she was a widow.

This young man and a second porter we sent on with our provisions to the Grotto of the Faulberg, where we were to spend the night. Between the Æggischhorn and this cave the glacier presents no difficulty which the most ordinary caution cannot overcome, and the thought of danger in connection with it never occurred to us. An hour and a half after the departure of our porters we slowly wended our way to the lake of Märjelin, which we skirted, and were soon upon the ice. The middle of the glacier was almost as smooth as a carriage-road, cut here and there by musical brooks produced by the superficial ablation. To Lubbock the scene opened out with the freshness of a new revelation, as, previously to this year, he had never been among the glaciers of the Alps. To me, though not new, the region had lost no trace of the interest with which I first viewed it. We moved briskly along the frozen incline, until, after a couple of hours' march, we saw a solitary human being standing on the lateral moraine of the glacier, near the point where we were to quit it for the cave of the Faulberg.

At first this man excited no attention. He stood and watched us, but did not come towards us, until finally our curiosity was aroused by observing that he was one of our own two men. The glacier here is always cut by crevasses, which, while they present no real difficulty, require care. We approached our porter, but he never moved; and when we came up to him he looked stupid, and did not speak until he was spoken to. Bennen addressed him in the patois of the place, and he answered in the same patois. His answer must have been more than usually obscure, for Bennen misunderstood the most important part of it. 'My God!' he exclaimed, turning to us, 'Walters is killed!' Walters was the guide at the Æggischhorn, with whom, in the present instance, we had nothing to do. 'No, not Walters,' responded the man; 'it is my comrade that is killed.' Bennen looked at him with a wild bewildered stare. 'How killed?' he exclaimed. 'Lost in a crevasse,' was the reply. We were all so stunned that for some moments we did not quite seize the import of the terrible statement. Bennen at length tossed his arms in the air, exclaiming, 'Jesu Maria! what am I to do?' With the swiftness that some ascribe to dreams, I surrounded the fact with imaginary adjuncts, one of which was that the man had been drawn dead from the crevasse, and was now a corpse in the cave of the Faulberg; for I took it for granted that, had he been still entombed, his comrade would have run or called for our aid. Several times in succession the porter affirmed that the missing man was certainly dead. 'How does he know that he is dead?' Lubbock demanded. 'A man is sometimes rendered insensible by a fall without being killed.' This question was repeated in German, but met with the same dogmatic response. 'Where is the man?' I asked. 'There,' replied the porter, stretching his arm towards the glacier. 'In the crevasse?' A stolid 'Ja!' was the answer. It was with difficulty that I quelled an imprecation. 'Lead the way to the place, you blockhead,' and he led the way.

We were soon beside a wide and jagged cleft

which resembled a kind of cave more than an ordinary crevasse. This cleft had been spanned by a snow bridge, now broken, and to the edge of which footsteps could be traced. The glacier at the place was considerably torn, but simple patience was the only thing needed to unravel its complexity. This quality our porter lacked, and, hoping to make shorter work of it, he attempted to cross the bridge. It gave way, and he went down, carrying an immense load of *débris* along with him. We looked into the hole, at one end of which the vision was cut short by darkness, while immediately under the broken bridge it was crammed with snow and shattered icicles. We saw nothing more. We listened with strained attention, and from the depths of the glacier issued a low moan. Its repetition assured us that it was no delusion—the man was still alive. Bennen from the first had been extremely excited; and the fact of his having, as a Catholic, saints and angels to appeal to, augmented his emotion. When he heard the moaning he became almost frantic. He attempted to get into the crevasse, but was obliged to recoil. It was quite plain that a second life was in danger, for my guide seemed to have lost all self-control. I placed my hand heavily upon his shoulder, and admonished him that upon his coolness depended the life of his friend. 'If you behave like a man, we shall save him; if like a woman, he is lost.'

A first-rate rope accompanied the party, but unhappily it was with the man in the crevasse Coats, waistcoats, and braces were instantly taken off and knotted together. I watched Bennen while this work was going on; his hands trembled with excitement, and his knots were evidently insecure, The last junction complete, he exclaimed, 'Now let me down!' 'Not until each of these knots has been tested; not an inch!'* Two of them gave way, and Lubbock's waistcoat also proved too tender for the strain. The *débris* was about forty feet from the surface of the glacier, but two intermediate prominences afforded a kind of footing. Bennen was dropped down upon one of these; I followed, being let down by Lubbock and the other porter. Bennen then descended the remaining distance, and was followed by me. More could not find room.

The shape and size of the cavity were such as to produce a kind of resonance, which rendered it difficult to fix the precise spot from which the sound issued; but the moaning continued, becoming to all appearance gradually feebler. Fearing to wound the man, the ice-rubbish was cautiously rooted away; it rang curiously as it fell into the adjacent gloom. A layer two or three feet thick was thus removed; and finally, from the frozen mass, and so bloodless as to be almost as white as the surrounding snow, issued a single human hand. The fingers moved. Round it we rooted, cleared the arm, and reached the knapsack, which we cut away. We also regained our rope. The man's head was then laid bare, and my brandy-flask was immediately at

---

* 'Ach, Herr, he replied to one of my remonstrances, 'Sein Sie nicht so hart.'

RESCUE FROM A CREVASSE.

his lips. He tried to speak, but his words jumbled themselves to a dull moan. Bennen's feelings got the better of him at intervals; he wrought like a hero, but at times he needed guidance and stern admonition. The arms once free, we passed the rope underneath them, and tried to draw the man out. But the ice-fragments round him had regelated so as to form a solid case. Thrice we essayed to draw him up, thrice we failed; he had literally to be hewn out of the ice, and not until his last foot was extricated were we able to lift him. By pulling him from above, and pushing him from below, the man was at length raised to the surface of the glacier.

For an hour we had been in the crevasse in shirt-sleeves—the porter had been in it for two hours—and the dripping ice had drenched us. Bennen, moreover, had worked with the energy of madness, and now the reaction came. He shook as if he would fall to pieces; but brandy and some dry covering revived him. The rescued man was helpless, unable to stand, unable to utter an articulate sentence. Bennen proposed to carry him down the glacier towards home. Had this been attempted, the man would certainly have died upon the ice. Bennen thought he could carry him for two hours; but the guide underrated his own exhaustion and overrated the vitality of the porter. 'It cannot be thought of,' I said; 'to the cave of Faulberg, where we must tend him as well as we can.' We got him to the side of the glacier, where Bennen took him on his back; in ten minutes he sank under his load. It was now my turn, so I took the man on my back and plodded on with him as far as I was able. Helping each other thus by turns, we reached the mountain grot.

The sun had set, and the crown of the Jungfrau was embedded in amber light. Thinking that the Märjelin See might be reached before darkness, I proposed starting in search of help. Bennen protested against my going alone, and I thought I noticed moisture in Lubbock's eye. Such an occasion brings out a man's feeling if he have any. I gave them both my blessing and made for the glacier. But my anxiety to get quickly clear of the crevasses defeated its own object. Thrice I found myself in difficulty, and the light was visibly departing. The conviction deepened that persistence would be folly, and the most impressive moment of my existence was that on which I stopped at the brink of a profound fissure and looked upon the mountains and the sky. The serenity was perfect—not a cloud, not a breeze, not a sound, while the last hues of sunset spread over the solemn west.

I returned; warm wine was given to our patient, and all our dry clothes were wrapped around him. Hot-water bottles were placed at his feet, and his back was briskly rubbed. He continued to groan a long time; but, finally, both this and the trembling ceased. Bennen watched him solemnly, and at length muttered in anguish, 'Sir, he is dead!' I leaned over the man and found him breathing gently; I felt his pulse—it was beating tranquilly. 'Not dead, dear old Bennen; he will be able to crawl home with us in the morning.' The prediction was justified by the event; and two days afterwards we saw him at Laax, minus a bit of his ear, with a bruise upon his cheek, and a few scars upon his hand, but without a broken bone or serious injury of any kind.

The self-denying conduct of the second porter made us forget his stupidity—it may have been stupefaction. As I lay there wet, through the long hours of that dismal night, I almost registered a vow never to tread upon a glacier again. But, like the forces in the physical world, human emotions vary with the distance from their origin, and a year afterwards I was again upon the ice.

JOHN TYNDALL, *Hours of Exercise in the Alps.*

IX.

THE PIC DU MIDI OF THE PYRENEES.

ASCENT IN 1797 BY R. DE MIRBEL.

We waited with a sort of impatience for the melting of the snows off the slopes of the Pic du Midi de Bigorre, in order to attempt a journey to this celebrated mountain. Ramond had approached it in the beginning of July, but he had found the road impracticable, and had not been beyond the Lake of Oncet. From that date to the 22nd, the sun had been only hidden at intervals by light clouds. Its heat, concentrated in the valleys, had warmed the atmosphere; the frost was gone, and now no obstacle stood in our way.

We formed a party of thirteen or fourteen persons, and we set out at four o'clock in the morning. The greater part of my companions took horses to the foot of the Pic, but as for me I went on foot, according to my usual custom, carrying on my back the tin box in which I meant to put all the rare plants which I might find. I was armed with a long stick tipped with iron, and shod with nailed shoes.

We followed the valley of Baréges, along the Bastan, and gained the slopes of the Tourmalet. At its base, opens towards the north a little lateral valley, from which flows a stream, which afterwards joins its peaceful waters to those of the impetuous Bastan. The valley of Baréges here softens a little

The Pic du Midi.

the roughness of its frowning slopes, for its soil, somewhat less arid, is covered with verdure, and its meadows are decked with flowers. The bushy asphodel, with its stem and leaves of brilliant green, and its white flowers streaked with rose, grows here abundantly, and raises its head above the more modest though not less beautiful flowers. The saxatile veronica, clinging by its ligneous stalk to the rocks, whose sharp points crop up here and there in the meadow, seems to wish to hide them from the traveller. Its pretty deep blue flowers, with their two white anthers, enable one to recognize it from a distance. We also found here the yellow gentian and the Alpine plantain.

The valley which leads to the Pic ends at the Lake of Oncet, where we stopped to breakfast. Those who have not climbed mountains cannot form an idea of the pleasure which there is in making the most frugal repast beside a limpid stream, after a long and weary journey. It seems as if the keen air led one back naturally to primitive habits; and truly the amateur mountaineer in visiting a new clime seems to gain altogether a new life.

The borders of the lake are adorned with the violet biflorus, whose golden flowers are interspersed amidst the bright green soil; here and there also we perceive, on the sides of the banks, the yellow arnica bending over the lake; while the scented ourge-laurel showed itself near the precipices, its eeping stems covered with pink flowers, and scenting the air with its perfume.

On the west of the lake high mountains rose perpendicularly from the water; on the north, the rocks were not practicable; but they were rather lower on the east, and allowed us to get glimpses of the Pic du Midi. This, then, was the way which we must take, and the ascent was gentle and easy.

The sun was already gilding the summit of the mountains, and it warned us to be on the march. We left one of the guides in charge of our horses, and set forward slowly towards the top of the Pic. The rarefaction of the air, the appearance of the vegetation, the silence of nature, the solitude in which we found ourselves, all told us that we were approaching high regions. A dry turf, parched and shining, covered the rocks, and a few alpine plants were visible here and there. Among them we noticed the spring gentian, and the stemless gentian, those two inseparable companions, which, born in the same latitude, are always found in the same spot, whether that be the water-side, or the barren rock, the grassy lands, or the leafless mountain. Sometimes, also, pretty tufts of silenas refreshed the eye, and near them the drasa with its grey flax flowers spread its delicate foliage and blossoms to view. Further on, in the midst of fallen heaps and ruins of all sorts, the monuments of the power of time, grew in the interstices of the stones some pale flowers which seemed to find life even in the bosom of destruction; and around them fluttered the most brilliant butterflies.

After an hour and a half's march, we arrived at the summit of the Pic. The vapors of night were dissipated, the sky was clear, and the sun shone brightly. The entire chain of the Pyrenees lay like an amphitheatre around us. On the right rose Néouvielle, a granite rock crowned with eternal snow; on the left, the Brèche de Roland, the tower of Marboré, and the Mont Perdu, whose distant peak towered above all the others. Turning towards the opposite side, we discovered an immense plain, which seemed at length to lose itself in the horizon. The view embraced at once mountains, precipices, glaciers, ancient snows, ærial lakes, the immense and silent workshops of nature, and fruitful fields watered by fertilizing streams of the mountain torrents. Those peaks, which once seemed to me only a useless chaos, and the result of some strange caprice of Nature, now appeared as the sublime work of a beneficent Hand. I gazed intensely on this marvellous world of which my imagination could hardly take in the extent, and the contemplation of which filled my soul with enthusiasm.

Flowers also still adorned the plateau. The snapdragon of the Pyrenees inserted its slender roots in the clefts of the rock, and the light blue of its flowers only set off the purple of the saxifrage. By its side were seen the golden corollas of the Alpine poppy. The saxifrage is a rare ornament of mountains, but here the precipices sheltered it; and it rivalled the snow itself in the purity of its whiteness.

B. DE MIRBEL.

X.

THE BRECHE DE ROLAND.

ASCENT IN 1797, BY B. DE MIRBEL AND J. PASQUIER.

I WOULD not have undertaken such an expedition as this had I not found in M. Jules Pasquier a man made, as it were, to share its fatigues, and full of zeal in the search after the secrets of nature. He had admired the beauties of the Pic du Midi; but they had only kindled his ardor and increased his longing for further adventures. He knew that through snows and glaciers some intrepid men had found a way even to the highest point of the Pyrenean chain; and that was enough to stimulate his ambition and to make him despise the dangers.

We set out from Baréges on the 8th of August, 1797, at six o'clock in the morning. Arriving at Luz, we took a guide, and continued our route towards the valley of Gavarnie. Through this one almost trembles as one passes. All is grand, magnificent, sublime; and man, surrounded by these august monuments, acknowledges his own littleness and the might of a sovereign Hand. Such was my first thought when I penetrated into this valley;

the second was more pleasing to my *amour propre.* I could not see without admiration or without pride that road, constructed on the edge of a frightful precipice, which the noise of the Gave renders still more terrible. Here, indeed, man has employed at once his powers of mind in the conception, his strength and address in the working, and his perseverance in the execution. The valley ascends from north to south. To the east and west rise sharp rocks formed of calcareous banks sloping almost perpendicularly to the south, and running from the east to the west. Often the rock, rising from the bottom of the water towards the heavens, only presents a wall which seems to defy human efforts; sometimes it is more inclined, and yet more difficult to cross, on account of the long slippery places formed of schistose *débris,* of loose stones fallen from the peaks, and of loose soil, too, which was always ready to roll downwards. Yet here they have managed to make a road, which is safe, commodious, and wide enough to reassure the most timid horseman. One cannot see this road without astonishment, now rising with the mountains, then falling with its descent; now avoiding it altogether, then joining it again, and even sometimes passing from one bank to the other, as an arch over the torrent, and thus opening a passage across the rocks from the plains of France to those of Spain. If the daring character of this great work excites the curiosity of the traveller, the variety of its ground, and the originality of the whole, do so much more.

The valley also everywhere presents different aspects. The verdant carpet, which adorns the rich basin of Luz, is prolonged far on to the mountain. Carelessly thrown over gentle slopes, crowned with a rich vegetation, and embellished with picturesque cottages, it seemed to say, 'This is the Vale of Tempe.' But all at once this green turf disappears, and to the rounded knolls succeed sharp rocks, while vigorous trees give place to trunks torn by tempests and nipped by frosts, which bend over the precipice. The grove, enclosed between rocks, storms and foams, boils and tumbles, while roaring cascades precipitate themselves on all sides, and the threatening rocks hang over the traveller's head.

When I saw this valley for the first time I seemed to proceed from marvel to marvel; but what struck me most, was the view from the bridge of Sia. Some time before we reached this, the banks of the Gave were clothed in less rude forms; its waters slackened their course; there they seemed almost to drag themselves through thick pastures, and under trees, whose branches met at the top and hid the river from sight. We had thus gone nearly a quarter of a league when a deafening noise was heard, and soon, as if by magic, we found ourselves on the bridge which, until then, had remained concealed. It is partly covered with ivy; its buttresses are supported on the rock; and the Gave rolls its waters at more than a hundred feet below the arch. On the left, the mountain again resumes its frowning aspect; on the right, on the contrary, it retains its graceful form. In the front of the picture you perceive the torrent, which, narrowed by the sides of the rocks, rises gradually, swells and falls with violence whenever there is a fall in the ground, then suddenly becoming calm again, it slowly continues its course.

We soon arrived at Gèdres. This village is situated at the foot of the Coumélie, a granite rock, which is the point of division between the valley of Héas and the valley of Gavarnie.

The nearer we approached to the end of our journey, the more imposing did the view become. Strange and twisted forms had now given place to shapes more grave and regular; and lively and brilliant colors to soft and uniform tints, which blended the aerial summits with the azure sky.

We saw, in passing, the beautiful cascade of Saousa, which falls in fine rain into the Gave, and which one might take for a light gauze agitated by the wind. Further on is the frightful solitude of La Peyrade, of which no one could form an idea until he has seen it. Picture to yourself a mountain whose broken peaks have crumbled one over the other, accumulating in the bottom of the valley in such high lumps of rock, that their size astonishes the eye and fatigues the imagination. The rest of the peak which felt this frightful concussion has for ages threatened to bury these immense *débris* under fresh ruins. Enormous blocks were first precipitated into the torrent, and thus they stop the smaller masses which pile one over the other. These blocks are separated by great inter-

THE BRÈCHE DE ROLAND.

stices, of which the engineer has made use in constructing the road.

It was only two o'clock when we arrived at Gavarnie. We were not tired and therefore continued our way towards the valley of Ossau, in order to profit by the evening. This valley is divided into several branches; we chose that which leads to the lake of the Espessières. On the banks of this lake young horses were grazing: they are sent into the mountains during the fine season. Alarmed at our approach, they quickly mounted the sides of the mountain, and gained with ease the steepest summits, where they seemed to defy us to get at them. But we managed to allure them into the plain again by holding out to them some handfuls of salt. Whilst we were engaged in stroking them the Marboré and the Brèche de Roland became covered with clouds; a violent clap of thunder resounded among the mountains, and the frightened horses escaped from our hands. Trembling for the success of our enterprise we again took the road to Gavarnie. But soon the sky cleared, the clouds dispersed, the setting sun colored the peaks with a bright carnation color, and the rainbow arched the whole with its brilliant colors.

We recommenced our ascent at four o'clock in the morning, conducted by an excellent guide named Rondo, whom a friend had sent us. Towards five o'clock we began to discover the summits of the Marboré, which one might take, at a distance, for towers, for their forms are so regular. After three quarters of an hour's march we found ourselves in front of the amphitheatre of Gavarnie, whose majestic appearance is beyond all description. At first sight one might be tempted to think it a work of man, on account of the regularity so seldom seen in the great works of nature. But the boldness of the design, the richness of the forms, the enormous masses of rock heaped one on the other, the grandeur of the architecture, at once simple and elegant, and, above all, the abundance and the variety of forms in the different parts, soon admonish the beholder—even while he admires the wonderful symmetry of the whole,—of the presence of a superior Agent. Immense layers, each retiring further back as the mountains rise, form steps covered with snow, and glaciers from whence fall numerous cascades. On the left of the amphitheatre, an impetuous torrent rushes from the mountain, strikes in its fall a projection of rock, and from thence rebounds into the circus. This magnificent cascade, measured geometrically by Reboul, is about 1266 feet high. One might be tempted to doubt this fact, if the learned mathematician who affirms it, did not inspire entire confidence. Nearly all strangers who visit Gavarnie think it an exaggeration to give 300 or 400 feet to its cascade! Most of them, it is true, have never travelled among mountains, and do not consider how each particular object loses in consequence of the imposing grandeur of the whole. This celebrated place offers, perhaps, all that is most astonishing in the structure of mountains. It presents to the naturalist great problems to solve and new systems to establish ; to the painter a sublime whole in which are found united grace and vigor in the forms, vivacity and richness in the coloring, and harmony and unity in all the parts.

The sun already gilded the summit of the towers of the Marboré, when we took the road to the Brèche de Roland. Rondo marched first, leading the way. M. Pasquier followed him, and I, sometimes before, sometimes behind, gathered plants or examined the structure of the rock. I had told Lagunier, our guide from Luz, not to go far off, in order that he might come to my aid in case of need. We had to climb the rocks in front of the cascades; and we travelled by a road that was frightfully steep. Formed by the fall of rounded and moveable stones, it lay along the perpendicular rock, against which we clung, and by the side of a frightful precipice. Such was the road which we had to follow for half an hour. Another soon presented itself which was more dangerous still. But the intrepid Rondo advanced first. The rock was exactly perpendicular; all parts of our body were placed against it; we placed the points of our feet over the little juttings formed by the slipping of the layers, and we supported ourselves by clinging with our hands to the projections above us. This painful attitude became almost intolerable when Rondo was obliged to stop before some new obstacles. Then each of us stiffening himself against the rock which repulsed him behind, remained suspended on weak supports, having under him a precipice of 2000 fathoms in depth. Happily this situation did not last long. We soon arrived at a delicious plateau, on which we found a large flock of sheep and goats watched by Spanish shepherds. They were taking their first meal, and their dog came up to us and seemed, by his caresses, to invite us to join them. Milk was offered to us which we gratefully accepted.

At some paces from thence we crossed a little valley of snow, and soon perceived before us the Brèche de Roland, which had long been hidden from us by the peaks which came between it and us. But we were separated from it by great glaciers, and no way of avoiding them presented itself. Lagunier, alike frightened by the danger which he had run, and by the obstacles which remained to be conquered, declared positively that he would not go a step further; and we felt that we had better not urge him, thinking that he would be rather a charge than a help.

We went on into a new snow valley, much larger than the first, and of a more exquisite appearance. On the north, the Taillon raises its perpendicular strata to a prodigious height. On the south, the first steps of the wall of the Brèche are clearly to be seen; but on the west, the brilliant carpet of snow, in its dazzling whiteness, follows softly the sinuosities of the rock, falls and rises with it, folds itself in a hundred ways, and mounts slowly towards the region of eternal ice, where a bluish tint modifies its whiteness. Whilst we were admiring the magic beauty of these places, a troop of izards, with straightened necks, heads raised, noses in the air, and their feet firm and sure, rushed from a neighboring rock, stopped on the snow, astonished at our presence, and all at once, with the rapidity of lightning, cleared the icy plain, and jumped from rock to rock, and from peak to peak, appearing and disappearing before our eyes twenty times in a minute, until they stopped at last perfecty quiet on the steep crest of the Taillon.

After having marched for some time in this snow valley, we directed our steps towards the glaciers which were on our left. A Spanish smuggler accompanied us. More accustomed than we to this sort of march, he cleared, with great rapidity, the first belts of the glaciers, and already had left us far behind, when, on a sudden, the ice opened under his feet, and he sank, uttering a piercing cry. We thought him lost, and ran to help him if there were yet time. He was wedged between the walls of ice, and thus suspended over the gulf, when M. Pasquier arrived. We helped him to disengage himself and get out, while the dangers into which the slightest imprudence might throw us came forcibly to our minds. Rondo was full of care for us. He cut the ice with a hatchet, and thus formed steps for us, which became every moment more useful as the ice became harder and harder and resisted our iron-pointed sticks. We walked on silently, looking carefully at our feet, and casting our eyes from time to time over the gulf into which the smallest accident would have precipitated us, and over the passage which remained for us to make, This painful ascent lasted for nearly a quarter of an hour, during which, in the most perilous parts, we could not sometimes prevent a little quaking of fear, which, however, we soon repressed.

We came at last to the end of our journey; the precipices were left far behind, and the dangers which we had run were only thought of in contrast with our present security, and as they led us to attach a higher value to the sublime spectacle which was presented to our view. An immense wall rises between France and Spain; it is formed, like the Marboré, of perpendicular beds and horizontal layers. A breach, cut at right angles, is the door of communication for the two countries. Standing on the threshold of this magnificent portal, you see on the east and on the west the insurmountable barrier raised by nature between the two peoples: while, on the north and south, you look over the lands subject to their respective dominions.

It was nearly one o'clock when we quitted the Brèche. We descended the glaciers with great precaution, and got out from these dangerous regions without accident. The same evening, at ten o'clock, we were back at Baréges.

B. DE MIRBEL, *Extract from an unpublished narrative.*

XI.

MONT PERDU.

ASCENT IN 1797 BY M. RAYMOND.

WE set out from Barèges on the 25th Thermidor of the year V., corresponding to the 11th of August, 1797, precisely ten years after my journey to the Monts Maudits, and twenty years after my first journey in the Swiss Alps. I must be pardoned for recalling dates of which the memory is so pleasant to me; they have left remembrances of which no disagreeable idea breaks the charm.

Our party was numerous on this occasion. La Peyrouse was accompanied by his son, one of his pupils, citizen Frizac of Toulouse, and by citizen Ferrière, the gardener to the central schools of this town. I was accompanied by Mirbel and Pasquier, who had just made the ascent of the Brèche de Roland, and by Corbin and Massey of Tarbes, both my pupils, and of whom the latter will often be mentioned with praise in the work which I am about to publish on the plants of the High Pyrenees.

Once down in the basin of Luz, we filed along

that highroad of naturalists, the Valley of Gèvres, so justly admired, yet so often described that it is almost superfluous to enumerate its singularities. Its precipices and cascades, and the difficulty of the road which leads through it are well known. Of what materials its walls are constructed along which one walks, as it were suspended over a precipice, is well known also.

We ascended the Coumélie by a tortuous and yet steep pathway, by which the flocks of Gèdres pass over the pastures of the middle region. A number of barns are scattered over these rich spots. and form three hamlets dependent on Héas, Gèdres, and Gavarnie. We only found there a small number of inhabitants and of flocks, for at this time of year they are still in the higher mountain regions.

We passed the night in a barn, rather disturbed by the uncertainty of the weather. However, the south wind which had covered the Marboré with clouds from Spain, at last yielded to the north wind which brought down the clouds from France. The former are always high, and cover the peaks; the latter are low, and creep over the bases of the mountains. By degrees they filled the valleys in which we were, forming an immense sea through which the different peaks pierced just about our level. I hoped for a fine day.

The best part of the night was employed in providing myself with guides. I had brought from Baréges the two men in whom I have most confidence, my Laurens, who scarcely ever leaves me, and Antoine Mouré, who supplies his place sometimes. These are mountaineers of proof; but in the places which we were going to examine, they were as much strangers as I was. I had then to seek at Héas an isard-hunter, who had been much recommended to me for the knowledge of Mont Perdu which he possessed, though, as it turned out, he knew no more than we did. I added to him two inhabitants of the Coumélie, who served me much better, though they did not know any more about the locality; and at dawn of day we took the road of the Valley of Estaubé, keeping over the pastures of the Coumélie, which may be traversed as easily as a floor.

We had hardly turned from the east towards the south when we were struck with the imposing appearance of the valleys of Héas and of Estaubé, encircling, as they do, enormous mountains, although only the secondary parts of them; of which the equally grand and simple forms contrast singularly with the horny ruins and dismembered granites which we had left behind us. From hence the summit of Mont Perdu is visible. It is very apparent and nevertheless not very noticeable to those who are not on the look-out for it. It consists of an oblique and blunted cone, and glistens with the eternal snows which rise above the high walls of the valley of Estaubé. I pointed it out to my young companions, who, seeing it so clearly, thought themselves already nearing the end of their journey. Yet it did not take us less than four or five hours to reach just the foot of the wall; and of this wall which we had either to turn or to climb, I took the measure with an uneasy eye.

But we were entering the valley of Estaubé, and in silence we contemplated its quiet solitudes. It possesses, at the same time, the calm of the upper regions, and of the secondary grounds. Some mountains which appeared considerable, even without having regard to their elevation, astonished us still more by the simplicity of their forms, which is noticed usually only on the borders of great chains, and in the neighborhood of places where they degenerate into mere pillars. The masses, boldly modelled, present smooth, yet striking contours, which no strange accident has caused to pass the limits of the beautiful. All rise and fall in just proportions. Nothing spoils the harmony of a design both severe and bold ; and the color, too, so transparent and pure,—it is light grey a little warmed with pink,—suits equally the light or shade, and softens the contrast between them. This color is continued up to the very azure of the sky.

There were very few fallen masses, and especially recent ones. Vegetation flourishes up to the very foot of the rocky ridges. It has even, here and there, taken possession of some old rocks. A little river with grassy banks flows peacefully over a stony bed, and afterwards, further on, it becomes a torrent. There, the service-tree overshadows Solomon's seal, which is rare in our mountains, though it here acquires uncommon dimensions. Over the declivities of the lateral mountains may be seen the red pine which here defies the axe. All the blocks

MONT PERDU.

are adorned with the light plumy bunches of the superb long-leaved saxifrage. In uncultivated ground there is sometimes found the carline of the Pyrenees, and sometimes the beautiful panicaut described by Gouin, and which here changes sometimes trom amethyst to crimson. On the turf there are those two carlines particularly mentioned by Allioni and Villars, the second of which, described under the name of acanthus-leaved carline, may be known by the golden color of its calyx crown.

There can be nothing more brilliant or more splendid than a piece of turf bedizened with those two carlines.

We pressed on, and at length we all sat down before these mountain walls of Estaubé, which seemed to rise higher as we advanced towards them. Already we could see that fine glaciers lay under the fields of snow which in some parts diversified the landscape. At last, after four hours' march we found ourselves just under the intermediate glacier; and we stopped to gaze on those walls which seemed to tower up to the very skies. The place in which we were is the highest to which shepherds go. The name of *couilas* is given to their temporary encampments; and this one was called the *couila* of the Abassat-dessus. We here met two Spanish shepherds belonging to that set of them who rent the highest pastures of the Pyrenees for their travelling flocks. These two men were stretched by the side of a hut, made of dry stones, just large enough to contain them sitting or lying. That was all the shelter that these two nomades, or rather half-savages, who inhabit this region only for some days in the fine season needed. Sometimes they dispensed with a hut of any kind, and made shift with the shelter of some overhanging rock.

To have met two men of this sort, two real *habitués* of the environs of Mont Perdu, appeared a most fortunate adventure in our ascent up the mountain, and we were all eager to ask them questions. But the shepherds had only passed a few days in this region of eternal snow; and their replies were only half satisfying me, when a smuggler of their nation came up and joined them. This latter was quite an authority. Forced to avoid the beaten roads, and to trust to the chances of the most dangerous paths, we felt that he must know Mont Perdu almost better than any one; and, as it proved, his advice differed greatly from that of the shepherds. Whilst he and they were discussing the question of the route we took a little repose, and I, according to my custom, formed my plan.

The unanimous result of their consultation was, that we must pass the 'Port de Pinède,' descend into the valley of Béousse, and remount on the right by some very steep rocks which they said were always practicable. But to ascend again for two hours just to have to descend one,—then to climb rocks which must occupy us for four or five more—this plan would just bring us up to Mont Perdu when it would be time to leave it again. I had been considering the glacier below which we stood. It was still covered with snow; and this snow must,

I imagined, make it practicable ; the inclination was great, but not an insuperable difficulty ; and the glacier led to a breach which seemed to open right on the face of Mont Perdu. So I declared that I was resolved to try the chances. This the shepherds thought outrageous, for though they allowed that these snows are sometimes practicable, yet they did not believe them to be so when grey spots showed the surface of the glacier to be visible through them. At first the smuggler alone applauded me, though my faithful Laurens afterwards took my side. The others smiled, and our local guides were just the most incredulous and the least courageous. It was necessary, however, to put an end to this state of indecision ; so I declared that I should ascend the glacier with whoever would follow me ; and as obstinacy never fails to decide irresolution they all came. As to the smuggler, he had already followed his own plans ; and very soon we lost sight of him.

We went directly towards the mouth of the glacier by slopes that were steep enough, certainly; yet they were grassy, and seemed to have only lately emerged from the snow which covers them for seven or eight months of the year. The fresh green was in its spring, and the ground covered with Alpine flora.

However, we approached the steep sides of the mountain, and then what had seemed the smallest objects acquired enormous dimensions. At last we reached the *débris* which comes down from the mountain, and which forms the moraine of the glacier. We were obliged to step on to the snow and face the threatening *couloir* at the top of which we expected to find Mont Perdu. At first this was a mere game; the snow had a good consistency and a moderate inclination; and we went on with all the confidence which experience of mountains gives. But we had not gone fifty steps when the inclination increased; and we could see that it continued to do so. We looked above our heads, and still the ground became steeper. Our pace slackened; we stopped and consulted what was to be done. I saw that La Peyrouse remained behind, and got him to try the cramping irons which I used, and which my pupils had adopted after my example; they were those which De Saussure had used in his most perilous journeys. But the help was as strange to him as the place which obliged him to have recourse to them. Nothing, at his age, could give him the requisite mountaineering habits. So I conjured him not to load me with the responsibility of his safety; he consented to leave us, and thus we parted at the moment on which I had most reckoned on the assistance of his learning.

I left him then at the bottom of the glacier with my brave Antoine, whom I had attached to his service; and they seated themselves on a rock from whence they could see us slowly continuing our way. We had not proceeded a quarter of an hour when the snow became so hard that our footsteps made no impression on it. So we had to think carefully of our footing and to help ourselves with our hatchets. Then we settled ourselves into a file and took care to plant our feet in the steps cut by the three first of the column, a work in which the gardener, Ferrière, distinguished himself, his heartiness contrasting strangely with the *sang-froid* of our other mountaineers. During the first hour all went well. We carefully avoided the uncovered part of the glaciers, and by means of numerous zigzags, prudently managed, we were avoiding the difficulty of a slope which varied from thirty-five to forty degrees, when all at once we perceived a man distractedly clinging to a rock from whence he called to us for aid! It was our smuggler, and a long track in the snow told his story. The unfortunate man had ventured without cramping irons, without a hatchet, without any of the means of safety which men of his trade never fail to carry; and he had slipped down more than two hundred paces, from being too near the edge of the rock. And, once launched, it was inconceivable how he had ever succeeded in stopping himself. We should have liked to fly to his assistance, but could only move slowly. However, we succeeded in rescuing him at last, and then we placed him in our ranks. He had lost his hat, his waistcoat, his pack of merchandise, and he had had a greater loss still; for he had lost his stick which had preceded him down the precipice, and which we could not restore to him. The other things were scattered about, and we soon recovered the waistcoat and the goods. But the hat had stuck in a dangerous place; it cost us a quarter of an hour's labor, although it was within twenty steps.

It was in vain, however, that we had put the poor

fellow in the very middle of our party; he could not recover his composure. Our assurance acted less on him than his uneasiness did on my companions. I saw already on the faces of two of them signs of fear of which I dreaded the consequences. At every step they asked me to measure the inclination of the glacier, which was as much as sixty degrees. It was now, therefore, a question whether we should change our route, and try the rocks at the side of the ice. This was not, in my opinion, desirable; but the general uneasiness increased. Twice we waited while our two guides from the Coumélie attempted the escalade. Each time they were constrained to come down again. It was necessary to return to the snow, where, by means of our old manœuvre, there was really nothing to fear except the discouragement of the party. The glacier was here at its greatest inclination, and we were also at our last effort. Above, the slope became visibly more gentle, and the ice was hidden under snows of a whiteness so pure as to indicate the summit of the ridge, standing out against the deep blue of the sky. The only question now was, how to triumph over an obstacle beyond which our imaginations showed us the top of Mont Perdu. We gathered up all our remaining strength. We mutually animated and encouraged one another. At each step that we took, we saw the distance lessening. The breach which had long been hidden from us by the edge of the glacier, reappeared in gigantic proportions, and already we felt the cold wind which rushed through the great opening. We hastened on; we pushed forward, and, out of breath, we reached the desired point. An exclamation of delight was uttered by all; but a deep silence succeeded at the sight of a new world, of the depths which separated us from it, of the glaciers which girded it round, of the clouds which covered it; a frightful and yet sublime spectacle by which our senses seemed overpowered. A single instant had sufficed to develop it in all its majesty; but for several moments we could not collect our senses. 'There is Mont Perdu! There is Mont Perdu!' said one to another, and still no one could single it out from the chaos of rocks, snows, and vapors.

And it was not without reason that we saw Mont Perdu everywhere; everything here belongs to it, everything is a part of it, even the ridge which we had reached, and which was only separated from the highest point by a depression or erosion of a part of its sides. This peak was before us, a little to the left, white shaded with grey, and apparently retreating in the midst of a thick cloud of haze which moved slowly round it. On the right stood out the Cylindre, more sombre than this cloud, more menacing than Mont Perdu itself, set up on its enormous pedestal about the level of which we stood, and so near us, that it appeared as if we could touch it with our hands. It signified nothing that I had seen it a hundred times at a distance; it appeared to me more fantastic than ever. Always invisible from the intermediate stations, it had suddenly grown into a colossus which was magnified in my eyes by the remembrance of its first appearance.

This figure of a truncated tower which recalls the idea of known dimensions, contrasting with proportions to which nothing is comparable, its situation, color, proximity, the vapor in which it was enveloped, all concurred to make this enormous rock the most extraordinary object in the picture. It was to this that all eyes constantly returned. It was this that the guides persisted in calling 'Mont Perdu.'

But what was still more unexpected, if possible, than these strange sights, what no former view had prepared us for, what we could only look on from the height of the observatory on which we were placed, was the indescribable appearance of the majestic support of these two summits. Cut out by the same scissors which have fashioned the flights of the Marboré, it presents a succession of steps sometimes draped in snow, sometimes covered with glaciers which at times overflow and pour themselves one over the other in large and motionless cascades, even to the borders of a lake of which the surface, still frozen, but freed from the snows, shone with a quiet brightness which heightened the dazzling whiteness of its banks.

This lake, the desolate area in which it reposed, the mass of ice which bounded it on the south, the black walls which surmount it, the Cylindre and Mont Perdu towering up into a stormy sky, and that rocky, naked, and rugged enclosure, from one of the battlements of which we were contemplating the most imposing and frightful scene in the Pyrenees; all and everything defied comparison; nothing at first presented itself by comparison with the known dimensions of which we could estimate the size of the whole; and we should have been reduced to a vague notion of heights and distances if accident had not furnished us with a determinate object in a troup of izards which wandered over the ice of the lake and drank in the crevasses. At the first cry they fled over the rocks, leaving us alone in these vast deserts, the extent of which they had enabled us to measure.

It was time to settle what we should do in order to visit the attainable points. I had not been slow to perceive that the way to the peaks was closed to us by the chaotic state of its glacier, and the steepness of its sides. Even the izards had avoided them in their flight, although that would have been the shortest way to escape from our view; and they had gone the whole length of the lake in order to take refuge in the more accessible heights which separate the Cylindre from the region of the Marboré. But we might descend into the basin. The slope, though rapid, was absolutely free from danger; and once on the level of the lake and its icy surface opened communications with several parts, and nothing hindered us from following the paths taken by the izards up to the western ridge of the Cylindre, and over the last steps of Mont Perdu.

But we had to think of returning; it was midday, and the state of the sky indicated an approaching change in the weather. If we spent the rest of the day here, we should have no longer a choice of the way to retreat, and our only resource would be to go back by the same way that we had come. But those of my companions who had trembled at the perils of the ascent, could not without imprudence be exposed to the more real danger of that descent. In default of convenient roads we must at least choose dangers not so well known to them. I remembered the declivity of the valley of Béousse, which the Spanish shepherds regard as the natural road from the lake. According to them, this way communicated with the back of the Port de Pinède. It was a long *détour*, certainly, and if we took it we must give up, from that time, any new enterprise; but, on the other hand, the smuggler assured me that these rocks were very practicable, and that he was going part of the way himself to get to the valley of Faulo. I could then recross the lake the next day, and possibly conduct La Peyrouse into these extraordinary places where I had already regretted his absence so many times. So I quickly decided to inform him of my movements. I wrote to him to pass the Port de Pinède directly, and to wait for us at the bottom of the valley of Béousse in a ruined house which I described to him from the smuggler's description of it. I told him of my design of returning next day, and of my hope that he might be able to go with me. I gave the note to one of the guides from Coumélie, who decided to carry it over the valley of snow at the bottom of which he must still be. The departure of my courier was not the least affecting episode of the journey. We had to watch him clambering through the snow, helping himself with his hands, and going with the greatest care, that he might not miss the track of our steps. All these delaying obstacles which he encountered were bad auguries for the success of his embassy; and the event justified the foreboding: it was again in vain that I had hoped to conduct La Peyrouse to Mont Perdu.

However, I gave a last look at the rocks of the beach, and my companions, whose predilection was for plants, drew my attention to the few specimens of vegetation which managed to resist even the bitter winter of a region of 9000 feet at least above the level of the sea. The northern exposure only offered us one plant; but it was the glacial ranunculus, which is so rare in the Pyrenees that I had only found two specimens at the top of Néouville, and of them I had been obliged to send one to La Peyrouse, in order to persuade him that it was there. In this place it was abundant and superb, but suspended to rocks which were exceedingly steep, and which were themselves suspended over such a formidable precipice, that in order to get some, all our zeal for science was called forth. Mirbel and Pasquier first seized some, and their example encouraged the others. No one had made such a bold step before; and none had been made so heartily. From the bosom of the lake rose a chain of rocks, which formed a long promontory. The shapes of this chain indicate a perfect similitude between its structure and that of the bases of the Cylindre: this, therefore, offered to me an object of comparison which must take away all my doubts.

I descended quickly. The lake was covered with a thick ice, the crevasses of which it was easy to jump; and I soon gained the promontory. I found the rock divided into horizontal layers, like the steps of the Marboré, the walls of the Brèche de Roland, and the Cylindre and its platform. But then these layers? Were they only on the external edges, or strata running through? The first stroke of the hammer answered the question: they were only external, and the strata were vertical. I was going to strike a second time into the body of the rock when I perceived on its surface a reddish projection. I looked nearer, and recognized a piece of a polypary. I looked again, and I saw the upper valve of an oyster; then some fragments of a madrepore, then of other broken zoophytes, of which I could not determine the species. . . . . I cried out, called my companions, and assembled them on the rocks, which were all clammy with the remains of various organisms. And I showed them these venerable remains, which on the sides of Mont Perdu had a very peculiar importance. They spread themselves over the promontory, and eagerly tore up everything which could be distinguished from the substance of the stone; and working myself with a new ardor in the midst of these ardent workers, I enjoyed a pleasure which no one could share with me—that of having opened so fine a field of observation to future travellers, who perhaps will find there some day what the actual state of our scientific knowledge did not permit us to see.

It was a pleasant thing to see the pupils of two rising schools in possession of a field of which the learned would envy us the discovery; and I could not unmoved see these young men gaining from this first success a passion for research and a thirst for learning. They themselves felt the influence of the place, and gave themselves up to transports which almost amounted to delirium.

'Let us stay here,' they said: 'to-morrow perhaps we shall accomplish the ascent to the peak.'

'But the cold of the night?'

'What is a night with such a hope before us?'

'But what about food?'

'Oh, they would do without that;' fatigues, fears, dangers—all were forgotten: prudence and foresight were at a discount. The ice was no longer terrible; the thick clouds which encircled the summit were no longer threatening, when all at once there was heard from these very clouds a fearful peal, which echoed and thus multiplied itself many times among the rocks. The most determined turned pale; they thought that they could already see the storm breaking over these frightful solitudes, and that it would shut us in: it was, nevertheless, nothing but a fall of snow from the upper steps of the mountain; but the impression was made, and now they only thought of getting away.

Hardly had we passed the lake when we found ourselves on the edge of a precipice, of which no other would give any idea. It seemed as if the earth had altogether on a sudden escaped from beneath our feet. On whatever side we turned there seemed nothing but a precipitous declivity and steep walls. On the left the mountains of Estaubé, on the right Mont Perdu, plunging into an immense profundity, and forming two long parallel chains, which were made of the same rock, cut out by the same model, and which enclosed between these enormous boulevards the valley of Béousse, over which we stood, as from some height on the airy regions, and which gradually disappeared from view.

Truly this valley was ravishing, lying in the midst of the rocks, which serve as battlements to it, and of the snows which fertilize it. Rich in the luxury of nature, and lovely in its wild beauty, it is just the earth in the first days of its birth, and before man had subjected it to cultivation. I sought in vain for any traces of the region being frequented: but neither stronghold, nor road, nor pathway, nor inn could be seen; travellers avoid this wild region, which they either cannot or dare not face, and which whoever approaches may easily think himself the first who has done so. Those meadows without flocks, those shades which have never been planted, those virgin forests, those box-hedges which have never been clipped, and that torrent which rises in Mont Perdu, the Cinca, so proud of its origin, so impetuous, so ungovernable, coursing along in a cutting full of ruins—all these things must be seen to be imagined. The eye follows this river in its course, and wanders with it in the desert, where it travels without obstacle and without witness. It seems to flee, and you follow it still; the eye seeks on the edge of the horizon the last rippling of its waves. The ear catches eagerly the last murmur which the wind brings back. It escapes all the senses at last in the deep valleys where it runs; and then the imagination still pursues it to the distant banks where the Ebro receives those waters of which we here saw the secret springs. But, after all, what is the great hidden charm of these deserts? What involuntary, deep, and imperious feeling holds me in these places where my fellows have not established their empire? What irresistible inclination ceaselessly draws back my thoughts and my steps, and holds and amuses my fancy in the vain desire there to build my cottage and bring up my family? What is civilization if it still leave in our hearts an imperishable regret for our old independence? What is society if man, whom she has fashioned to her will, and attached to her by habit and necessity, cannot escape an instant from the crowd which constrains him without shedding a tear at the thought of the necessity which plunges him back into it?

RAMOND, *Voyages au Mont Perdu.*

XII.

NORTH CAPE.

VOYAGE OF JOSEPH ACERBI, IN 1798.

WE set out for Alten on Monday, the 15th of July, at two o'clock in the afternoon, and we did not arrive at the Cape till the night between the Friday and Saturday following. Three miles from Alten we passed on our right a mountain, called in Norwegian Himellar, or Heaven-man, from which there fell into the sea five or six cascades, two or three hundred yards of perpendicular height. Further onward was another grand cataract, where we quenched our thirst. We went up into the mountains to see the place where it had its source, and were surprised to find at their summit very beautiful natural meadows. Still further off we again saw a fine cascade running down from another mountain. All these waterfalls were supplied, no doubt, by the melting of the snow on the distant mountains, which formed, as it were, the back-ground of the picture. The cascade last mentioned was precipated from a hill, adorned on three sides with a wood of birch, spread in the manner of an amphitheatre, so that it

THE NORTH CAPE.

appeared as if it had been planted by the hand of man. In the midst of this pleasure-ground stood a wooden house, covered with turf, and inhabited by a family of fixed Laplanders. I wished to pay them a visit. One of our guides, however, besought me not to go there immediately by myself, but to send him on before me, because, said he, the family will perhaps be frightened at the sight of a stranger of so different an appearance to their own. He went into the house, but found nobody there; it was completely deserted; the family had either gone on a fishing excursion, or were in the mountains tending their reindeer. . . . We returned with regret to our boats, and it was not without pain that we bade adieu to so charming a prospect, which bore a striking resemblance to all that is most romantic and beautiful in the natural scenery of Switzerland.

There was not a breath of wind, and our boatmen were much fatigued with rowing in so great a heat. In order to give them some respite, and to gratify our own curiosity, we visited all the Laplanders settled on this coast, who generally lived at the distance of a Norwegian mile, or a mile and a half from one another. Abundance and contentment reign in all their dwellings. Each Laplander is the proprietor of the territory around his little mansion, to the extent of a Norwegian mile, or eight English, in every direction. They have some cows, which furnish them excellent milk, and meadow-land, which yields hay for their fodder in winter. They have every one a store of fish, dried in the sun, not only for their own use, but wherewithal to purchase luxuries—that is, salt, oatmeal, and some woclen clothes. Their houses are constructed in the form of tents—a hole in the middle, which gives them light, serves also as an aperture for letting out the smoke of the fire, which is always placed in the centre of the cabin, and around which they sleep quite close to one another. In winter, besides the heat of the fire, they have the benefit of the animal warmth of the cows, with whom they share the shelter of their roof, as the inhabitants of Scotland do in the Highlands and the northern isles. The doors of their houses in summer are always open, and although in that season there is no night, they are accustomed to sleep at the same time as other Europeans. . . . They not only sleep with their doors wide open, but so soundly that it is not easy to rouse them. The fact is, that they are not to be exposed to any kind of danger or disturbance. They are far removed from the anxieties of fear that attend envied possession; and the only wild beasts that could possibly give them any alarm or uneasiness are the wolves and bears. But these animals never attack houses, as they procure sufficient nourishment by following the wandering Laplanders with their reindeer. . . .

In one of the families we visited we witnessed a very tender and affecting scene, which convinced us that sensibility is not banished from those northern latitudes. At three o'clock after midnight we entered a cabin, in which there were, besides the master of the house, his mother, his young wife, and two infant children. They were fast asleep, and we waited for some time that we might awake them gently: they all of them lay on the ground, which they had covered with the branches and leaves of the fragrant and aromatic birch; over these were spread some reindeer skins. They slept, as the maritime Laplanders do in general, with their clothes on; but these, being very large and loose, occasion no inconvenience by impeding in any degree the

Island of Lofoden, North Cape.

circulation of the blood. The wife awoke first, and casting her eyes on one of our boatmen, whom she knew, she was glad to see him, and entered into conversation with him in Lapponese. The husband and his aged mother also awoke soon after, but the children continued in their sound sleep. The old woman perceiving our Laplander, burst into a flood of tears; the young woman likewise wept, so did the boatman; and so by instinctive sympathy did we all, without knowing why. For a moment we preserved a dead silence, when our interpreter having entered the cabin, and found us in tears, asked in Finnish the reason of all this sorrow. The occasion was this: the old woman had seen the boatman about a year before, when she was in perfect health, but since that time she had been seized by a fit of apoplexy, which had totally deprived her of the use of speech. After this general emotion had subsided, we asked for some reindeer milk and cheese. Our landlady immediately went out of the cabin and conducted us to the store, which was a little wooden box or shed raised upon beams to a certain height from the ground, that the provisions it contained might not be damaged by the snow of winter. We were astonished at the quantity of things this good and provident woman had in her magazine. There was great plenty of dried fish and dried reindeer flesh, cheese, and tongues of the reindeer, oatmeal, reindeer skins, fur and woolen clothes, and other articles. Everything bespoke riches and comfort; and what was most remarkable, our kind hostess gave us whatever we wanted in the most liberal manner, and without the least idea of receiving aught in return; on the contrary, she persisted in refusing to accept any money when we offered it. I have seen few places where the people live in so easy and happy a simplicity as in the maritime districts of Lapland. . . .

We left this cabin to pursue our voyage, but after proceeding five or six English miles, we were obliged by the wind again to land.... We travelled seven or eight English miles on foot, and found here and there among those mountains delicious spots and valleys, enclosed by hills that were covered with birch and some other trees. We came at last to a mountain Laplander's tent, and our curiosity was satisfied: this tent was of a conical form, and not shaped as tents are in general. In the middle was the fire, and around the fire sat the Laplander's wife, a boy, who was his son, and some inhospitable and surly dogs, which never ceased barking at us all the time we remained near them. Fast by the tent was erected a shed, consisting of five or six sticks or posts that were fastened to one another near the top, in the same manner as the tent, and covered with skins and pieces of cloth: under this canopy the Laplanders kept their provisions, which were cheese of the reindeer, a small quantity of milk of the same, and dried fish.

A little further on was a rude enclosure or parting, made in haste, which served as a fold or yard for the reindeer when they were brought together to be milked. Those animals were not near the tents at the time of our visit; they were in the mountains, from whence they would not descend till towards night. As we did not feel ourselves disposed to ramble about in quest of them, at the hazard of losing ourselves among a series of mountains, we judged it more advisable to offer some brandy to the Laplanders, on condition that they would go with their dogs and bring the reindeer home, or as near as they could to the tent. Scarcely had they swallowed the brandy which we had given them as an earnest of more, when we heard the shrill barking of the dogs resounding through the mountains. The Laplanders then told us that the reindeer were coming, and very soon after we beheld a troop of not less than three hundred deer descending from the mountains in a direction towards the tent. We then insisted that they should drive the reindeer within the enclosure near the tent, that we might have an opportunity of seeing and examining them better, and tasting the milk fresh from the does. They did as we desired, but not without very great difficulty, because the animals, not being accustomed to be shut up in the fold at that hour of the day, were unwilling to be confined; and it was not till after repeated efforts that the Laplanders were able at last, with the assistance of the dogs, to compel them to enter. We then had time to view them at our leisure. These poor animals were lean, and of a sad and melancholy appearance: their hair hung down, and their excessive panting indicated how much they suffered at this season from heat; their skins were pierced here and there, and ulcerated by the mosquitoes, and the eggs of the fly, called in Lapponese *kerma*, which tormented them in the most cruel manner. I made a collection of those insects and their eggs, intending them as presents for my entomological friends. As to the milk which we tasted, it is not so good at this time as in winter. In summer it has always a kind of strong or wild taste, and too much of what the French call *haut goût*.

THE ISLAND OF MAGEROE, NORTH CAPE

Our guides advised us to return to the boats, and avail ourselves of the favorable breeze that had sprung up for pursuing our voyage, and we took leave of our Laplanders, whose only regret at our departure seemed to be mortification at the removal of the brandy. We passed in our boat the Whaal-Sund, or Sound of Whales, which was agitated at the same time by the current that sets in here very strong, and by the wind, which blew contrary to the current. Whales resort to this strait in great numbers, and are, as we were told, very common in all these seas. Although we were assured by our mariners that they never passed this strait without seeing eight or ten whales, we were so unfortunate as not to get a sight of one. We went on shore to the house of a merchant, situated on an island near Havesund; this was perhaps the most dismal habitation on the face of the earth. The whole land around it did not produce one tree or shrub; no, not so much as a blade of grass; there was nothing to be seen but naked rocks. The inhabitant of that house had not anything but what he brought from a distance, not even fuel. The sun for three months of the year is not visible; and if during that space of time the atmosphere were not illuminated by the *aurora borealis*, he would be buried in profound darkness. Dreadful place to live at! The only attraction in these abodes is fishing, and the love of gain. The nearer one approaches to the North Cape the more nature seems to frown: vegetation dies, and leaves behind it nothing but naked rocks.

Proceeding on our voyage, we left on our right

the strait formed by Mageröe, or Bare Island, of the continent. The vast expanse of the Frozen Ocean opened to our left, and we arrived at last at the extremest point of Europe, known by the name of the North Cape, exactly at midnight.

The North Cape is an enormous rock, which projecting far into the ocean, and being exposed to all the fury of the waves and the outrage of tempests, crumbles every year more and more into ruins. Here everything is solitary, everything is sterile, everything sad and despondent. The shadowy forest no longer adorns the brow of the mountain; the singing of the birds, which enlivened even the woods of Lapland, is no longer heard in this scene of desolation; the ruggedness of the dark grey rock is not covered by a single shrub; the only music is the hoarse murmuring of the waves, ever and anon renewing the assaults on the huge masses that oppose them. The northern sun, creeping at midnight at the distance of five diameters along the horizon, and the immeasurable ocean in apparent contact with the skies, form the grand outlines in the sublime picture presented to the astonished spectator. The incessant cares and pursuits of anxious mortals are recollected as a dream; the various forms and energies of animated nature are forgotten; the earth is contemplated only in its elements, and as constituting a part of the solar system.

JACOB ACERBI, *Travels through Sweden, Finland, and Lapland, to the North Cape, in the years* 1798 *and* 1799.

XIII.

THE BROCKEN.

THE Brocken is the name of the principal mountain of the picturesque chain of the Hartz mountains, in the kingdom of Hanover. From its summit, raised about 10,500 feet above the level of the sea, may be seen a plain of 70 leagues in extent, occupying nearly the twentieth part of Europe, and having a population of more than 5,000,000 of inhabitants.

From the most remote historical epochs, the Brocken has been the theatre of the marvellous. On the top of it there may still be seen blocks of granite, called the Seat and the Altar of the Sorceress; a spring of limpid water is named the *Magic Fountain;* and the common name of the anemone which grows on this mountain is the *flower of the fairies.* We may presume that these names owe their origin to the worship of the great idol which the Saxons secretly worshipped on the summit of the Brocken, when Christianity was already dominant in the plain. And as the place in which this worship was celebrated must have been much frequented, no doubt this spectre which so often haunts it at the rising of the sun was taken notice of in these long past times. So tradition says that this spectre had its share in the tribute paid by the superstitious.

If all who constantly live in sight of the Brocken desire to ascend it at least once in their lives;—if all other Germans, who, though it lies out of their

The Brocken.

horizon, have often heard of it and aspire also to enjoy the spectacle in question, which, living as they do in the plains, their imagination is unable to represent to them by any analogous image, it is easy to conceive what an influence this mountain has in the fine season. Still it has only been since the beginning of this century that the fashion of visiting the Brocken has become an established one. It appears that all the exaggerations of the eighteenth century were necessary to interest men in its beauties. Before that there were few, besides the woodcutters, who were eager enough about it to attempt a difficult ascent. Towards the end of the last century, the number of the curious increasing, the Count of Vernigerode, whose principality lies under the sides of the mountain, and embraces the mountain itself, taking pity on those who suffered from tempests on these heights, and sympathizing with those who wished to pass the night there, in order to witness the rising and setting of the sun,—caused a hotel to be constructed on the top. It was finished on the 10th of September, 1800. One of the servants of the Count's household, an excellent man, who will be remembered by all who visited the Brocken during his lifetime, was installed as innkeeper, at the height of 3500 feet, under the strange condition that he should always live there, even during the winter,—no doubt in order that it might be said that the goodness of the Count never fails in any weather. So this brave man allowed himself to be buried in the snow all the year round with his wife and daughter; for it often accumulates even to the top of the roof; and they could only breathe and see the sky through a little tower in the middle of the house. Thus he passed thirty-three years in perfect serenity. And from this elevation he could, in one sense, command all Germany. I must be permitted this remembrance of a simple-minded, honest soul. The contrast between his patriarchal hospitality and the often stormy majesty of the mountain, is striking, and, at the same time, resting and pleasant. When I ascended the Brocken for the first time as a young man, I reached the top at eleven o'clock at night, having lost my way, and being pierced through and through with the cold; but some dogs, in answer to my call, signalized my approach, and the good Gerlach came running to meet me with a lantern and some brandy. Next morning, when I left, he would descend with me as far as the forests, and his eyes were full of tears. I was, no doubt, the last visitor whom he would see that year; for the snow already threatened to entomb them. This year I did not find him there; and I could not help mourning for him, for his name is attached to the history of the mountain.

The Brocken is now a sort of necessity to the people of Lower Germany. They love to contemplate from its summit that fatherland which seems so parcelled out and divided to those who do not view it from above. Students, above all, go there in numbers. There are universities all around,—Marburg, Gottingen, Jena, Leipzig, Halle, Berlin; and the ascent of the Brocken is a sort of exercise which the students feel obliged to take.

It is not, however, only on account of this singular spectacle which is seen from the summit, but from the nature of its rocks and firs, that the Brocken has become famous among the poets. It is here that, for a long time, if we are to believe the tradition all the witches in Germany have held their rendezvous. They even assert that the devil himself hailed down the rocks which cover the cupola of the mountain.

For some years past the ascent of this mountain has been wonderfully facilitated. I have related with what difficulty I formerly mounted. In order to understand this, it is necessary to know that the Brocken is not a mountain, but literally a heap of stones. It is probable that originally it was composed of high needles of granite, of which some are still to be seen in other parts of the Hartz. In course of time these needles have become divided into enormous blocks, which have fallen and accumulated around the base, so that, at length, nothing but ruins remain of the primitive edifice. It is amidst these blocks that the fir-trees have rooted themselves. The waters filter through and roar below, and every moment after you quit the regular paths, you run the risk of falling into some bog, which is half covered with moss and large plants. Otherwise, there is scarely a precipice, I may say scarcely a ravine, into which one could fall. It is a squat monster, on the round back of which a man may easily climb. This time I ascended it, not on foot, not on a mule, not in a chair carried by porters; I went up in a post-chaise. They have made an excellent road, as sure and safe as the gravel path of a park, without any danger, without any difficulty, without even a jump; and by just paying a very moderate toll, every one is free to avail himself of it. I could not believe my eyes when I found myself in my carriage, with my Hanoverian postilion smacking his whip and blowing his horn on this height, which had cost me so dear at my first ascent. Add to that, that I had travelled from Dresden to Harzburg during the day, and had reached the foot of the Brocken after a journey of 300 miles by railway.

THE HEXENTANZPLATZ.—THE ILSENSTEIN.

It was in the midst of a wild and desert place, among heaps of naked and sombre rocks, between which the Bode winds its course, that in former times the sorceresses of the north held their solemn meeting every year on the first of May. The place was well chosen, and few persons were likely to have the indiscretion to trouble their rendezvous. Even in our civilized times, in full daylight, under the azure of a fine sky, and in the glad rays of the sun, these dark shapeless masses, so rugged and so strange, arrest the smile on the lips of the traveller, and cause him to think that, however little superstitious he may be, he would feel rather strange about midnight, on some peak, or in some dark passage of this convulsion of nature, which has the appearance of a petrified tempest. Let him suppose, to increase the effect, that heavy clouds were hanging over the summits, that pale lightnings and heavy thunders were seen and heard, and there would be wanting few favorable conditions to any one who wished to assure himself that he was at all times master of his nervous system.

It is on the Hexentanzplatz that Goethe has placed

THE BROCKEN, HEXENTANZPLATZ.

the scenes of the witches' meeting (the Walpurgis night) in the drama of 'Faust:'—

'How strangely across these abysses shines a northerly and dim light, which penetrates even into the depths of the gulf! There rises a vapor; further off an unhealthy exhalation. Here, through a veil of mists, flashes a warm brightness, sometimes like a light thread, sometimes breaking out as from a living source. Here, it winds in a thousand streaks across the valley, and further on, in a narrow gorge, it collects all at once. Near us falls a rain of sparks, which cover the soil with a gold dust; but look there, in all its heights, the wall of rocks is in a blaze.'

MEPHISTOPHELES.—'Does not Lord Mammon light up his palace splendidly for the feast?'

We can now ascend quite easily on to the Plateau of the Witches, thanks to a staircase of eleven hundred steps. There we are almost opposite to the granite rocks of the Rossetrappe (Horse's Hoof-print). From the one side you command the valley of the Bode; from the other a vast plain towards the west.

The Ilsenstein, like most part of the Hartz Mountains, is isolated, and terminates the chain of mountains which go towards the east, towards the plateau of Thuringia. It is in front of the Brocken, and is an immense block of granite, which rises to a peak at more than 300 feet above the valley, in which flows the little river Ilse, forming an innumerable number of cascades, which are particularly charming, from their bright and smiling appearance in the midst of such stern scenery.

According to tradition, there was at the summit of the Ilsenstein an enchanted palace, inhabited by a king of the Hartz, named Ilsan; and he had a daughter of remarkable beauty, named Ilse. A wicked fairy caused this charming princess to die of jealousy. She is still to be seen sometimes, as the superstitious people think, bathing in the river which bears her name. If she meets a traveller, she conducts him to the interior of the mountain, where she loads him with riches. Perhaps the meaning of this legend is, that this mountain contains, like the Rammelsberg, precious mines. The summit is reached by a steep pathway, which passes over blocks of naked rock of the most singular forms.

From the Ilsenstein you gain the top of the Brocken by an easy and picturesque road. This mountain, the usual end and aim of excursions in the Hartz, is estimated very differently by persons who have made the ascent. As on the Righi, the common desire of tourists is to see the sun rise; but though a pure sky is favorable for the spectacle, there are also unexpected moments which answer the traveller's wishes as perfectly. We had started in the evening from Ilsenstein in very bad weather; but we had the good fortune next day to witness one of the curious sights which leave a much stronger impression than that of a splendid and vast panorama stretched out beneath one's feet. The clouds which were crowded over the valley in a compact and heavy mass, resembled a sea formed of immense and motionless waves ; electric currents passed from one to another from time to time, but without producing the least noise. At this moment the sun rose, and, by a strange contrast, lighted up, in a reddish tint, the upper part of the mountain on which we were, without communicating any of this lively color to the lower mass of clouds, which retained their leaden hues : it seemed as if all the bright rays were broken one by one, and decomposed on their surface. The effect was magical : it appeared like two different worlds seen the one from the other,—the earth seen from some superior planet. To describe faithfully what we felt at this moment would require the genius of Milton or of Dante.

Magasin Pittoresque.

XIV.

PARNASSUS.

Castri is the name of a miserable village perched on a rock, like the nest of a bird of prey; it is also the name borne in the present day by the site of Delphos, the ancient sanctuary of Apollo.

At a little distance from Arakhova, ascending by roads where the Klepht alone can venture without trembling, you arrive at excavations worked in the rock and consecrated formerly to the god Pan and the nymph Gorycia. A long inscription, all defaced, indicates the Gorycian cave, to which access for horses was practicable in the time of Pausanias, who declares that he had never seen a grotto more spacious, or more beautiful; but now a great part of it is filled up by water and ruins. It was at the Gorycian cave that the Thyades, priestesses of Athens, used to assemble at one time of the year, calling to them the women of Phocis and foreign women, whom devotion brought to Delphos. Becoming excited at last, by their mysterious practices, and; for the time being, in a state of delirium, they then mounted the most impracticable paths, and reached the highest peak of Parnassus. There, lost in the clouds, they gave themselves up to strange madness in honor of Apollo.

Some ruins of marble sarcophagi, hidden under the vines which on this side cover the stony and rapid slope of the valley; a subterranean chamber into which it is easy to penetrate; the impression of the hinges and of the enormous nails of a door in the rock; a door which closed, as they say, a secret road leading to the tripod of the Sibyl; some little columns sustaining the external vestibule of a poor church; a basement wall, which they regard as indicating the place of the temple of Apollo, in which the god used to be, and on which may be read an inscription well preserved, recording the decrees made in honor of the benefactors of the temple, the names of several architects employed in constructing or enlarging it, and the enfranchisement of a slave by his consecration to the god; lastly, all along the only path which traverses the valley, niches of various sizes cut in the rock, and in which the image of a Madonna has taken the place of the rich oblations of the Pagans:—this is all which is left to remind us of the existence of proud Delphos. No temples nor statues covered with gold, and shining in the sun; no longer any. dances, or games, or solemn processions, or assemblies of the people; no Amphictyons regulating the destinies of Greece; no more conquerors eager to tear from heaven the secret of their future lives; no longer any philosophers bowing before the sagest and truest device which the genius of Paganism ever brought forth: 'Know thyself.'

All has disappeared, just as on the day after a *fête*, the splendid scaffolding, the music, the dances, and the pleasure-seeking people, are gone. The pale and sorrowful Sibyl seems alone to inhabit these sombre and desert places. In a dream into which the imagination easily falls, one sees her pass, unhappy in her glory and in her involuntary science, and conducted by inflexible priests, who force her to sit on the fatal tripod, where the god awaits her with his furies, his delirium, his tortures, and his obscure lies. This recollection is the only one which vividly strikes the mind when you stop at Delphos. All around are abysses, half open and yawning gulfs, resounding echoes, rocks blackened as if by fire: such was, and such is still, the valley of Delphos.

If the riches and the magnificence destined to veil the terrible mysteries have disappeared, Nature is there just the same. Now, as formerly, the Phocean, who comes to dream, to seek the shade, or to gather flowers, must pass over to the other side of Parnassus, in order to find the green and melodious forests of Daulis. Some olive-trees grow in the hollow of the valley at the outlet from which they become more abundant, until they form a great wood on the plain, which extends to the gulf. In the night, if you awake, you hear the wind which comes ceaselessly from the sea, and beats against the sides of the rocks, making most lugubrious noises; and yet, at some paces from thence,

MOUNT PARNASSUS.

in the bay and on the banks of Crissa, the same wind sings or sighs in soft and melancholy tones. At Delphos, it becomes a dull groaning, a prolonged plaint, which fills the soul with sadness, and makes you fear, when you listen to it, that the ancient oracle may have recovered its voice, in order to reveal to you the future which lies before you.

Y. Gemeniz, *Voyage en Greece.*

The Greeks have placed the dwellings of the Muses, that is to say, the source of poetical inspiration, as well as the dwelling of the gods, on the highest summits,—there where earth seems to touch heaven. The Muses haunted Olympus, Pieria, Helicon, and, above all, Parnassus.

Parnassus is one of the most beautiful mountains of Greece; on its snowy summits walked the chaste Muses in their purity! The summits of Parnassus are often enveloped in clouds. 'Who ever saw Liakoura without clouds?' said Lord Byron. This peculiarity agrees with the destiny which ancient mythology attributed to the holy mountain. The poetical creation is a mystery; it was becoming to envelop it in mysterious clouds.

Among the Greeks, all inspirations were sisters: Parnassus consecrated the alliance of poetical and religious enthusiasm. Whilst the Thyades celebrated there those dances which the madness of Bacchus had animated, the Pythian, seated on the tripod, breathed in the prophetic emanations of the mountain, Apollo had his temple there, in the place of which there now flourishes a laurel, an emblem of the inspiration which does not die. The Muses bathed there in the stream of Castalia, which is still flowing, and whose remarkably pure and light water is a charming emblem of the limpid poetry of the Greeks. Ingenious in linking the natural peculiarities of places with ideas, such as the fables connected with those places express, the ancients had placed the temple of Apollo at the foot of the peaked rocks named the Brilliants (Phedriades), which reflect even now with so much power the arrows of the god. In their eyes the god of light and heat was the god of verse; and they dedicated to him a steep and inaccessible peak. The perfection of art is a warm and luminous summit, up which no pathway leads, and to which only the flight of a divine will carries any one.

Above the site of the ancient Delphos rises the double summit so often invoked by poets. It stands over against the very picturesque grotto, from which flows the spring of Castalia. M. Ulrichs points out that certain Latin poets, such as Ovid and Lucan, who never were at Delphos, seem to believe that the two peaks, at the foot of which the town was built, form the culminating point of Parnassus, whilst Parnassus has really only one peak, and that is true in every sense, at least of the ancient Parnassus.

One evening, at Drachmani, finding myself at the foot of the Parnassus, and following with my eye the vultures which hover over its sides, I recalled the famous line,—

"C'est en vain qu'au Parnasse un téméraire auteur."

I found an immense effort of reflection necessary to convince me that this proud mountain, which stood erect before me, bathing its rocks, its firs, and its abysses in the violet tints of evening, was really the Parnassus of Boileau.

On the other hand, I really found the Parnassus which was before me in the ancient poets, and above all, in Euripides. And while gazing on those rocks, glittering, as they were, in all the brightness of a southern sun, I did not feel the words of the poet in the 'Phenician Virgins' at all too strong :—

'Thou rock irradiate with the sacred flame,
That blazing on thy artful brow,
Seems double to the vale below.'

J. J. Ampere, *La Poésie Grecque en Grèce.*

The route from the monastery of St. Luke, at Delphos, turns along the sides of the Kirphis or Xero-Vouni, just where it joins the Parnassus or Liakoura. After ascending for about half an hour, you come to a little chapel situated in the most delicious position, close to a spring of water shaded by plantains. There was probably here in old times a religious station for the pilgrims who came to Delphos, for the road seemed to follow the old route. When once you have passed these ravines of the chain of the Kirphis you perceive the entrance to the deep gorge from which old Delphos was visible. Just at the entrance of this gorge, high up in the mountain, on the extreme bounds of the cultivated ground, and at the foot of those snowy cones which give an imposing physiognomy to the frowning brow of the Liakoura, appears like a vigilant watch, the city of Arachova. Some black pine forests seem placed near the edge of this sort of glacier like a dyke intended to stop the invasion of the snows. At the other extremity of this gorge, also very high up, at the foot of the porphyry rocks, is the village of Castri, built on the ruins of Delphos.

There remained still two hours on horseback to turn all the hills and re-ascend as far as to Castri, which one always keeps in view; but in proportion as we neared it the sight became at each step more beautiful. In the lower parts of the hills one has to cross short well-watered and well-planted valleys, keeping in your eye the fresh valley of the Plistus. As soon as the top of the hills is reached, the bay of Salona, the gulf of Corinth, and in the distance the mountains of the Peloponnesus, become visible. Going a little further, we found the sea disappear again, and we were in an enclosure of high mountains, and as it were isolated from the rest of the world. It must have been a fine spectacle when on the solemn feast days the ancient processions used to wind away from the two opposite sides, arriving by sea at Crissa, and by land on the coasts of Arachova. From the time of first stepping on this sacred ground the traveller passed over tombs; some had been erected on this part of the route, just as a Christian of ancient days might have caused his to be erected near Jerusalem, or in the valley of Jehoshaphat; others have been brought down by the fall of the upper rocks, whose enormous fragments lie dispersed around. Nothing less than one of those violent earthquakes, which are so common here, is necessary to precipitate them.

The tombs continue as far as the monastery of St. Elias. At some steps from the monastery flows a little river which comes from the spring of Castalia, situate a little above, on the right of the road. A torrent descends from the Parnassus by a fissure between two steep rocks, the rock Naplia and that of Hyampeia, down which they say the fabulist Æsop was precipitated by the inhabitants of Delphos. When it reaches the extremity of this narrow fissure, the torrent is received into a short arched passage, and flows into a square basin dug by nature itself in the rock, but increased a little by the hand of man. This basin, which is about 30 feet long by 10 wide, encloses the celebrated fountain of Castalia. Below the fountain, on the side of a rock a hundred feet in perpendicular height, are scooped out three niches. That in the middle, which is the largest, probably contains a statue of Apollo, and the two others the statues of the god Pan and of the nymph Castalia. A fourth niche, placed on the right, is shut in by walls, and transformed into a chapel dedicated to St. John, which has, no doubt, succeeded to the

Héroüm* dedicated to Antinoüs. The Christian religion has all over Greece established its altars in the very places sanctified by ancient feelings of reverence. . . . Seated on a rock in the sound of the murmurs of this torrent, on the edge of the Castalian fountain, which two formidable rocks shut in on one side, whilst the other opens on to a deep valley—a real solitude enclosed on all sides by mountains, I could conceive without difficulty the impression of religious feeling which must seize on the imagination of visitors, and dispose them to receive the decisions of the oracle.

J. A. BUCHON. *La Grèce continentale et la Morée.*

---

* A little temple erected by the Greeks in honor of deified heroes.

XV.

MOUNT ATHOS.

BY DR. HUNT.

ON Easter Monday, after a stay of five days, we set out with mules provided for us by the convent to the town of Chariess, in the centre of the Peninsula, where the Turkish Aga and the council of deputies from all the convents reside for the disposal of public business. It was necessary to make this visit, in order that our imperial firman and our letter from the Greek Patriarch might be examined, and that we might be informed how to make the tour of the convents with the greatest ease and security. The distance from Batopaidi to Chariess is two hours and three quarters. About three miles from the former we had a most striking view of the summit of Athos. The whole ride furnishes a succession of sublime Alpine scenery. Instead of the usual salutations which are exchanged between travellers who meet on the road, the only one we now heard was the Easter congratulation, 'Christ is risen;' to which the answer is, 'He is the true God.'

Chariess is the only town in the Peninsula.

situated nearly in the centre of it, on the side of a natural amphitheatre, clothed with the richest verdure, and cultivated in a manner to render it highly picturesque. The meadows are so luxuriant as to be cut thrice in a year, owing to the richness of the soil, the complete shelter they enjoy, and the judicious manner in which the water is distributed by irrigation. The vineyards and filbert-gardens are also dressed with uncommon care. Excepting the

Mount Athos.

houses where the Aga and the council of deputies reside, it contains only a few shops, which furnish the monasteries with cloth, sugar, tobacco, snuff, and cordials. Every Saturday a bazaar or market is held there, to which the hermits repair in order to sell what they have manufactured in their solitary huts. Knit stockings, pictures of saints, a few simple oils and essences distilled from plants, common knives and forks, on the horn-handles of which they engrave, with aqua-fortis, a serics of ancient Greek moral adages, compose their principal labors. The trade of making manuscripts is still practised by them ; many devout pilgrims preferring a psalter or prayer-book written by a hermit on the holy mountain to the clearest printed copy. Women are prevented from coming to the town, as well as from visiting any of the convents; nor is any Mussulman permitted to have a shop there. . . .

As the road we were now about to take towards Santa-Laura and the hermitages would conduct us amongst crags and mountains, and to places where there are few mules to be procured, we left the greatest part of our baggage to be sent across the Isthmus, to the convent of Xeropotamo, there to await our arrival. . . .

The natural scenery here is particularly striking, and the summit of Mount Athos, once consecrated by the fame and altars of the Athoan Jove, rears itself with awful grandeur above the surrounding mountains. The manner in which the torrents, breaking from the cliffs above St. Anne's, are distributed by a thousand little wooden aqueducts, so as to water every spot of garden or vineyard, is worthy of being remarked. The woods and thickets in the neighborhood are extremely luxuriant, and the Arachne arbutus flourishes in such profusion as to supply the common fuel. The season was unfavorable for our visiting the summit of Athos, whence the monks assured us that all the islands of the Cyclades may be seen, and even Constantinople, in clear weather. They reckon it a journey of five hours from the hermitage to the top of Mount Athos.

When the learned Greeks fled from Constantinople in 1453, they took with them to Western Europe their most valuable manuscripts; those which they left were probably secreted in the monasteries. The libraries in the islands of the sea of Marmora and of Mount Athos, of the Patriarch of Constantinople, and of St. Saba, near Jerusalem, were carefully examined by Mr. Carlyle and myself. . . .

On taking leave of Father Gerasimos of Chiliantari, we congratulated him on the grace and tranquillity which his little religious commonwealth enjoyed in the midst of the wars and revolutions of Europe; but he replied that, on the contrary, they were in a state of perpetual conflict with three most powerful enemies—the devil, their own lusts, and the travelling caloyers, who embezzle the alms by which the convent should be supported. He accompanied us to the gate, and shaking us affectionately by the hand, said he hoped he had left such an impression of himself on our hearts that we might be mutually glad to see each other if Providence ever brought us again together, quoting a Turkish proverb, 'That mountain never approaches mountain, nor island island; but that man often unexpectedly meets fellow-man.'

We had an escort assigned to us of six well-armed Albanians; our road conducted us through the most picturesque and magnificent scenery; but in some places so dangerous from the precipices which beetle over the sea that a false step of our mules might have been fatal. Six miles from Chiliantari we came to the ruins of a castle called Callitze; and two miles further we halted to breakfast under the shade of some Oriental planes near a fountain, and the bed of a river filled with scarlet oleanders and agnus castus. The spot is called Paparnitz; here we saw once more* cows and ewes with their young, a proof that we had passed the holy precincts.

From Dr. Hunt's *papers.* (*Extract from* '*Memoirs relating to European and Asiatic Turkey,*' *edited from MS. Journals by* Robert Walpole.)

---

* No woman is allowed to enter the gates of any convent on the holy mountain; nor is any female animal permitted to come upon the peninsula. The caloyers, or lay brothers, tell every traveller that no female animal could live there or upon Mount Athos, although they see doves, swallows, and other birds building their nests and hatching their young in the thickets.

XVI.

MOUNT ELBURZ IN THE CAUCASUS.

SIR R. K. PORTER, OCTOBER 1817.

Early in the morning we descended the northern side of the town into a plain, keeping for a considerable way along the foot of some high, well-wooded ground, after which we ascended again over a succession of lands until we reached the village and post of Zergifskoy, a place situated on the slope of a considerable hill, conspicuous even as far as Stavrapol, from its being composed of whitish sand, which from that distance has the appearance of snow. Here two Cossacks were given me for an escort; but how different were they, both in person and costume, from my friends of the Don! Their stature was low, their visages rugged, and their garb of the wildest and most savage fashion. These people belong to the foot of the Caucasus; and, as I proceeded further, I found most of the inhabitants habited in a similar manner. A small cloth cap, bound with sheepskin or fur, fits almost close to their head; while a short vest covers their body, and, falling as far as the knee, meets a pair of loose trousers, which, stuffed into

MOUNT ELBURZ.

boots, completes the uncouth but picturesque habiliment. Their arms are a musket slung across the shoulder, protected from the damp by a hairy case; a straight sword fastened to the left side by the belt round their waist; a dagger of great breadth, and also a large knife, pendent from the same. On the right and left of their breast is sewn a range of narrow pockets, each large enough to hold a wooden case containing a charge of powder; the range usually counts six or eight of these charges. Independent of this magazine, few go without a light cartouche-box attached to another belt which covers the right shoulder. Their saddle and the rest of their horse accoutrements differ little from the fashion of most other Cossacks. But both man and horse are, in some measure, protected by their "*bouka*," a sort of cloak made of the hair of the mountain-goat, and only manufactured by the mountainers. This forms an excellent defence against rain or wind, when brought round the body, but in mild weather it is merely tied on behind. In addition to the cloak they wear a hood for the protection of the face and ears, called a "*bashlick*." No fixed color marks the uniform of the military branch of the imperial Cossacks, but brown, grey, and white, seem the favorite hues.

On quitting Zergifskoy we mounted the height, and continued travelling over a country similar to that we had passed the preceding day. We hoped to gain the town of Alexandroff before night, but were disappointed, and obliged to halt at the village of Severnaia, finding it impossible to proceed on so dangerous a road after dusk. We set off, however, be-times in the morning; and, after traversing a rather uneven country, at the distance of eight or ten versts from our lodgings, reached the brow of a very steep hill, from whence, for the first time, I beheld the stupendous mountains of Caucasus. No pen can express the emotion which the sudden burst of this sublime range excited in my mind. I had seen almost all the wildest and most gigantic chains in Portugal and Spain, but none gave me an idea of the vastness and grandeur of that I now contemplated. This seemed Nature's bulwark between the nations of Europe and of Asia. Elborus (Elburz), amongst whose rocks tradition reports Prometheus to have been chained, stood, clad in primeval snows, a world of mountains in itself, towering above all, its white and radiant summits mingling with the heavens; while the pale and countless heads of the subordinate range, high in themselves, but far beneath its altitude, stretched along the horizon till lost to sight in the soft fleeces of the clouds. Several rough and huge masses of black rock rose from the intermediate plain; their size was mountainous, but being viewed near the mighty Causasus, and compared with them, they appeared little more than hills; yet the contrast was fine, their dark brows giving greater effect to the dazzling summits which towered above them. Poets hardly feign when they talk of the genius of a place. I know not who could behold Caucasus and not feel the spirit of its sublime solitudes awing his soul.

After a description of a ten-days' journey, Sir R. K. Porter continues:—The road lay over a continuation of the extensive plain, part of which we had crossed the day before; it bore a direction due east. On our right rolled the Terek, breaking over its stony bed, and washing with a surge, rather than a flowing stream, the rocky bases of the mountains which rise in progressive acclivities from its bold shores. The day had begun to clear about noon; and the dark curtain of vapors, which had so long shut these stupendous hills from my sight, broke away into a thousand masses of fleecy clouds; and, as they gradually glided downwards, exhaled into ether, or separated across the bows of the mountains, the vast piles of Caucasus were presented to my view; a world of themselves; rocky, rugged, and capped with snow; stretching east and west beyond the reach of vision, and shooting far into the skies. It was a sight to make the senses pause; to oppress even respiration, by the weight of the impression on the mind of such vast and overpowering sublimity. The proud head of Elborus was yet far distant; but it rose in hoary majesty above all, the sovereign of these giant mountains finely contrasting its silvery diadem, the snow of ages, with the blue misty brows of its intermediate subject range; and they, being yet partially shrouded in the dissolving masses of white cloud, derived increased beauty from comparisons with the bold and black forms of the lower mountains nearer the plains, whose rude and towering tops and almost perpendicular sides sublimely carry the astonished eye along the awful picture; creating those feelings of terrific admiration to which words can give no name.

After a ride of two versts,* we reached the key of the celebrated pass into Georgia, where I rejoined my companions.

There is a tradition here that, during the subsiding of the Deluge, the Ark of Noah, while floating over these mountains in the direction of Ararat, its place of final rest, smote the head of Elborus with its keel, and the cleft it made in the mountain has remained ever since. To give any color of feasibility to the legend it had better have represented that the ark struck off the top of the one mountain in its passage to the other; for, otherwise, Elborus, towering as it is, being at present much lower than Ararat, it could not have been touched at all by the sacred vessel floating towards so much higher a region. But this oral tradition of some junction having taken place between Elborus and the earliest personages of Holy Writ, is not the only honor of the kind attached to the history of this celebrated mountain. Heathen tradition and classical writers affirm that Elborus was the huge and savage rock of the Caucasus to which Prometheus was bound. And who but Æschylus has drawn its picture? In his pages alone we find the magnitude, sublimity, and terrors of that "stony girdle of the world," that quarry of the globe, whence all its other mountains may seem to have been chiselled; such are its wonderful abysses, its vast and caverned sides and summits of every form and altitude mingling with the clouds. There is still a tradition amongst the natives who

* Two English miles comprise about three versts Russian.

reside in the valleys of Elborus that the bones of an enormous giant, exposed there by divine wrath, are yet to be seen on its smaller summit. Indeed the story is so much a matter of firm belief with the rude tribes in that quarter of the Caucasus that people are to be found amongst them who will swear they have seen these huge remains.

SIR R. K. PORTER, *Travels in Georgia, Persia, etc.*

XVII.

THE TAURUS MOUNTAINS OF CILICIA (BULGHAR-DAGH).

BY ÉLISÉE RÉCLUS.

THE appearance of the Bulghar-Dagh differs singularly according to the seasons. In autumn, a season unfortunately chosen by the greatest number of travellers, Nature has already lived its rapid and fugitive life, and burnt up by the heat, it is preparing for the long sleep of winter. The fields are yellow like straw, and only narrow lines of verdure are visible along the banks of the rivers; even the hills which rise above the narrow plain seem to hide their shrubs under an immense grey veil. Beyond extends, it is true, on the sides of the mountains, the green zone of the conifers; but the high peaks are covered with dried-up pasture; all vegetation has faded, even to the herbs watered by the snows. It might be supposed that a fire had passed over this chain of mountains, whose only beauty consists in the boldness and severity of its forms. But the traveller who looks on Bulghar-Dagh in the joyful season of spring, or even in the beginning of summer, will have no Arabia Petrea before his eyes; he will behold a marvellous paradise of freshness and beauty exposed in all its splendor to a southern sun. A plain, which is narrow on the west, but rather wide in the direction of Tarsus, extends to the base of the mountain heights, and is covered with luxuriant vegetation, interrupted here and there by many cultivated fields, which appear almost like a chess-board. Beyond rise the first hills which set off the verdure of the plain by their chalky sides; but whose summits are also crowned by clumps of trees. Higher up, the spurs of the mountains stretch out their promontories, which are remarkable for their red ochre notches, and cut up by steep fissures. The slopes which flank these spurs are clothed with vast forests of cedars, firs and junipers. A line, often indistinct to the naked eye, but which the telescope reveals in all its clearness, separates this zone of forests from the pastures of emerald green which stretch into all the valleys their fresh verdure, dotted with patches of dazzling snow. Higher still rise in towers the peaks of Bulghar-Dagh, like gigantic black crytals separated one from the other by plates of silver. The entire chain forms, as it were, an immense cone, whose base is bathed by a sea of blue, and whose summit loses itself in an atmosphere no less azure than the streams.

M. Kotschy, who had ascended to the highest peak of Bulghar-Dagh in 1836, in company with Russegger, wished to do so again in 1856. Full of admiration of this proud mountain, Russegger had given it the name of Allah-Tepessi, or mountain of God; but the real name under which it is known in the country is Metdesis. It may be reached from Gullek, by the valley which stretches out to the west of the village; and in no part of Syria or of Anatolia, not even on the slopes of Lebanon, are cedars to be found so fine as those which cover the slopes of this valley, even to a height of more than 6000 feet. Many thousand of these beautiful cedars grow in splendid groups above the sea of pines, firs and junipers. But, unhappily, in spite of the positive prohibitions of the Pacha, the shepherds have a habit of firing the brambles of the high mountains, and often these fires spread even as far as the forests. During the night these conflagrations resemble a flaming flood, rolling its waves along the slopes; and by day they veil the mountain in their sombre smoke; so that soon nothing is to be seen but blackened trunks where there once stood splendid groves.

Above the zone of the cedars, one enters into that of the brambles, which takes the place of what in Europe would be pasture land. In the Cilician Taurus, except by the banks of its streams, one seldom sees grassy slopes; even to the foot of barren rocks and wastes of snow, grow ligneous plants, and bushes with foliage of a fine green. At a height where on our mountains there extends a uniformly grey pasture land, tufts of brilliantly-colored flowers adorn the soil, introducing thus into these regions a variety and a brightness of which our Alps can give us no idea.

The ascent of the Metdesis resembles that of most other snowy mountains; one has to walk along the edge of precipices, to pass through *couloirs*, which are frightful in appearance, assisting oneself with one's hands in the steepest parts, and trying the depth of the snow before placing the feet upon it. When a man goes straight up, as Russegger did in 1836, he finds the ascent very difficult; but much of the fatigue may be avoided by making a *détour* towards the east, and climbing first to the point of the Tchubanhuju, or the Shepherd's Call, a mountain so named because the young shepherds, as soon as they have arrived at the summit, never fail to shout their triumph to their companions who are below in charge of the flocks. On the western side of the Tchubanhuju, may be remarked in the midst of a field of snow, a vast extent of ice which might make one believe in the existence of a glacier similar to those of the Alps; but these transparent and bluish masses are due to the action of a considerable stream, which, during cold nights, melts the snows near it; then afterwards this melted snow turns into ice.

The peak of the Metdesis, which is 10,800 feet high, commands a very extensive horizon, "a panorama of divine beauty," said Russegger. In the first place, all the great peaks of the chain are visible; each of them being more than 10,400 feet high, covered with snow on the side exposed to the north wind, and showing their sombre-colored rocks on the slopes which are turned towards the south. On the north side the inclination of the Metdesis is suddenly interrupted by a frightful precipice; a field of eternal snow, dotted with enormous stones, fills up a high valley. Spots of quiet color scattered about like islands, tell of gardens and orchards; and on the north side, in one place, they form a sort of archipelago. This is where the industrious population of Orte-Boor live. Beyond this, quite on the horizon, like distant mirrors, the waters of two great lakes, and the snows of Erdchich, the highest point of Asia Minor, glitter in the sun. Beyond all this region rise other mountains as numberless as the waves of the sea; while on the south inferior chains are to be seen, as well as the plain of Tarsus, and the blue Mediterranean. By crossing the chain of mountains through one of the two passes which lead over to the northern side, Gejek-Deppe and the pass of Kochan, and following a road which has been daringly cut over the edge of the precipices, the argentiferous lead-mines of Bulghar Maaden will be reached. These mines have been worked since 1842 by a hundred industrious Greeks. From this charming modern village, you descend into the paradise-like valley of Al-Chodcha, with its innumerable orchards. It is in this valley, according to the natives, that the marvellous plant grows whose flowers shine like a number of sparks during the night. The sheep and cattle which browse on this fairy plant, chew gold, and soon their teeth are covered with thin sheets of the precious metal. Those travellers who are happy enough to meet with this flower of light gather it with care, and almost immediately afterwards they see at their

A GORGE IN THE TAURUS

feet another plant, whose roots are attached to ingots of gold. "May you find the flower of light!" the Persians say to travellers. M. Kotschy, however, great botanist as he is, has not been able in all his researches to discover in the Bulghar-Dagh this plant with its luminous flowers.

ELISÉE RECLUS. *Paysages du Taurus cilicien. Revue Germanique.*

MOUNT TAURUS. BY W. G. BROWNE, 1802.

The route from Kara-Bignar to Erakli employed us about twelve hours; the road is over a sandy plain, which is little cultivated. Erakli, however, is agreeably situated in the midst of gardens full of fruit and forest-trees. About forty minutes from the city begins the ascent of the mountainous ridge, a continuation of Taurus. It employed us nearly five hours to reach the summit. The Kaludjis, not knowing the road, were obliged to take guides from Erakli to conduct them. A little further we came to a small village, near which I saw, perhaps, an acre or two of cultivated land. The Turkmans with their flocks, dwelling under tents, inhabit this almost inaccessible region. A series of stupendous bare rocks succeeds to the first summit. The air is cool and salubrious, even in the hottest season; and pellucid springs give spirit and animation to the scene. The summit of this primitive ridge is composed of a large grained marble; other calcareous substances recline on its ample sides, or are upheaved by its frequent asperities. They are all of them massy rocks, without any appearance of strata. A number of very ancient cedars, whose stunted growth and fantastic branches cast a gloomy shade, diversifying the rugged sides of the mountain.

In my visit to the Turkman tents, I remarked a strong contrast between their habits and those of the Bedouin Arabs. With the latter, the rights of hospitality are inviolable; and while the host possesses a cake of bread, he feels it a duty to furnish half of it to his guest; the Turkman offers nothing spontaneously, and if he furnishes a little milk or butter, it is at an exorbitant price. With him it is a matter of calculation whether the compendious profit of a single act of plunder, or the more ignoble system of receiving presents from the caravans for their secure passage, be most advantageous. The Arab values himself on the *hasb-we-nasb*, that is, his ancient pedigree; the Turk on his personal prowess. With the former civility requires that salutations be protracted to satiety; the latter scarcely replies to a salam aleikum.

The muleteers, who had preferred this devious path to the highroad to avoid the Dellis, were now alarmed at the frequent visits of the Turkmans. They described me to them as an officer of Chappan Oglon's retinue, employed to communicate with the English fleet on the coast, an explanation which appeared to satisfy them; and fortunately I was able to support that character. It is to be observed that Chappan Oglon has a large military force at his disposal, and administers justice with a rod of iron. His vengeance pursues on eagle's wings the slightest transgression against his authority. Our precautions at night were redoubled; and I divided the time into two watches, which I ordered my servant to share with me, but the disposition to sleep having speedily got the better of his vigilance, a pipe, although carefully placed under the carpet on which I slept, was stolen unperceived before morning.

The dress of the Turkmans consists of a large striped and fringed turban, fastened in a manner peculiar to themselves; or sometimes of a simple high-crowned cap of white felt. A vest, usually white, is thrown over the shirt; the Agas superadd one of cloth; and in general, and in proportion to their rank and wealth, they approximate to the dress of the capital. But the common people wear a short jacket of various colors. A cincture is indispensably required, in which are fixed an enormous yatagar and pistol.

Many of them wear half boots, red or yellow, laced to the leg; the dress of the women is a colored vest, and a piece of white cotton cloth on the head, covering part of the face. They are masculine and active, performing all the harder kinds of labor required by the family. Their features are good, but not pleasing. The men are generally muscular, and well proportioned; tall, straight, and active. Their teeth are white and regular; their eyes are often extremely piercing; and there is an air of uncommon boldness in their countenances and mode of address. Their complexions are clear, but sunburnt. In a word, they have everything that denotes exhaustless health and vigor of body. A great resemblance is visible between them and the populace of Constantinople ; but the latter appear effeminate by the comparison. Every action and every motion of the Turkman is marked by dignity and grace. Their language is clear and sonorous, but less soft than that of the capital ; expressing, as may be conceived, no abstract ideas, for which the Turkish is indebted to the Arabic alone ; but, fitted to paint the stronger passions, and to express in the most forcible manner and laconic terms, the mandates of authority. Their riches consist of cattle, horses, arms, and various habiliments. How lamentable to think that with persons so interesting, and a character so energetic, they unite such confirmed habits of idleness, violence, and treachery. From the rising of the sun till his disappearance the males are employed only in smoking, conversing, inspecting their cattle, or visiting their acquaintance. They watch at night for the purpose of plunder, which, among them, is honorable in proportion to the ingenuity of the contrivance or the audacity of the execution. Their families are generally small, and there is reason to think that their number is not increasing.

The destructive locust has not spared even the solitary domain of these wandering tribes. An infinity of junipers and cedars overspread the first descent of the mountain, which is long and steep, and covered with loose stones. Those near the summit are granite and hornblende ; lower down, limestone is the prevailing substance. The dwarf elder, whose odor is very agreeable, skirts the mountain to a certain height. The route from Erakli to Tarsus occupied in the whole about twenty-nine hours. On the third day we rode for about a mile through the bed of a torrent, now dry, but occasionally flowing between lofty and tremendous rocks. We soon after ascended another range inferior in height to the first; having crossed it we continued our journey through a beautifully wooded valley in which there are a great variety of ornamental trees and shrubs. On one side is a precipice descending to the dry bed of a torrent, and on both, lofty and almost perpendicular rocks shaded with the most luxuriant verdure. A few spots might be remarked which were capable of cultivation; but the valley contained many fragments of granite, micaceous schistus and limestone.

From the last resting-place another descent ensued, which at length brought us into an extensive plain, shortly afterwards to Tarsus, distant about three hours from the sea.

W. G. Brown, 1802. *From Walpole's Turkey.*

XVIII.

MOUNT LEBANON.

ASCENT BY LORD LINDSAY IN 1837.

STARTING from Deir el Akhmar, at a quarter past four in the morning, and ascending through woods of prickly oak and vælonidi, we reached in three hours the ruined village Ainnet, from which begin the steep ridges of Lebanon. All the trees ceased now, except a species of dwarf cedar, emitting a delicious fragrance, which replaced them, and continued, though diminishing in number, almost to the summit. The rocky slope of the mountain is covered with yellow, white, red, and pink flowers, affording delicious food to the bees of Lebanon: their honey is excellent. At eight we came in sight of Lake Leman of the East, or Yemouni, as every one pronounced it, lying to the south, embosomed between the upper and lower ridges. An hour afterwards, we reached an immense wreath of snow, lying on the breast of the mountain, just below that summit; and from that summit, five minutes afterwards, what a prospect opened before us! Two vast ridges of Lebanon, curving westwards from the central spot where we stood, like horns of a bent bow or the wings of a theatre, run down towards the sea, breaking in their descent into a hundred minor hills, between which, unseen, unheard, and through as deep, and dark, and jagged a chasm as ever yawned, the Kadisha, or Sacred River of Lebanon, rushes down to the Mediterranean, the blue and boundless Mediterranean, which, far on the west horizon, meets and mingles with the sky. Our eyes coming home again, after roving over this noble view, we had leisure to observe a small group of trees, not larger, apparently, than a clump in an English park at the very foot of the northern wing or horn of this grand natural theatre :—these were the far-famed cedars. We were an hour and twenty minutes in reaching them, the descent being very precipitous and difficult. As we entered the grove, the air was quite perfumed with their odor, "the smell of Lebanon" so celebrated by the pen of inspiration.

We halted under one of the largest trees, inscribed with De La Borde's name on one side, and De La Martine's on the other. But do not think that we were sacrilegious enough to wound these glorious trees; there are few English names comparatively, I am happy to say,—I would as soon cut my name on the wall of a church.

Several generations of cedars, all growing promiscuously together, compose this beautiful grove. The younger are very numerous; the second-rate would form a noble wood of themselves, were even the patriarchal dynasty quite extinct,—one of them, by no means the largest, measures nineteen feet and a quarter in circumference, and, in repeated instances, two, three, and four large trunks spring from a single root, but they have all a fresher appearance than the patriarchs, and straighter stems,—straight as young palm-trees. Of the giants, there are seven standing very near each other, all on the same hill; three more, a little further on, nearly in a line with them, and, in a second walk of discovery, after my companions had lain down to rest, I had the pleasure of detecting two others low down on the northern edge of the grove, twelve therefore in all, of which the ninth from the south is the smallest, but even that bears tokens of antiquity coeval with its brethren.

The stately bearing and graceful repose of the young cedars contrast singularly with the wild and frantic attitude of the old ones, flinging abroad their knotted and muscular limbs like so many Laocoons, while others, broken off, lie rotting at their feet; but life is strong in them all, they look as if they had been struggling for existence with evil spirits, and God had interposed and forbidden the war, that the trees He planted might remain living witnesses to faithless men of that ancient "Glory of Lebanon,"—Lebanon, the emblem of the righteous,—which departed from her when Israel rejected Christ; her vines drooping, her trees few, that a child may number them, she stands blighted, a type of the unbeliever! And blighted she must remain till her second spring, the day of renovation from the presence of the Lord, when, at the voice of God,

Israel shall spring anew to life, and the cedar and the vine, the olive of Carmel and the rose of Sharon, emblems of the moral graces of God, reflected in His people, shall revive in the wilderness, to beautify the place of His sanctuary and to make the place of His feet glorious, to swell the chorus of Universal Nature to the praise of the living God.

We had intended proceeding that evening to Psherré, but no, we could not resolve to leave those glorious trees so soon, the loveliest, the noblest, the holiest, in the wide world. The tent was pitched, and we spent the rest of the day under their "shadowy shroud." Oh, what a church that grove is! Never did I think Solomon's Song so beautiful, and that most noble chapter of Ezekiel, the thirty-first, I had read it on the heights of Syene, Egypt on my right hand, and Ethiopia on my left, with many other denunciations (how awfully fulfillèd!) of desolations against Pathros, and judgments upon No,—but this was the place to enjoy it, lying under one of those vast trees, looking up every now and then into its thick boughs, the little birds warbling, and a perpetual hum of insect life pervading the air with its drowsy melody. Eden is close by,—these are "the trees of Eden," "the choicest and best of Lebanon," these are the trees (there can be none nobler) which Solomon spoke of, "from the cedar of Lebanon to the hyssop on the wall," the object of repeated allusion and comparison throughout the Bible,—the emblem of the righteous in David's Sabbath hymn, and, honor upon honor, the likeness of the countenance of the Son of God in the inspired Canticles of Solomon.

Our encampment was very picturesque that night, the fire throwing a strong light on the cedar that o'ercanopied us: those enormous arms, of ghastly whiteness, seemed almost alive and about to grasp and catch us up into the thick darkness they issued from.

The direct road from the cedars to the village of Eden is little more than two hours; we were desirous, however, of seeing the famous Convent of Canubin (or Anubin, as they pronounced it, always dropping the initial C), and accordingly, on arriving at Psherré, after an hour and twenty minutes' ride, we sent on the baggage direct under Allwyn's care, who was not well enough to accompany us.

The descent to Psherré (the Beshirai of the maps) was very precipitous, but nothing to what awaited us beyond it; the village lies in a lovely valley, all verdant with vines and fruit-trees, and musical with cascades; and the breezes of Lebanon, —who that has ever quaffed can forget them? To the east, on the slope of the valley, stands the Convent of Mar Serkis, almost concealed among thick groves, with a very remarkable pointed rock arising over it. Our route lay westwards, along the edge of the ravine, broken every now and then by deep gullies, descending from the northern Lebanon, each with its torrent dashing down from the mountains, and sometimes forming beautiful cascades over the rocks, light clouds of spray hovering over their descent. We passed the village Hatsheit at nine, and

MOUNT LEBANON, CASCADE OF NAHR-EL-LEBEN.

that of Belansi at ten, both situated on the edge of the chasm; looking eastwards from this point towards its head, we saw the river Kadisha, like a silver thread descending from Lebanon. The whole scene bore that strange and shadowy resemblance to the wonderful landscape delineated in "Kubla Khan," that one often feels in actual life, when the whole scene around you appears to be re-enacting after a long interval, your friends seated in the same juxtaposition, the subject of conversation the same, and shifting with the same "dream-like ease," that you remember at some remote indefinite period of pre-existence; you always know what will come next, and sit spell-bound as it were in a sort of calm expectancy. One would almost have thought Coleridge had been here in some such vision, or at least that some such description of the valley had been unconsciously lingering on his memory,—the general resemblance between the scene he has painted and that before us is so striking. I dare not insist on the coincidence of there being "a sacred river" in both landscapes, in proof of their identity, "there is a river in Macedon, and there is a river at Monmouth; it is called the Wye at Monmouth; it is out of my province what is the name of the other river, but it is all one, and so like as my fingers is to my fingers, and there is salmon in both!"

Beyond Belansi we began the descent to Canubin by a very difficult path, occasionally hewn into rude steps. This magnificent ravine (I speak of it generally, as we viewed it from different points) is of immense depth, broken into vast hollows, overhung with trees, chiefly prickly oaks, and shooting into pinnacles, between which the mountain torrents rush down on all sides, some of them forming beautiful cascades, many hundred feet in height. At Canubin, however, the voice even of the Kadisha is scarcely heard; a profound silence reigns, all is grandeur, but grandeur in repose,—the choicest place in the world for dreaming away one's life in monastic inactivity. The convent hangs about two-thirds down the precipice, partly built up against, partly excavated in the rocks; it looks as if held by cramping irons in its present position, so deep is the abyss below, so menacing the rocks that overhang it.

Here, in winter only, resides the Batrah, or Patriarch, of the Maronites: we had expected to see him, but were disappointed to hear that he had flown off with all the brethren to Adiman, their summer residence on the top of the mountain opposite.

Several leaves of the Syriac Bible alighted at our feet as we rode up to the gate, and a lay-Maronite, who made his appearance at the window above it, seemed quite indifferent to their fate. He informed us, in addition to the unwelcome news of the Batrah's absence, that there was nothing in the convent for man or beast. This did not at all coincide with our plans, which were to rest there a few hours, feed our horses and ourselves, and then proceed in the afternoon to Eden; we, therefore, the gate being open, took possession of the monastery, searched and discovered corn in abundance, fed our horses, established ourselves in the pleasantest place we could find, and then tried to persuade the Maronite that food for man was also producible, assuring him, as we did from the first, that we had feloush enough to pay for it. All persuasion was in vain till a sort of major-domo arrived, to whom intelligence had been sent of the capture of the convent; from that moment all was cordial hospitality, —he unlocked a small room, furnished with mats, produced some of the sweet red wine of Lebanon, and, by degrees, the most sumptuous *déjeûner à la fourchette* we had seen for many a day made its appearance,—salad, cheese, grapes honey, and dibs, a syrup expressed from grapes, and delicious Arab bread,—a meal for princes!

During the glow of victory, for we virtually resigned our conquest the moment that hospitable thoughts were evinced by the rightful proprietors, we explored the convent as thoroughly as a lingering respect for bolts and bars permitted. There is nothing worth seeing except the church, which is a large and beautiful grotto cut lengthways in the rock that overhangs the monastery. The portraits of the patriarchs mentioned by old travellers, no longer line its walls, but there are several paintings of a character superior to that one would expect to see in such an out-of-the-way place,—daubs, but done in Italy; the best of them was an assumption of the Virgin over the altar. In, and on a press in the church, lay many books and manuscripts, the former chiefly printed at Rome by the Propaganda, some of the latter most beautifully written,—all in Arabic, I suppose, but in the Syriac character. The Bible to which the leaves that flew out of the window with such *empressement* to welcome us belonged, lay in a small apartment at the end of a long gallery built up against the rock, and overlooking the gate.

After a hearty meal and comfortable siesta we remounted, and with the major-domo as guide, a merry and good-humored fellow, re-ascended the gorge we had come down by, but up its western side. We presently passed a small chapel cut in the rock; the whole valley, indeed, is full of the excavated dwellings of ancient hermits. The scenery was still more beautiful at this evening hour, the southern declivity all shadow, except the salient points of rock.

After about an hour's ascent we came in sight of the vale of Eden, with the village on the northwest side of it, so that we had to wind round the head of the valley to reach it,—there is no cutting across country in Mount Lebanon, and who would wish to do so, and abridge his enjoyment? Above, below, around you, wherever you cast your eyes, man and nature vie with each other in beautifying and enriching the landscape. Man affording nature a field to display her bounty upon, by terracing the hills to their very summits, that not a particle of their soil may be lost,—Nature in rewarding his toil by the richest luxuriance, pouring grain into his lap, and wine into his cup, without measure. The slopes, too, of the valleys one mass of verdure, are yet more productive than the hills, thanks "to the springs of Lebanon" that come gushing down so fresh and cool and melodious in every direction, —vines twine around and hang in garlands from every tree; mulberries are cultivated in immense quantities, with houses for the silk-worms, of dry branches or matting, bound with reeds, built between the trees; they never pluck off the leaves, but cut whole boughs off for the silk-worms; the trees, however, are little injured in appearance, as many boughs as are seen on a young fig-tree being left untouched on each. The fig-trees are beautiful, the apricots delicious, and as common as apples in England. Walnut-trees of majestic growth and beautiful produce, flourish beside the deep torrent-beds, along with the weeping willow and Lombardy poplar, the only unfruitful trees in this garden of Eden; for all I have said, though descriptive generally of the valleys of this part of Lebanon, applies strictly to that we have just descended to from Canubin. And then the cordial greeting of the country people, poor, but all seemingly happy and contented, and as like each other in features as brothers and sisters,—a smile on every woman's countenance, all of them unveiled, and some very pretty, the steeples of the village churches peeping out through the trees, and the bells answering each other across the ravines every morning and evening, were moral charms that doubled the attractions of the scenery; we felt ourselves in a Christian country and almost among brethren.

Eden is built on a lofty ridge, extremely precipitous, its sides supported by terraces, wherever it has been possible to introduce them, planted with vines, mulberries, and corn. A considerable torrent, augmented in its course by minor rills, flowing in cascades from the hills, rushes down a deep ravine towards the south. We reached the village after a quarter-of-an-hour's ascent from the bridge, and found our friend Allwyn encamped near a cascade in a magnificent grove of walnut-trees. Pell and I, pursuant to his advice, started off immediately on foot for the brow of a hill about twenty minutes distant to catch the sunset view of the western side of Lebanon; it was superb! Tripoli was concealed by the rising ground, but the headland, the part where the merchants reside, the vessels, the towers, remnants of the old fortifications of the knightly Berengers, were clearly visible, and the seaward course of Kadisha, distinguishable at intervals by its snow-white foam. More to the south, we saw the bold headland near Batroun, the mountain that hid Djibail, etc., etc., and, beyond all, the Mediterranean.

A crowd of villagers congregated under the trees in front of our tent that night: children were romping about, some one was modulating the shepherd's reed not unmelodiously, it was a more cheerful scene than I ever witnessed in the lowlands of Syria or Palestine, where the merry-hearted sigh and the mirth of the tabret has almost ceased in the land. * * *

We returned to Psherré, by the direct route, the following afternoon, with the intention of proceeding to Zachli, by Akoura and Afka, along the heights of Lebanon and thence to Damascus. Burckhardt is the only traveller I know of who has taken this route ; and a most sublime and beautiful one it is, so far as Akoura and Afka, beyond which I cannot speak of it, the guide having led us, either ignorantly or knavishly, into another road.

LORD LINDSAY. *Letters on Egypt, Edom, and the Holy Land.*

XIX

MOUNT ARARAT.

BY SIR ROBT. KER PORTER, NOV. 1817.

On leaving our halting-place, a fuller view of the great plain of Ararat gradually expanded before us, and the mountain itself began to tower in all its majesty to the very canopy of heaven. It bore southeast from the line of our caravansary. We now took a descending position, due east over a stony and difficult road, which carried us, for more than ten versts, through several close and rocky defiles, and over as many frozen streams, till we reached a small Mahometan village on the side of the Mosduan hills. We halted there for the night, and, for the first time, I slept under the roof of a Mussulman. My goodly escort had already made themselves acquainted with the substance of the honest people; for, in our way to the village, some of them spied a flock of sheep with their shepherd, at a little distance on the plain, and starting away scoured off immediately towards them. Not guessing their intentions, I supposed they were aware of the approach of some hostile band, and were charging to meet them. My surprise, therefore, was rather excited when I saw them plunge into the mass of the flock, the shepherd run for his life, and in a few minutes the troop return with their spoils,—two or three sheep with their throats cut, which were soon skinned, dressed, and eaten. This was nothing more, in their opinion, than a mere exercise of their horses; a *chappow* (or fray), as much their right as the air they breathe, and as little to be complained against by the owner of the sheep as the gathering of a few turnips in a neighbor's field might be by some of us, though it certainly was something new to an Englishman of the nineteenth century to find himself thus at the head of a band with such habits.

On the morning of the 17th of Nov. (O. S.) we left our hospitable Mussulmans; for whether they were so inclined or overawed by the fierce looks and glittering arms of my attendants, I will not pretend to say, but I had no reason to complain of their want of civility. We set forth over a road as hard as that of the day before, in a direction southeast, and gradually descending from a great height through a very extended sloping country, towards the immense plain of Ararat. In our way we passed the relics of a considerable town called Talish. A little further we saw the ruins of what had been a fine caravansary on the side of a mountain stream, and from amidst the mouldering walls, we observed a few half-starved wretches creeping to the air, as if that were their only aliment. Indeed, sterility seemed to have been the curse of this immediate spot. Not a trace of verdure was discoverable on the ground; all parts were covered with volcanic stones, or rather masses of cinders, as if thrown from an iron forge,—black, heavy, and honey-combed. Lower down, upon this long declivity, rises a mound of earth and rock, which in

Mount Ararat.

any neighborhood but that of Ararat, would be called a mountain. Here it appears scarcely a hill. Its form and substance are evidently those of an extinguished volcano; but in what age it has been at work, we have not means to guess; no authors of established verity, ancient or modern, having said one word of any known volcanic eruption in the region of Ararat. Besides the cinders above mentioned, I observed in several places during our downward march large portions of rock, of a soft red stone, bearing likewise the marks of calcination.

As the vale opened beneath us in our descent my whole attention became absorbed in the view before me. A vast plain, peopled with countless villages, the towers and spires of the churches of Eitch mai-adzan, arising from amidst them, the glittering waters of the Araxes, flowing through the fresh green of the vale ; and the subordinate range of mountains skirting the base of the awful monument of the antediluvian world. It seemed to stand a stupendous link in the history of man, uniting the two races of man, before and after the flood. But it was not until we arrived upon the flat plain that I beheld Ararat in all its amplitude of grandeur. From the spot on which I stood it appeared as if the largest mountains of the world had been piled upon each other to form this one sublime immensity of earth, and rock, and snow. The icy peaks of its double heads rose majestically into the clear and cloudless heaven; the sun blazed bright upon them and the reflection sent forth a dazzling radiance equal to other suns. This point of the view united the utmost grandeur of plain and height. But the feelings I experienced while looking on the mountain are hardly to be described. My eye, not able to rest for any length of time upon the blinding glory of its summits, wandered down the apparently interminable sides, till I could no longer trace their vast lines in the mists of the horizon; when an irrepressible impulse, immediately carrying my eye upwards again, refixed my gaze upon the awful glare of Ararat; and this bewildered sensibility of sight being answered by a similar feeling in the mind, for some moments I was lost in a strange suspension of the powers of thought.

Agridagh is the name given to this sublime mountain by the Turks; and the Armenians call it Malis; but all unite in revering it as the haven of the great ship which preserved the father of mankind from the waters of the deluge. The height of Ararat has never yet been measured with any satisfactory degree of accuracy; though Capt. Monteith, of the Madras Engineers, has gone nearer to the mark, perhaps, than any other traveller. . . These inaccessible summits have never been trodden by the foot of man since the days of Noah, if even then; for my idea is, that the ark rested in the space between these heads, and not on the top of either. Various attempts have been made, in different ages, to ascend these tremendous mountain-pyramids, but in vain. Their form, snows, and glaciers, are insurmountable obstacles, the distance being so great, from the commencement of the icy region to the highest point, cold alone would be the destruction of any person who should have the hardihood to persevere.*

* Nevertheless, this ascent was accomplished in 1850, by Col, Khodzko.

On viewing Mount Ararat from the northern side of the plain its two heads are separated by a wide cleft, or rather glen, in the body of the mountain. The rocky side of the greater head runs almost perpendicularly down to the northeast, while the lesser head rises from the sloping bosom of the cleft in a perfectly conical shape. Both heads are covered with snow. The form of the greater is similar to the lesser, only broader and rounder at the top, and shows to the northwest a broken and abrupt front, opening, about half-way down, into a stupendous chasm, deep, rocky, and peculiarly black. At that part of the mountain, the hollow of the chasm receives an interruption from the projections of minor mountains, which start from the sides of Ararat, like branches from the root of a tree, and run along in undulating progression till lost in the distant vapors of the plain.

The dark chasm which I have mentioned as being on the side of the great head of the mountain, is supposed by some travellers to have been the exhausted crater of Ararat. Dr. Benizzi even affirms it, by stating that, in the year 1783, during certain days of the months of January and February, an eruption took place in that mountain; and he suggests the probability of the burning ashes ejected thence at that time, reaching to the southern side of the Caucasus (a distance in a direct line of two hundred and twenty versts); and so depositing the volcanic productions which are found there. The reason he gives for this latter supposition is, that the trapp seen there did not originate in those mountains, and must, consequently, have been sent thither by volcanic explosions elsewhere. And that this elsewhere, which he concludes to be Ararat, may have been that mountain, I do not pretend to dispute; but these events must have taken place many centuries ago, even before history took note of the spot; for, since that period, we have no intimation whatever of any part of Ararat having been seen in a burning state. This part of Asia was well known to the ancient historians, from being the seat of certain wars they describe; and it cannot be supposed that, had so conspicuous a mountain been often, or ever (within the knowledge of man) in a state of volcanic eruption, we should not have heard of it from Strabo, Pliny, Ptolemy, or others; but, on the contrary, all these writers are silent on such a subject with regard to Ararat; while every one who wrote in the vicinities of Etna or of Vesuvius had something to say of the thunders and molten fires of those mountains. That there are volcanic remains, to a vast extent, around Ararat, every person who visits its neighborhood must testify; and, giving credit to Dr. Benigg's assertion, that an explosion of the mountain had happened in his time, I determined to support so interesting a fact, with the evidence of every observation on my part, when I should reach the spot. But, on arriving at the monastery of Eitch-mai-adza, where my remarks must chiefly be made, and discoursing with the fathers on the idea of Ararat having been a volcano, I found that a register of the general appearance of the mountain had been regularly kept by their predecessors and themselves, for upwards of eight hundred years; and that nothing of an eruption, or any thing tending to such an event, was to be found on any one of these notices. When I spoke of an explosion of the mountain having taken place in the year 1783, and which had been made known to Europe by a traveller declaring himself to have been an eye-witness, they were all in surprise; and, besides the written documents to the contrary, I was assured by several of the holy brethren, who had been resident in the plain for upwards of forty years, that during the whole of that period they had never seen even a smoke from the mountain. Therefore, how the author in question fell into so very erroneous a misstatement, I can form no guess.

Sir R. K. Porter, *Travels in Georgia, Persia, Armenia, etc.*

XX.

MOUNT SINAI.

ASCENT BY DR. ROBINSON, MARCH 1838.

THE lower and easier road from Wady-et-Taiyibeh to Sinai enters the Feiran from the head of Wady Mukatteb, and follows it up Wady-esh-Sheikh almost to the convent. From the point where we now were, this road is long and circuitous; while a shorter one strikes directly towards the convent, ascending in part by a narrow and difficult pass. We took the latter; and, crossing Wady-esh-Sheikh, proceeded on a course S.E. by S., up to the broad Wady, or rather sloping plain, Es-Seheb, thickly studded with shrubs, but without trees. Here and around Wady-esh-Sheikh are only low hills, lying between the rocky mountains behind us and the cliff of Sinai before us; and forming, as it were, a lower belt around the lofty central granite region. Over these walls,—low walls of porphyry or grünstein,—like those above described, run in various directions, stretching off to a great distance.

We came to the top of the plain at a quarter

MOUNT SINAI.

before eleven o'clock, where is a sharp, but rough, pass, full of *débris*, having on the right a low, sharp peak called El-Orf. From this point to the base of the cliffs of Sinai there is a sort of belt or track of gravel or sand, full of low hills and ridges.

The black and frowning mountains before us, the outworks, as it were, of Sinai, are here seen to great advantage, rising abrupt and rugged from their very base, eight hundred to a thousand feet in height; as if forbidding all approach to the sanctuary within.

At half-past twelve o'clock we began gradually to ascend towards the foot of the pass before us, called by our Arabs Mukb Hâwy, Windy Pass, and by Burckhardt Mukb-er-Râhah, from the tract above it. We reached the foot at a quarter past one o'clock, and, dismounting, commenced the slow and toilsome ascent along the narrow defile, about S. by E., between blackened shattered cliffs of granite, some eight hundred feet high, and not more than two hundred and fifty yards apart; which every moment threatened to send down their ruins on our heads. Nor is this at all times an empty threat; for the whole pass is filled with large stones and rocks, the *débris* of these cliffs. The bottom is a deep and narrow watercourse, where the wintry torrent sweeps down with fearful violence. A path has been made for camels along the shelving piles of rocks, partly by removing the topmost blocks, and sometimes by laying down large stones side by side, somewhat in the manner of a Swiss mountain road. But although I had crossed the most rugged passes of the Alps, and made from Chamounix the whole circuit of Mont Blanc, I had never found a path so rude and difficult as that we were now ascending. The camels toiled slowly and painfully along, stopping frequently; so that, although it took them two hours and a quarter to reach the top of the pass, yet the distance cannot be reckoned at more than one hour. . . . Higher up the path lies in the bed of the torrent, and became less steep. As we advanced the sand was occasionally moist, and on digging into it with the hand, the hole was soon filled with fine sweet water. We tried the experiment in several places. Here, too, were several small palm-trees, and a few tufts of grass, the first we had seen since leaving the borders of the Nile. Burckhardt mentions a spring, called Kaneitan, in this part of the pass; but it was now dry; at least we neither saw nor heard of any. In the pass we found upon the rocks two Sinaitic inscriptions, one of them having over it a cross of the same date.

It was half-past three o'clock when we reached the top, from which the convent was said to be an hour distant, but we found it two hours, as did also Burckhardt. Descending a little into a small Wady, which has its head here, and runs off through a cleft in the western mountains, apparently to Wady Rudhwâh, we soon began to ascend again gradually on a course S.E. by S., passing by a small spring of good water, beyond which the valley opens by degrees, and its bottom becomes less uneven. Here the interior and loftier peaks of the great circle of

Sinai began to open upon us, black, rugged, desolate summits; and as we advance, the dark and frowning front of Sinai itself (the present Horeb of the monks) began to appear. We were still gradually ascending, and the valleys gradually opening, but as yet all was a naked desert. Afterwards a few shrubs were sprinkled about, and a small encampment of black tents was seen on our right, with camels and goats browsing, and a few donkeys belonging to the convent. The scenery through which we now passed reminded me strongly of the mountain around the Mer de Glace in Switzerland. I had never seen a spot more wild and desolate.

As we advanced, the valley still opened wider and wider, with a gentle ascent, and became full of shrubs and tufts of herbs, shut in on each side by lofty granite ridges with rugged, shattered peaks a thousand feet high, while the face of Horeb rose directly before us. Both my companion and myself involuntarily exclaimed, 'Here is room enough for a large encampment!' Reaching the top of the ascent, or water-shed, a fine broad plain lay before us, sloping down gently towards the S.S.E., enclosed by rugged and venerable mountains of dark granite, stern, naked, splintered peaks and ridges, of indescribable grandeur, and terminated at the distance of more than a mile by the bold and awful front of Horeb, rising perpendicularly in frowning majesty from twelve to fifteen hundred feet in height. It was a scene of solemn grandeur, wholly unexpected, and such as we had never seen; and the associations which at the moment rushed upon our minds were almost overwhelming. As we went on, new points of interest were continually opening to our view. On the left of Horeb a deep and narrow valley runs up S.S.E. between lofty walls of rock, as if in continuation of the S.E. corner of the plain. In this valley, at the distance of nearly a mile from the plain, stands the convent, and the deep verdure of its fruit trees and cypresses is seen as the traveller approaches—an oasis of beauty amid scenes of the sternest desolation. At the S.W. corner of the plain the cliffs also retreat, and form a recess or open place extending from the plain westward for some distance. From this recess there runs up a similar narrow valley on the west of Horeb, called El-Leja, parallel to that in which the convent stands, and in it is the deserted convent El-Arab'în, with a garden of olive and other fruit trees not visible from the plain. A third garden lies at the mouth of El-Leja, and a fourth further west in the recess just mentioned. The whole plain is called Wady-er-Bâhah; and the valley of the convent is known to the Arabs as Wady Shu'eib, that is, the vale of Jethro. Still advancing, the front of Horeb rose like a wall before us; and one can approach quite to the foot and touch the mount. Directly before its base is the deep bed of a torrent, by which in the rainy season the waters of El-Leja and the mountains around the recess pass down eastward across the plain. As we crossed it our feelings were strongly affected at finding here so unexpectedly a spot so entirely adapted to the Scriptural account of the giving of the Law. No traveller has described this plain, nor even mentioned it, except in a slight and general manner, probably because the most have reached the convent by another route without passing it, and perhaps, too, because neither the highest point of Mount Sinai (now called Jabel Mûsa), nor the still loftier summit of St. Catherine, is visible from any part of it.

As we approached the mountain our head Arab, Beshàrah, became evidently quite excited. He prayed that our pilgrimage might be accepted, and bring rain, and with great earnestness besought that when we ascended the mountain we would open a certain window in the chapel there, towards the south, which, he said, would certainly cause rain to fall. He also entreated, almost with tears, that we would induce the monks to have compassion on the people, and say prayers as they ought to do for rain. When told that God alone could send rain, and they should look to Him for it, he replied, 'Yes, but the monks have the book of prayer for it; do persuade them to use it as they ought.' There was an earnestness in his manner which was very affecting. From the Wady-esh-Sheikh to the convent is a distance of twenty-five minutes by a difficult path along the rocky bed of the narrow valley. We had come on in advance of the loaded camels, and reached the convent at half-past five o'clock. Under the entrance were many Arabs in high clamor, serfs of the convent, who were receiving a distribution of some kind of provision from above; we did not learn what. The only regular entrance at present is by a door, nearly thirty feet (or more exactly twenty-eight feet nine inches) from the ground, the great door having been walled up for more than a century. On making known our arrival, a cord was let down with a demand for our letters, and we sent up the one we had received from the branch convent in Cairo. This proving satisfactory, a rope was let down for us, in which seating ourselves, we were hoisted up one by one by a windlass within to the level of the floor, and then pulled in by the hand. The superior himself—a mild-looking old man with a long white beard—received us with an embrace and a kiss, and conducted us to the strangers' rooms. While these were preparing, we seated ourselves in the adjacent piazza upon antique chairs of various forms, which have doubtless come down through many centuries, and had a few moments of quiet to ourselves in which to collect our thoughts. I was affected by the strangeness and overpowering grandeur of the scene around us; and it was for some time difficult to realize that we were now actually within the very precincts of that Sinai on which from earliest childhood I had thought and read with so much wonder. Yet, when at length the impression came with its full force upon my mind, although not given to the melting mood, I could not refrain from bursting into tears.

We were soon put in possession of our rooms, and greeted with kindness by the monks and attendants. . . . Here all travellers have lodged who have visited the convent for many generations, but they have left no memorials behind except in recent years. . . . The garden was now suffering from drought, but it looked beautifully verdant in contrast with the stern desolation that reigns all around. Besides the tall dark cypresses which are seen from afar, it contains mostly fruit trees, few vegetables being cultivated in it. Indeed the number and variety of fruit trees is surprising, and testifies to the fine temperature and vivifying power of the climate, provided there be a supply of water. The almond-trees are very large, and had been long out of blossom. The apricot-trees were also large, and like the apple-trees, were now in full bloom. There were also pears, pomegranates, figs, quinces, mulberries, olives, and many vines, besides other trees and shrubs in great variety. The fruit produced is said to be excellent.

The name of Sinai is now given by the Christians in a general way to this whole cluster of mountains. The peak of Jebel Mûsa has commonly been regarded as the summit of Mount Sinai, the place where the Law was given. . . . We measured across the plain, where we stood, along the watershed, and found the breadth to be at that point 2700 English feet or 900 yards, though in some parts it is wider. The distance to the base of Horeb, measured in like manner, was 7000 feet, or 2333 yards. The northern slope of the plain, north of which we stood, we judged to be somewhat less than a mile in length by one-third of a mile in breadth. We may, therefore, fairly estimate the whole plain at two geographical miles long, and ranging in breadth from one-third to two-thirds of a mile, or as equivalent to a surface of at least one square mile. This space is nearly doubled by a recess on the west, and by the broad and level area of Wady-esh-Sheikh on the east, which issues at right angles to the plain, and is equally in view of the front and summit of the present Horeb.

The examination of this afternoon convinced us that here was space enough to satisfy all the requisitions of the Scriptural narrative, so far as it relates to the assembling of the congregation to receive the Law. Here, too, one can see the fitness of the injunction to set bounds around the mount that neither man nor beast might approach too near. The encampment before the mount, as has been before suggested, might not improbably include only the head-quarters of Moses and the Elders, and of a portion of the people, while the remainder, with their flocks, were scattered in the adjacent valleys.

E. Robinson. D. D., *Biblical Researches in Palestine and the adjacent regions.*

XXI.

GUNGOOTREE, THE SACRED SOURCE OF THE GANGES.

BY EMMA ROBERTS.

HAVING recovered from the fatigues and bruises attendant on our journey to the source of the Jumna, to the great dismay of a portion of our followers, we determined to proceed to Gungootree, whence the sacred river Ganges takes its rise. The nearest route from Kursalee to Gungootree may be traversed in four days, but the natives always endeavor to dissuade travellers from taking it at any season of the year, recommending in preference a lower, more circuitous, and therefore longer way. The more direct road leads over a great arm of the Bundurpooch mountain which separates the valleys, or rather channels through which the sacred rivers hurry from their icy birthplace. The greater part of this tract is desert and uninhabited, conducting the wayfarer through regions of rock and snow, destitute of the dwellings of man, or of supplies for his use; there is danger also that fuel may be wanting for that necessary solace to the weary, a blazing fire; while the necessity of dispensing with everything like superfluous baggage must oblige the party to rest at night in caves and clefts of the rocks.

Amidst the most formidable evils reported of this route is the *bis-ka-kowa*, or poisonous wind, said to blow over the highest ridge, and to exhale from noxious plants on the borders—a very natural supposition among a race of people ignorant of the effects produced on the atmosphere at so great an elevation. Yielding to the universal clamor, we consented to take the longer and safer path, but some friends who were obliged to forego the journey to Gungootree crossed into the valley of the Ganges by a very difficult and romantic route. After parting company at Banass, they descended to the banks of the Bhim, a roaring torrent, rushing beneath precipices upwards of 2000 perpendicular feet from the river; the eagles wheeling through the sky from their eyries near the summit, appearing not larger than crows. The ascent then led over a mountain covered with cedars, a noble forest, not uncheerful, though marked with sombre grandeur.

The next day's march conducted the party along the banks of a torrent which poured down the face of a mountain from a bed of snow near its summit. The day was cold, the ground hard with frost, but the air bracing, and the scenery wild and magnificent. A long and toilsome ascent over Unchighati followed; scrambling up the bed of a stream over rough stones, rendered slippery from being cased in ice, they reached the limit of the cedar forest, and subsequently came to birch and small rhododendrons. The scene then assumed a very wintry aspect, and soon everything like foliage was left behind. Attaining the crest of the pass, which was covered with snow, and at an elevation of some hundred feet above the limit of the forest, on looking back to Bundurpooch, Duti Manji, and Bachuncha peak and ridge, few scenes of more sublime grandeur could be found throughout the whole of

View in the Himalayas.

these stupendous regions. The prospect of range after range of the south and east was very extensive; an ocean of ridges in one wide amphitheatre, closed in by the line of the snowy mountains resting their fantastic peaks against the dark blue sky. Below the course of the Bhagirati could be traced, which, after issuing from its gigantic bed of snow, rejoicing in its escape from the wintry mountains, and their rugged and awful approaches, flows in tranquil beauty through a peaceful valley. In descending the southeast side of the pass, the birch which had clothed the previous path gave place to pines and evergreen oaks, which grew in great abundance in advance of the cedar; the rhododendron, which near the crest was merely a creeper, became a tree, a change in the nature of vegetation marking the different heights, which is exceedingly interesting to the traveller.

The descent of this mountain to Nemgâng was long and painful, and to Europeans a new route, the generality of travellers crossing the ridge from the Jumna to the Ganges, either higher up or lower down; but the next day's march compensated for all the fatigue incurred in its approach. Descending to the Bini-ke-Gârh, a torrent rushing down a high ridge to the northward, the glen which it watered proved of surpassing beauty; nothing could exceed the loveliness of the foliage which clothed this summer valley, or rather vista; for, opening on a view of the precipitous heights of the Unchi-Ghâti, it contrasted its romantic attractions with the sublime features of the mountains beyond. Reaching the junction of the Bini and the Bhagirati, the holy name given to the sacred river, the travellers found the Ganges a noble stream, much wider and deeper than the Jumna, at the same distance from its source, but not so tumultuous.

Descending to Nangâng by a different route to that already mentioned, we also were compelled to encounter many difficulties; the prospects, however, repaid them. Equally grand, though different in character to those last described, at a very considerable depth below, we looked upon a cultivated scene—the hanging terraces common to these hills, waving with grain, and watered by winding streams, and running along the base of high woody trees. Beyond, again, were the eternal mountains in all their varieties; snow resting on the crests of some, others majestically grouped with venerable timber, and others bleak, bare, and barren, rising in frowning majesty from the green and sunny slopes which smiled below. Between these different ranges ran deep ravines, dark with impenetrable forests, rendered more savage by the awful music of the torrents roaring through their fastnesses, while presently their streams issuing forth into open day, were seen winding round green spots bright with fruit-trees. Such, or nearly such, for every traveller sees them under a different medium, were the prospects which beguiled us as we slipped and slid down the steep side of the mountain-pass. Nangâng formed our halting-place; several days' march still lay before us, and there were more mountains to climb and more forests to thread. We now observed a diversity in the timber, chestnuts of magnificent growth being the prevailing tree. Our sportsmen found plenty of game: the monah, the feathered wonder of the Himalaya, and other varieties of the pheasant tribe, peopled these vast solitudes, and paid tribute to the guns of the invading strangers.

We met with some delightful halting-places on

the line of march, grassy terraces, carpeted with strawberry and wild flowers, where the cowslip, the primrose, and the buttercup, brought the pranked-out fields of our native country strongly to the mind. Many of the travellers in the Himalaya are moved even to rapture at the sight of the first daisy which springs spontaneously in their path; as an exotic in some garden of the plains it excites deep emotion; but growing wild, spangling the meadow-grass with its silvery stars, it becomes infinitely more interesting; and the home-sick, pining exile will often gather its earliest encountered blossom weeping.

Leaving this luxuriant vegetation, we arrived at a wild spot, the summit of a ridge of peaks covered with snow; and though the prospect was more circumscribed, and all of a greater sameness, we enjoyed it amazingly. We seemed to be hemmed in on all sides with thick-ribbed ice, transported to antarctic snows, imprisoned amid icebergs, vast, freezing, and impassable. Presently, however, we emerged, and descending through the snow, reached the boundary-line between the districts of the Jumna and the Ganges. The extreme limits of these river-territories were marked in the manner usually employed in rude and desolate places, by heaps of stone,—many raised by Europeans,—who thus commemorate their pilgrimage. These cairns being destitute of inscriptions, it is impossible to say who the adventurous architects were, since no European name has any chance of being retained in its primitive form by a native.

The next point of great interest is the summit

of a ridge, whence the first view of the Ganges is obtained, a sight which never fails to raise the drooping spirits of the Hindoo followers, and which excites no small degree of enthusiasm in the breast of the Christian travellers. The sacred river, as seen from this height, flows in a dark, rapid, and broad stream, and, though at no great apparent distance, must still be reached by more than one toilsome march. From a height about two miles from Gungootree, the first glimpse, and that a partial one, is obtainable of that holy place, which lies sequestered in a glen of the deepest solitude, lonely, and almost inaccessible, for few there are who could persevere in surmounting the difficulties of the approach. Considerable distances must be traversed over projecting masses of rough stones, flinty, pointed, and uncertain, many being loose, and threatening to roll over the enterprising individual who attempts the rugged way. Sometimes the face of the rock must be climbed from cliff to cliff; at others, where there is no resting-place for hand or foot, ladders are placed in aid of the ascent; while awful chasms between are passed on some frail spar flung across. These horrid rocks would seem indeed to form invincible barriers to the approach of the holy place, but religious enthusiasm on the one hand, and scientific research, stimulated by curiosity, on the other, render the barriers inadequate for resisting the invasions of man. The difficult nature of the access, however, prevents the concourse of pilgrims who resort to more easily attainable places esteemed sacred on this hallowed river.

The grandeur of the scene which opened upon us, as we at length stood upon the threshold of Gungootree, cannot be described in words. Rocks were piled upon rocks in awful majesty, all shivered into points, which rise one upon another in splendid confusion, enclosing a glen of the wildest nature, where the Ganges, beautiful in every haunt, from its infancy to its final junction with the ocean, pours its shallow waters over a bed of shingle, diversified by jutting rocks, and every leaf shadowed by the splendid foliage of some fine old trees. The devotee who undoubtingly believes that every step he takes towards the source of that holy river, which, from his infancy, he has been taught to look upon as a deity, will lead him into beatitude, is content to seek its origin at Gungootree, but the real source of the sacred stream lies still higher, in more inaccessible solitudes; and it was reserved for the ardor of those who measured the altitude of the highest peaks, and penetrated to the utmost limits of man's dominion, to trace the exact birthplace of the holy river. Captains Hodgson and Herbert, in 1818, found at the height of 13,800 feet above the sea-level, the Bhagarati, or true Ganges, issuing from beneath a low arch at the base of a vast mass of frozen snow, nearly three hundred feet in height, and composed of different layers, each several feet in thickness, and, in all probability, the accumulation of ages. Neither here, nor at Gungootree, is there anything resembling a cow's mouth to support the popular fallacy, which must have been invented by persons utterly unacquainted

GUNGOOTREE, THE HIMALAYAS.

with the true features of the scene in which the sacred river gladdens earth with its ever-bounteous waters.

A pilgrimage to Gungootree is accounted one of the most meritorious actions which a Hindoo can perform; and in commemoration of his visit to this holy place, a Ghoorka chieftain has left a memorial of his conquests and his piety, in a small pagoda, erected in honor of the goddess, on a platform of rock, about twenty feet higher than the bed of the river. The Brahmins who have the care of this temple are accommodated with habitations in its close vicinity; there are a few sheds for the temporary residence of pilgrims, many of whom, however, are content with such shelter as the neighboring caves can afford. The usual ceremonies of bathing, praying, and marking the forehead, were gone through at this place, the officiating Brahmin taking care that the fees should be duly paid. Notwithstanding the stern and sullen nature of his retreat at some periods of the year, he may be said to lead a busy life, conversing with devout pilgrims and carriers of water to distant lands who require his seal to authenticate their burdens; and making the most out of all his visitors, whatever their country or their creed may be. Though dispensing with his orisons we paid him for his services, and it seemed a matter of indifference to him on what account he received the cash.

E. ROBERTS, *Hindostan, the shores of the Red Sea, and the Himalaya Mountains.*

XXII.

ADAM'S PEAK, CEYLON.

ASCENT BY DR. DAVY, 1817.

THE first excursion which I made into the interior after my arrival in Ceylon, was to Adam's Peak, the highest mountain in the island, and one that cannot fail to excite the interest of the traveller; its name being known, and its fame spread all over the world, and being an object of veneration almost equally to the Buddhist and the Hindoo, to the Mahometan and the nominal Christian of India, each of whom considers it a sacred mountain, and has attached to it some superstitious tale.

On the 15th of April, 1817, at dawn, I set out from Colombo in company with my friends, the Rev. G. Bisset, William Granville, Esq., and Mr. Moon: on the 17th we reached Ratnapoora, and on the evening of the 19th, the summit of the Peak, distant from Colombo only sixty-six miles.

Our mode of travelling varied with the nature of the road and country. The first sixteen miles we went expeditiously in gigs, over an excellent road, through a populous country, delightfully shaded the

ADAM'S PEAK, CEYLON.

greater part of the way by the rich and beautiful foliage of extensive groves of cocoa-nut trees, which form a deep belt round the southwest part of the island.

On leaving the great maritime road at Pantara to strike into the interior, we exchanged our gigs for the indolent Indian vehicles, palanqueens, in which we were carried as far as Ratnapoora, in Saffragan, about forty-three miles from Colombo, over a pretty good new road, through a country low and yet hilly, in general overgrown with wood, very thinly inhabited (having been a border region) and little cultivated; and excepting here and there, exhibiting few objects and little scenery of an interesting nature. At Horima, where we slept the first night in our palanqueens, we noticed the remains of a Hindoo building of the simplest kind of architecture, the style of which has already been alluded to. The next morning at dawn, just before sunrise, from a hill over which we were passing, we had a splendid view of a tropical wilderness; hills, dales and plains, all luxuriantly wooded, bounded by blue mountains, fleecy clouds resting on the low ground, and a brilliant sky overhead. The charms of the prospect were heightened by the coolness and freshness of the air, and by the animation of the scene, produced by the notes of a variety of birds, some of them reminding one of the blackbird, others of the song of the thrush, and others of that of the red-breast; with which were mixed the harsh cries of the wild peacock, jungle-fowl and parrot, the soft cooing of doves, and the shrill sounds of innumerable insects.

.... Though not eight miles from Adam's Peak, the river here is hardly fifty feet above the level of the sea.....At Ratnapoora we left our palanqueens and proceeded towards the mountains, each in a chair lashed to two bamboos, and carried on men's shoulders. In this manner we travelled about nine miles as far as Palabatula..... Four miles from Ratnapoora we stopped to breakfast at Gillemallé, a beautiful spot..... The latter half of the way is almost one continued ascent by a narrow, rocky path, shaded either by an impenetrable jungle, or by trees so covered with parasitical plants, that each resembles a bower. This kind of luxuriant vegetation is probably connected with the dampness of the climate, and the frequent and heavy showers which fall in this part of the country. Owing to the same cause, the country is infested with leeches, from which the naked legs of our bearers suffered not a little, and from which we did not escape completely. Patabatula is the last inhabited station on the peak. We gladly sought shelter there from a heavy thunderstorm which had deluged us with rain for more than two hours. There is a little Wilharè at this spot, and two open amblams, or rest-houses, one small, where we took up our quarters, and the other pretty large, where we found assembled at least two hundred pilgrims of both sexes and of all ages, either going to, or returning from the Peak.

At dawn, the next morning, we started for the summit on foot, the mountain-path we had to ascend admitting of no other mode of travelling.....After toiling up this steep, gloomy path about two miles, we came to a halting-place on a little platform above a precipice, from which we had a prospect of the country below, that was at once grand and beautiful.

About half-way up the mountain we crossed a small torrent that flows over an immense tabular mass of rock; and about a mile further, to the bed of a much larger torrent, the Setagongola, which may be considered the parent stream of the Kalu-ganga. This river scene was a very impressive one, and extremely picturesque; the torrent, with fine effect, rushed from a wooded height down a channel obstructed by great masses of rock, on which were assembled numerous groups of pilgrims variously employed, some bathing, some making a frugal repast on cold rice, and others resting themselves lying at full length, or sitting cross-legged in the Indian fashion, chewing betel. About half a mile from the river we crossed a little glen. The descent, which is very steep, was facilitated in the most difficult parts by rude wooden ladders. The opposite ascent was in appearance of a much more formidable nature, but the danger is removed by steps having been cut in the rock. About half-way up the rock, on the left-hand side, is the figure of a man rudely cut, and an inscription in Singalese, both commemorating the being by whom the steps had been made. From the top of this bare rock we were once more gratified with an extensive view. A thunderstorm was gathering; the scene was magnificent and awful, and of a nature to baffle description.....Very soon after leaving the rock, the storm commenced, attended with very heavy rain, and with thunder and lightning extremely loud and vivid. There being no shelter, it was useless to halt; we continued ascending without intermission, the difficulty of the path increasing with the height.

The storm lasted till about half-past two, when we had reached a little flat, covered with stunted wood. Whilst we stopped here to rest ourselves for a few minutes under a rude shed made for the use of pilgrims, the weather rapidly improved; the rain nearly ceased, the thunder was to be heard only rolling at a distance, the mists and clouds were dispersing, and we presently had the pleasure of seeing the object of our toil immediately above us, the Peak, of a conical form, rising rapidly and majestically to a point.

We arrived at the top of the mountain a little after three o'clock. The rain was over, the air clear, and the sun shining. The magnificent views of the surrounding scenery amply repaid us for a laborious march, and all the difficulties we had to contend with.

From the surrounding scenery our curiosity soon led us to examine the summit of the mountain. It is very small; according to a measurement made by Lieut. Malcolm (the first European who ascended the Peak), its area is seventy-four feet by twenty-four. It is surrounded by a stone wall five feet high, built in some places on the brink of the precipice. The apex of the mountain is a rock, which stands in the middle of the enclosure, about six or eight feet above the level ground. On the top is the object of worship of the natives, the Sree-pada, the sacred impression, as they imagine, of the foot of Boodhoo, which he stamped on his first visit to the island. It is a superficial hollow, five feet three inches and three quarters long, and between two feet seven inches and two feet five inches wide. It is ornamented with a margin of brass, studded with a few gems, of little value; it is covered with a roof, which is fastened to the rock by four iron chains, and supported by four pillars; and it is surrounded by a low wall. The roof was lined with colored cloths; and its margin being decked with flowers and streamers, it made a very gay appearance. The cavity certainly bears a coarse resemblance to the figure of the human foot.

We passed the night on the mountains; and it was the first time since I had entered the tropics that I had occasion to complain of cold. The next morning before sunrise, we were awoke by the shouts of a party of pilgrims just arrived. They consisted of several men and women, all native Singalese, neatly dressed in clean clothes. They immediately proceeded to their devotions. A priest, in his yellow robes, stood on the rock close to the impression of the foot, with his face to the people, who had ranged themselves in a row below, some on their knees, with their hands uplifted and joined palm to palm, and others bending forward with their hands in the same attitude of devotion. The priest, in a loud, clear voice, sentence by sentence, recited the articles of their religious faith and duties, and, in response, they repeated the same after him. When he had finished, they raised a loud shout, and he retiring, they went through the same ceremony by themselves with one of the party for their leader.

An interesting scene followed this; wives affectionately and respectfully saluted their husbands, and children their parents, and friends one another. An old grey-headed woman first made her salams to a really venerable old man; she was moved to tears and almost kissed his feet; he affectionately raised her up. Several middle-aged men then salamed the patriarchal pair; these men were salamed in return by still younger men, who had first paid their respect to the old people; and, lastly, those nearly of the same standing slightly salamed each other, and exchanged betel leaves. The intention of these salutations, I was informed, was of a moral kind, to confirm the ties of kindred, to strengthen family love and friendship, and remove animosities. The Mahometans, there is good reason to believe, first assigned the name to this mountain by which it is generally known amongst Europeans. The moormen of Ceylon still call it Adam Malay; they say that Adam, when turned out of Paradise, lamented his offence on the summit of the Peak standing on one foot (of which the impression remains) until he was pardoned by God.

From Dr. Davy's *Interior of Ceylon.*

XXIII.

ASCENT OF THE GUNUNG-TALANG, SUMATRA.

A CHAIN of mountains runs through the whole length of the island of Sumatra; and the ranges are, in many places, double and treble. Some near the equator attain the height of 15,000 feet; and among them are extensive plains of a great elevation. The mountains are mostly on the western side. One, which is an active volcano, is known in the island under the name of Sœlassie. It is upwards of 9000 feet above the level of the sea, and was in a state of eruption in the month of October 1845. Several Dutchmen were not afraid to make the ascent even during this period. Some extracts are given from the narrative of one of them.

On our way from Solok to Mocara Pamy, we had perceived from time to time, from the top of the hills, columns of smoke rising from the Sœlassie; and more than once this sight had awakened in us a desire to visit this mountain. We made our wishes known to the overseer, Mr. Van der Ven, who received us cordially, and fully approved of the project. He himself superintended the preparations, and the very next day, October the 21st, we were on horseback by five o'clock in the morning.

Scarcely had we been on the road a quarter of an hour, when we came to a deep cutting covered

The Sœlassie, Sumatra.

with loose flints which made the road so dangerous that we were obliged to descend and lead our horses. We crossed a little bamboo bridge without any parapet, and after having climbed up a steep slope we were rewarded for our trouble by a most magnificent view. And in the distance we saw the Sœlassie, which continued to throw out its columns of smoke.

Near Batol-Bandjak, where we stopped, we saw in abundance these trachyle flints. The inhabitants made us visit several mineral springs in the neighborhood; and we found that the water was bitter and sulphurous.

In the evening we reached the Batol-Bedjandjang at the foot of the volcano. We resumed our march at five o'clock in the morning in the midst of mist and very disagreeable fine rain. The thermometer pointed at 68°. And we had to climb successively three sufficiently steep ridges of more than 600 feet in height each. At the top of the last one, the view extended over a plateau covered with a rich vegetation of trees and shrubs, at the extremity of which we reached a new ascent of about 1300 feet. The soil, which is composed of a mixture of sulphurous and calcareous earth, had become hot; and here and there rose little clouds of smoke from the bottom of the crevasses.

It was eleven o'clock when we took a moment's repose at the bottom of the highest peak which still stood above us, and towered about 300 feet above our heads. And here, although a strong smell of sulphur indicated the neighborhood of the crater and the end of our journey, yet the activity of the volcano also became more evident. In the midst of the blocks of old lava which surrounded us, the vegetation had diminished, the brambles had dried up, and the trunks of the trees were blackened and burnt. We rapidly cleared the space which remained, and arrived at a crevasse situated between the two summits, from one of which the crater was to be seen in all its imposing grandeur.

What a majestic spectacle it was! Before us stood open the old crater by which all the activity of the volcano had developed itself for ages past, and further off the one then in a state of eruption. It appeared like a lake of recent formation environed by flames and clouds of smoke. The dead silence which reigned around us was only interrupted by the subterranean noises of the volcanoes.

On the southwest, at about 360 feet from the summit, the furnace was fully at work. The western side was formed by a vertical wall over which a part of the lava escaped. On the south side, a sloping ridge is lost in depths which the eye cannot penetrate. As far as can be seen, crevasses appeared from whence escaped clouds of smoke.

To get a nearer view of the lake, we descended the sloping sides, helping ourselves as much by our hands as by our feet, and never letting go our hold on one block of rocks until we could fix ourselves firmly on another. So we were witnesses of what was going on within; and we heard a continuous noise resembling that made by the paddle-wheels of many steamboats in motion.

Mr. Van der Ven here ran into the greatest danger. Having gone quite close to an opening, the hot lava gave way under his feet; but happily it rested on a mass which was already hardened; so that he had time to jump off backwards. The heat did not permit us to remain long in the crater; we were obliged to abandon it hastily in order to visit the little sulphur lake which was under the ridge on to which we had climbed. This lake, which is of a rounded form, is about 160 feet in diameter. Three of us descended an almost vertical wall, of perhaps twenty-two feet high, down to a quantity of boiling water. Clinging with one hand to the crevasses they could with the other get out some spoonfuls; but the strong smell of sulphur in this water obliged them to get up again very quickly.

We then recrossed the plateau to the point where we had commenced our examination in order to see about preparing a convenient lodging-place for the night. By ten o'clock in the evening we were wrapped in our cloaks and seeking to get some sleep on our stony beds when the rain came on again with great violence. Clouds from whence proceeded such lightning as illuminated the heavens succeeded each other in rapid succession; and three times our tent was nearly carried away. The water streamed in upon us; and we trembled with cold. The wind also put out our lights; but by the illumination of the lightning we managed after many efforts to fix our tent firmly; and then under its feeble shelter we waited for the day.

We had struggled for some hours against the unchained elements, and their fury might, for aught we knew, have been prolonged; so it was a great relief to us in the morning to see the sky become perfectly pure and cloudless before we set out on our return. We descended by the eastern side, whose slopes were less dangerous, right down to the bottom of the extinct crater, and up again on the other side to the summit, from whence we were able to enjoy a magnificent view over hills and valleys, lakes, rivers, and islands, which were spread out beneath our eyes.

Nouvelles Annales des Voyages.

XXIV.

PETER BOTTE, MAURITIUS.

ASCENT BY CAPTAIN LLOYD, LIEUTS. TAYLOR, PHILLPOTTS AND KEPPEL IN 1832.

You are no doubt aware, from my former letter, that the Peter Botte has always been considered inaccessible; and although a tradition exists of a man of that name having ascended it and losing his life in returning, it is seldom believed, no authentic account remaining of the fact. A Frenchman, forty years ago, declared that he had got on the top by himself, and made a hole in the rock for a flag-staff; and his countrymen naturally believed him; but the value of this assertion may also be judged of by the present narrative.

The ascent has been frequently attempted, and by several people, of late years: once by the officers of His Majesty's ship *Samarang*, who lost their way and found themselves separated from the Peter Botte itself by a deep cleft in the rock, and in consequence were compelled to return. Captain Lloyd, chief civil engineer, and your old friend Dawkins, made the attempt last year, and succeeded in reaching a point between the shoulder and the neck, where they planted a ladder which did not reach half-way up a perpendicular face of rock that arrested their progress. This was the last attempt. Captain Lloyd was then, however, so convinced of the practicability of the undertaking, that he determined to repeat the experiment this year, and accordingly made all his preparations by the beginning of this month. On the 6th he started from town, accompanied by Lieut. Phillpotts of the 29th regiment, Lieut. Keppel, R.N. (my old messmate), and myself, whom he asked to join him. He had previously sent out two of his overseers with about twenty-five Negroes and Sepoy convicts to make all necessary preparations. They carried with them a sort of tent, and ropes, crow-bars, a portable ladder, provisions, and everything we could possibly want for three or four days, as we intended to remain on the shoulder of the mountain, close to the base of Peter Botte, until we either succeeded, or were convinced of its impossibility. These men had worked hard, and on our arriving at the foot of the mountain we found the tent and all our tools, etc., safely lodged on the shoulder of Peter Botte. I may as well describe here the appearance of the mountain. From most points of view it seems to rise out of the range which runs nearly parallel to that part of the sea-coast which forms the Bay of Port Louis; but on arriving at its base you find that it is actually separated from the rest of the range by a ravine or cleft of tremendous depth. Seen from the town (as you will perceive by the sketch) it appears a cone

PETER BOTTE, MAURITIUS

with a large overhanging rock at its summit, but so extraordinarily sharp and knife-like is this, in common with all the rocks on the island, that when seen end on, as the sailors say, it appears nearly quite perpendicular. In fact, I have seen it in fifty different points of view, and cannot yet assign to it any one precise form. But to my tale.

We dined that evening and slept at the house of a Frenchman in the plain below, and rose early next morning much exhausted by the attacks of bugs. All our preparations being made, we started, and a more picturesque line of march I have seldom seen.

Our van was composed of about fifteen or twenty Sepoys of every variety of costume, together with a few Negroes carrying our food, dry clothes, etc. Our path lay up a very steep ravine formed by the rains in the wet season, which having loosened all the stones, made it anything but pleasant; those below were obliged to keep a bright look out for tumbling rocks, and one of these missed Keppel and myself by a miracle. From the head of this gorge we turned off along the other face of the mountain; and it would have been a fine subject for a picture, to look up from the ravine below and see the long string slowly picking their 'kittle' footsteps along a ledge not anywhere a foot broad; yet these monkeys carried their loads full four hundred yards along this face, holding by the shrubs above, while below there was nothing but the tops of the forest for more than nine hundred feet down the slope.

On rising to the shoulder a view burst upon us

which quite defies my descriptive powers. We stood on a little narrow ledge or neck of land, about twenty yards in length. On the side which we mounted we looked back into the deep wooded gorge we had passed up; while on the opposite side of the neck, which was between six and seven feet broad, the precipice went sheer down fifteen hundred feet to the plain. One extremity of the neck was equally precipitous, and the other was bounded by what to me was the most magnificent sight I ever saw. A narrow, knife-like edge of rock, broken here and there by precipitous faces, ran up in a conical form, to about 300 or 350 feet above us, and on the very pinnacle old 'Peter Botte' frowned in all his glory. I have done several sketches of him, one of which, from this point, I send by the same ship as this letter.

After a short rest we proceeded to work. The ladder (see sketch) had been left by Lloyd and Dawkins last year. It was about twelve feet high, and reached, as you may perceive, about half-way up a face of perpendicular rock. The foot, which was spiked, rested on a ledge not quite visible in the sketch, with barely three inches on each side. A grapnel-line had been also left last year, but was not used. A Negro of Lloyd's clambered from the top of the ladder by the cleft in the face of the rock, not trusting his weight to the old and rotten line. He carried a small cord round his middle, and it was fearful to see the cool, steady way in which he climbed, where a single loose stone or false hold must have sent him down into the abyss; however, he fearlessly scrambled away, till at length we heard him halloo from under the neck, 'All right!' These Negroes use their feet exactly like monkeys, grasping with them every projection almost as firmly as with their hands. The line carried up he made fast above, and up we went all 'shinned' in succession. It was, joking apart, awful work. In several places the ridge ran to an edge not a foot broad, and I could, as I held on, half-sitting, half-kneeling across the ridge, have kicked my right shoe down to the plain on one side, and my left into the bottom of the ravine on the other. The only thing that surprised me was my own steadiness and freedom from all giddiness. I had been nervous in mounting the ravine in the morning, but gradually I got so excited and determined to succeed, that I could look down that dizzy height without the smallest sensation of swimming in the head; nevertheless, I held on *uncommonly hard*, and felt very well satisfied when I was safe under the neck. And a more extraordinary situation I never was in. The head, which is an enormous mass of rock, about thirty-five feet in height, overhangs its base many feet on every side. A ledge of tolerably level rock runs round three sides of the base, about six feet in width, bounded everywhere by the abrupt edge of the precipice, except in the spot where it is joined by the ridge up which we climbed. In one spot, the head, though overhanging its base several feet, reaches only perpendicularly over the edge of the precipice, and most fortunately it was at the very spot where we mounted. Here it was that we reckoned on getting up; a communication being established with the shoulder by a double line of ropes, we proceeded to get up the necessary *matériel*, —Lloyd's ladder, additional coils of rope, crow-bars, etc. But now the question, and a puzzler, too, was how to get the ladder up against the rock. Lloyd had prepared some iron arrows with thongs to fire over; and, having got up a gun, he made a line fast round his body, which we all held on, and going over the edge of the precipice on the opposite side, he leaned back against the line and fired over the least projecting part. Had the line broken he would have fallen 1800 feet. Twice this failed; and then he had recourse to a large stone with a lead line, which swung diagonally, and seemed to be a feasible plan; several times he made beautiful heaves, but the provoking line would not catch, and away went the stone far below; till at length Æolus, pleased, I suppose, with his perseverance, gave us a shift of wind for about a minute, and over went the stone, and was eagerly seized on the opposite side.

Hurrah, my lads! steady's the word! Three lengths of the ladder were put together on the ledge, a large line was attached to the one which was over the head, and carefully drawn up; and finally, a two-inch rope to the extremity of which we lashed the top of our ladder, then lowered it gently over the precipice till it hung perpendicularly, and was steadied by two Negroes on the ridge below. "All right; now hoist away!" and up went the ladder, till the foot came to the edge of our ledge, where it was lashed in firmly to the neck. We then hauled away on the guy to steady it, and made it fast; a line was passed over by the lead-line to hold on, and up went Lloyd, screeching and hallooing, and we all three scrambled after him. The union-jack and a boat-hook were passed up, and old England's flag waved freely and gallantly on the redoubted Peter Botte. No sooner was it seen flying than the *Undaunted*, frigate, saluted in the harbor, and the guns of our saluting battery replied; for though our expedition had been kept secret until we started, it was made known on the morning of our ascent, and all hands were on the lookout, as we afterwards learnt. We then got a bottle of wine to the top of the rock, christened King William's Peak, and drank his Majesty's health, hands round the Jack, and then Hip! hip! hip! hurrah!

I certainly never felt anything like the excitement of that moment; even the Negroes down on the shoulder took up our hurrahs; and we could hear far below, the faint shouts of the astonished inhabitants of the plain. We were determined to do nothing by halves, and accordingly made preparation for sleeping under the neck. After dinner, as it was getting dark, I screwed up my nerves and climbed up to our queer little nest at the top, followed by Tom Keppel and a Negro, who carried some dry wood, and made a fire in a cleft under the rock. Lloyd and Phillpotts soon came up, and we began to arrange ourselves for the night, each taking a glass of brandy to begin with. I had on two pairs of trousers, a shooting waistcoat, jacket, and large flushing jacket over that, a thick woollen sail-

or's cap and two blankets; and each of us lighted a cigar as we seated ourselves to wait for the appointed hour for the signal of our success. It was a glorious sight to look down from that giddy pinnacle over the whole island, lying so calm and beautiful in the moonlight, except where the broad, black shadows of the other mountains intercepted the light. Here and there we could see a light twinkling in the plains, or a fire of some sugar manufactory; but not a sound of any sort reached us except an occasional shout from the party down on the shoulder (we four being the only ones above). At length, in the direction of Port Louis, a bright flash was seen, and after a long interval, the sullen boom of the evening gun. We then prepared our pre-arranged signal; and whiz went a rocket from our nest, lighting up for an instant the peaks of the hills below us, and then leaving us in darkness. We next burnt a blue light; and nothing can be conceived more perfectly beautiful than the broad glare against the overhanging rock. The wild-looking group we made, in our uncouth habiliments, and the narrow ledge on which we stood, were all distinctly seen; while many of the tropical birds, frightened at our vagaries, came glancing down in the light, and then swooped away, screeching into the gloom below, for the gorge on our left was as dark as Erebus. We burnt another blue light, and threw up two more rockets, when our laboratory being exhausted, the patient-looking, insulted moon had it all her own way again. We now rolled ourselves up in our blankets, and having lashed Phillpotts, who was a determined sleep-walker, to Keppel's leg, we tried to sleep; but it blew strong before the morning, and was very cold. We drank all our brandy, and kept tucking in the blankets the whole night without success. At day-break we rose, stiff, cold, and hungry, and I shall conclude briefly by saying that, after about four or five hours' hard work, we got a hole mined in the rock, and sunk the foot of our twelve-foot ladder deep in this, lashing a water-barrel, as a landmark, at the top, and, above all, a long staff, with a union-jack flying. We then in turn mounted to the top of the ladder to take a last look at a view such as we might never see again, and bidding adieu to the scene of our toil and triumph, descended the ladder to the neck, and casting off the guys and hauling-lines, cut off all communication with the top.

In order to save time and avoid danger, we now made fast a line from the neck to the shoulder, as tight as possible, and hanging on our traps by means of rings, launched them one by one from the top, and down they flew, making the line smoke. All were thus conveyed safely to the shoulder, except one unlucky bag, containing a lot of blankets, my spy-glass, and sundry other articles, which not being firmly fixed, broke the preventer-line, and took its departure down to Pamplemousses. We at length descended and reached the shoulder all safe and without any accident, except that of the blankets, not a rope-yarn being left to show where we got up. We then breakfasted, and after a long and somewhat troublesome descent, got to the low country, and drove in Lloyd's carriage to town, where we were most cordially welcomed by all our countrymen, though I believe we were not quite so warmly greeted by the French inhabitants, who are now constrained to believe that their countrymen alone did not achieve the feat, and that the British ensign has been the first to wave over the redoubtable Peter Botte.

LIEUT. TAYLOR, *Royal Geographical Society's Transactions.*

XXV.

THE PEAK OF TENERIFFE.

ASCENT BY BERTHELOT.

It was on the 8th of July that I determined to climb to the very Peak of Teyde, better known in Europe under the name of the Peak of Teneriffe. I intended to reach it by the southern slopes ; and I knew that before me no one had attempted it on that side, because the paths which lead to it are almost impracticable ; but then I thought I might possibly find there some plants which had escaped the learned researches of Broussonnet, and of Ch. Smith ; and this hope alone outweighed all the obstacles. I was, at this time, at Chasna, a village situated in a most picturesque position on the south of the peak, and at about 4600 feet above the level of the sea, although it was hardly three leagues distant from the southern side of the isle. I set out from thence at five o'clock in the morning, with Mr. Macgregor, then English consul at the Canaries, and with two guides, who were to accompany us. After two hours' march, we arrived at the base of the central mountains. The pines which covered almost all the land that we had crossed, gradually became more rare; and as we advanced into the gorge of Oucanca these beautiful trees insensibly disappeared, and were replaced by viscous brooms. Oucanca is a place which is worthy of a visit; a volcanic eruption, accompanied no doubt by violent commotions, overthrowing the base of the central mountains, gave birth to the gorge now existing there. The principal crater, which is easily recognized, vomits a torrent of vitrified lava which inundates the neighboring places, and follows its course towards the coast, traversing a space of more than two leagues. The wildness of this place is still more increased by the enormous rocks which seem to have become detached from the neighboring heights.

Emerging from the gorges of Oucanca, we continued to ascend the mountain in front of us; the white heaths, of which we had already found some bushes, then showed themselves in greater number, and soon extended so as to form a sort of belt of vegetation exclusively round the bases of the peak.

The place at which we had arrived was called *Degollada de Oucanca*. Teneriffe was in front of us; we could already count the torrents of black lava which marked its sides; and we could also see all the central mountains of Teneriffe. Indeed it is only from this point that a view can be obtained which embraces the whole group of these volcanic summits. This view is most imposing; and no description can give a just idea of it. These *Cañadas* mountains which may probably have once formed a

THE PEAK OF TENERIFFE.

perfectly circular chain, present now two great passages whose ruinous approaches plainly indicate the violent causes which have created them. Their high crests rise to more than 9000 feet above the level of the ocean; and all the space enclosed by their line of circumvallation round these trachytic mountains constitutes one immense crater, whose origin was probably prior to that of the peak itself which the geologist Escolar called *el hijo de las Cañadas* (the son of the *Cañadas*). It is nearly in the middle of this elliptical crater, of which the greatest diameter is about five leagues, that the Peak rises, still smoking, above all this agitated soil. The vast circle which surrounds it is known at Teneriffe by the name of the gorges of the Peak, (*Cañadas del Teyde*, or simply *Cañadas*).

The path which conducts to the *Degollada of Oucanca*, in the bottom of the gorges, is a very rugged one; the opposite slope of the mountain is almost perpendicular, and presents, in several places, precipices which are more than 900 feet deep. When we were descending into the interior of the *Cañadas* we could scarcely conceive how we should ever arrive there; but at last we succeeded. The level of these gorges is about 9000 feet above the sea; and the Peak rises about 3000 feet above this level. We had, on one side, the vast slopes of the great cone, and on the other the chain of mountains from which we had descended, and whose almost perpendicular side served of old as a division to the immense boiling crater. Truly an astonishing spectacle! If in imagination we go back to the ages of geological disturbance in which this frightful volcano was in all its activity we shall not be able to think without horror of that flaming gulf of more than nine leagues in circumference, and of 900 feet in depth. Yet only thus can we form an idea of the state of fermentation of this era of incandescence; and the formation of the Peak in the middle of this gulf will then appear only a secondary phenomenon.

After having admired these grand volcanic effects, and before we proceeded still nearer to the base of the Peak, we were obliged to rest ourselves at the source of La Piedra, for we were suffocated by the heat. In this elevated region, the air is always calm and clear, the heavens always of a brilliant azure; and the lightest cloud never comes to break its uniformity. The intensity of the solar rays in these gorges, their reflection from the layers of white gravel stone, their dazzling scintillation on the fragments of pumice-stone and obsidian, which cover the ground, are so many causes of the high temperature. From thence you look down on the clouds; and so there are none of those pleasant mists which in the lower regions, from time to time refresh the atmosphere, moisten the earth, and vivify the vegetation. The inhabitant of the plains, who crosses this belt, soon feels its influence; the extreme dryness of the air closes the pores, stops perspiration, and cracks his skin; an immoderate thirst ceaselessly torments him, and often he seeks in vain for some hidden spring which still could only quench his thirst for an instant. It is in vain also that to avoid the heat of the sun, he tries to take refuge under the bushes of broom or the shadow of some rock; the earth everywhere is burning, everywhere the heat is insupportable, everywhere there reigns this depressing stillness, and he is speedily forced to quit the shelter in which no breath of air can be felt.

The source of La Piedra suplies a deliciously cool water, to which the goats that are left to wander in these gorges, and the bees whose hives are placed in its neighborhood, come to quench their thirst. A quantity of white broom grows near it; and indeed this useful shrub is the ornament of these *Cañadas*. The goats browse, too, on its stems, whilst the bees ceaselessly suck the perfumed flowers. So, even in the most desert places, Nature seems to have provided for the wants of all. Without the broom, which is so abundantly spread over this valley, how could these flocks and precious swarms subsist? and yet the latter form one of the most important branches of rural economy to the inhabitants of the south.

We now continued our way along the defile of *Cañada Blanca;* and our guides made us afterwards cross a torrent of lava which was on our right, then another, and soon after a third. They call all these places which have been invaded by the eruptions *mal pais* (mauvais pays). In proportion to the height we attained, did the obstacles seem to become more and more insurmountable; and every minute we had to scramble over the heaps of scoria, or the masses of obsidian, which lay in our way.

We had marched for more than two hours over this terrible ground, when our guides, who had already stopped several times to consult together, began to appear uncertain as to the road which they ought to follow; and very soon one of them came to announce to us that we had wandered from the right way, and that we must give up our enterprise. We were not of his mind; we had gone too far to give up; but somehow we felt that we must get out of that particular spot, for night was coming on; and besides this place, to which our ignorant guides had conducted us, was a discouraging one. The lava heaped up in blocks surrounded us on every side, and further on it appeared to be spread in sheets; so we did not know which way to turn. However, at all hazards, and by main force we managed to clear a way for the unfortunate horse that carried our provisions, and which had almost been killed over and over again during this journey.

We were nearly worn out with fatigue when we arrived at the foot of a mountain of pumice, leaning against the Peak. On getting clear of this pumice our shoes and stockings were in rags; but we had already reached one of the slopes of the Peak, and we took courage. I knew this place too, for it was the way I had gone in 1825 on my first expedition. Certain now of wandering no more, we pushed on boldly towards *La Estancia*, where we at length arrived about nine o'clock, in the light of a fine moon.

In spite of the height of this station, we found the temperature very supportable; we breathed the purest air, and some light gusts of north wind brought to us the perfume of the broom. Our people had no sooner arrived than they collected a quantity of the neighboring bushes, which they heaped together and lighted. On this they laid to roast an unfortunate goat, which they had killed in the *Cañadas*. Soon after supper they grouped themselves round the fire; and each fell asleep in his place. As for me, I could not do much in that way, for the forced march of the day had heated my blood; and in such a state of irritation one sleeps but ill, especially on rocks. The spectacle beneath my eyes was likewise too full of attraction for me; the serenity of the heavens, the solitude of the place, the strange forms of the rocks heaped around our bivouac, and those grand shadows which veiled the gorges, out of which we had just come—all these things formed an imposing tableau.

It was three o'clock in the morning when we left the place of our bivouac in order to advance towards the point of the Peak. The pathway which we followed first, although very much inclined, is notwithstanding practicable enough; but on approaching the *Altavista*, the irregularity of the ground became frightful on account of the incumbrance of the various matters which the volcano had vomited; and one could not walk too cautiously amidst so many crevasses and roughnesses. After having got clear of this *mal pais del Teyde*, as our guides call it, we arrived at the course of *La Rambleta*. Everything seemed to point out the existence in this place of a crater anterior to that of the summit of the Peak; for it is from hence that all the numerous torrents of lava flowed which have inundated the *Cañadas.* The Teyde or Peak must have had intervals of rest; and it was probably after one of them that a new eruption produced the Peak. This volcanic head which has covered up the old opening really rises in the midst of *La Rambleta;* now it crowns the mountain, and the slopes of its summit which we saw beneath us, were lighted up by the rays of the rising sun. Sulphureous exhalations were already perceptible; and we saw that we were near the end of our enterprise; but this little cone remained still to be ascended, and its height was about 440 feet. The pumice-stones and the remains of lava rendered this ascent very fatiguing; however, after we had rested and taken breath several times we at length reached the summit.

The view which one enjoys at this elevation is perfectly grand; it would be imposible for me to give an exact idea of it; to explain the impression which this sublime spectacle produced on me would be still more difficult. I felt at the same time a sort of giddiness and yet of ecstasy; I was dumb with admiration. From that culminating point whence the eruptions burst forth at 12,000 feet above the level of the sea, our view embraced seven islands. On the east, the high peaks of the grand Canary pierced through the clouds that were gilded by the rays of the sun; further on, we discovered Lanzerote and Forteventura; on the west, the shadow of Teneriffe extended in an immense triangle as far as

Gomera; and not far off were to be seen Palma and the isle of Ferro. Below us lay Teneriffe, with the whole circuit of its coasts, the different chains of its mountains, its plateaux, and its picturesque valleys. Our eyes wandered long over this multitude of hollows and risings which the play of the shadows, showed to us; we could have wished to make out all the localities, and to recognize every object; but the panorama was too distant for it to be possible to seize all its details; it was but a plan in relief; we could not properly appreciate the heights and the distances, for from thence even the hills seemed to sink under the Peak. We were almost beside ourselves with admiration at the immensity of this picture; but the scene soon changed its aspect. As the sun advanced in its course, so the vapors rose on all sides; gradually we saw condensed masses floating about, and white clouds forming themselves over the places where a great quantity of vegetation sucked in and constantly reproduced new mists. Thus insensibly the whole surface of the island became covered, over which we stood as over an ocean of clouds.

BERTHELOT, *Bulletin de la Société de Géographie.*

XXVI.

THE SIERRA NEVADA.

CLIMBING A PRECIPICE.

Around the head of the lake were crags and precipices in singularly forbidding arrangement. As we turned thither we saw no possible way of overcoming them. At its head the lake lay in an angle of the vertical wall, sharp and straight, like the corner of a room; about three hundred feet in height, and for two hundred and fifty feet of this a pyramidal pile of blue ice rose from the lake, rested against the corner, and reached within forty feet of the top. Looking into the deep blue water of the lake, I concluded that in our exhausted state it was madness to attempt to swim it. The only other alternative was to scale that slender pyramid of ice and find some way to climb the forty feet of smooth wall above it. . . . Upon the top of the ice we found a narrow, level platform, upon which we stood together, resting our backs in the granite corner, and looked down the awful pathway of King's Cañon, until the rest nerved us enough to turn our eyes upward at the forty feet of smooth granite which lay between us and safety.

Here and there were small projections from its surface, little protruding knobs of feldspar, and crevices riven into its face for a few inches.

As we tied ourselves together, I told Cotter to hold himself in readiness to jump down into one of these in case I fell, and started to climb up the wall, succeeding quite well for about twenty feet. About two feet above my hands was a crack, which, if my arms had been long enough to reach, would probably have led me to the very top; but I judged it beyond my powers, and, with great care, descended to the side of Cotter, who believed that his superior length of arm would enable him to make the reach

I planted myself against the rock, and he started cautiously up the wall. Looking down the glare front of ice, it was not pleasant to consider at what velocity a slip would send me to the bottom, or at what angle, and to what probable depth, I should be projected into the ice-water. Indeed, the idea of such a sudden bath was so annoying that I lifted my eyes toward my companion. He reached my farthest point without great difficulty, and made a bold spring for the crack, reaching it without an inch to spare, and holding on wholly by his fingers. He thus worked himself slowly along the crack toward the top, at last getting his arms over the brink, and gradually drawing his body up and out of sight. It was the most splendid piece of slow gymnastics I ever witnessed. For a moment he said nothing; but when I asked if he was all right, he cheerfully repeated, 'All right.' It was only a moment's work to send up the two knapsacks and barometer, and receive again my end of the lasso. As I tied it round my breast, Cotter said to me, in an easy, confident tone, 'Don't be afraid to bear your weight.' I made up my mind, however, to make that climb without his aid, and husbanded my strength as I climbed from crack to crack. I got up without difficulty to my former point, rested there a moment, hanging solely by my hands, gathered every pound of strength and atom of will for the reach, then jerked myself upward with a swing, just getting the tips of my fingers into the crack. In an instant I had grasped it with my right hand also. I felt the sinews of my fingers relax a little, but the picture of the slope of ice and the blue lake affected me so strongly that I redoubled my grip and climbed slowly along the crack, until I reached the angle, and got one arm over the edge as Cotter had done. As I rested my body on the edge and looked up at Cotter, I saw that, instead of a level top, he was sitting upon a smooth, roof-like slope, where the least pull would have dragged him over the brink. He had no brace for his feet, nor hold for his hands, but had seated himself calmly, with the rope tied round his breast, knowing that my only safety lay in being able to make the climb entirely unaided; certain that the least waver in his tone would have disheartened me, and perhaps made it impossible. The shock I received on seeing this affected me for a moment, but not enough to throw me off my guard, and I climbed quickly over the edge. When we had walked back out of danger we sat down upon the granite for a rest.

In all my experience of mountaineering I have never known an act of such real, profound courage as this of Cotter's. It is one thing, in a moment of excitement, to make a gallant leap, or hold one's nerves in the iron grasp of will; but to coolly seat one's self in the door of death, and silently listen for the fatal summons, and this all for a friend—for he might easily have cast loose the lasso and saved himself—requires as sublime a type of courage as I know. . . .

It was about two o'clock when we reached the summit and rested a moment to look back over our new Alps, which were hard and distinct under direct unpoetic light; yet with all their dense grey and white reality, their long, sculptured ranks, and cold, still summits, we gave them a lingering farewell look, which was not without its deep fullness of emotion, then turned our backs and hurried down the *débris* slope into the rocky amphitheatre at the foot of Mount Brewer, and by five o'clock had reached our old camp-ground. We found here a note pinned to a tree informing us that the party had gone down into the lower cañon, five miles below, that they might camp in better pasturage.

The wind had scattered the ashes of our old camp-fire, and banished from it the last sentiment of home. We hurried on, climbing among the rocks which reached down to the crest of the great lateral moraine, and then on in rapid stride along its smooth crest, riveting our eyes upon the valley below, where we knew the party must be camped.

At last, faintly curling above the sea of green

tree tops, a few faint clouds of smoke wafted upward into the air. We saw them with a burst of strong emotion, and ran down the steep flank of the moraine at the top of our speed. Our shouts were instantly answered by the three voices of our friends, who welcomed us to their camp-fire with tremendous hugs.

After we had outlined for them the experience of our days, and as we lay outstretched at our ease, warm in the blaze of the glorious camp-fire, Brewer said to me, "King, you have relieved me of a dreadful task. For the last three days I have been composing a letter to your family, but somehow I did not get beyond, 'It becomes my painful duty to inform you.'"

CLARENCE KING, *Mountaineering in the Sierra Ne. ada.* (*Atlantic Monthly*).

XXVII.

DISCOVERY OF AN ANCIENT VOLCANO.

BY H. DE SAUSSURE IN 1855.

YOU have often asked me to communicate some details relating to my journey in Mexico; but until the present time I have not found it possible to begin the relation of my observations on the geography of this interesting country. I shall now confine myself to speaking of the discovery of an ancient extinct volcano, about which there are remarkably curious points, worthy of the attention of the geographer as well as of the geologist. But when I talk of the discovery of this mountain, I do not pretend that it had never been visited by any one, for the inhabitants of the surrounding district knew it very well; but no traveller has ever suspected its existence, and even the inhabitants of the Mexican towns are quite in ignorance about it.

On the southwest of the valley of Mexico, extends the green province of Michoacan, which with good reason passes for the garden of Mexico, and which unites the advantages of a broken-up soil, furrowed by a great number of water-courses, and of a temperate climate. When the traveller gets into one of these green meadows, after having travelled a long time in the sandy plains of Anahuac and the marshes of the basin of Mexico, he experiences a peculiar delight at the sight of these wooded hills between which stretch verdant meadows, rivers with their pure, clear waves, and enchanting lakes on the bosom of which float islets covered with a rich vegetation. In the other districts of this country some wild and rugged mountains conceal veins of precious metal which, at the present time, are the sole riches of these Spanish republics. The most flourishing of these districts is that of Angangeo, situated on the confines of the State of Mexico. I quitted this locality on the 6th of August, 1855, and directed myself to the west towards the village of Taximaroa. I had received some vague intimation of the existence in this region of a great mountain bearing the name of San Andres, but I had some trouble in finding a guide who should conduct me to it.

All the volcanoes of Mexico are easy of access. The slope of their sides is so gentle that one can ascend on horseback to a considerable height; but they are always covered with forests which hide the horizon and the summit of the mountain. Everywhere the visual ray is arrested by the trunks of venerable trees which seem to dispute the ground, or which lie heaped together in masses of rottenness, where all living nature seems to retire into shade from the eye of the passer-by. This vigorous and gigantic vegetation, the fruit of a tropical

THE SAN ANDRES, MEXICO.

climate, and remarkably fertile soil, excites for a length of time the imagination of the traveller; but all this ends at last in fatigue, and its monotony fills the soul with *ennui* and sadness. Here, however, the uniformity is broken by great openings among the trees; and the horizontal ground appears to me to have belonged to a series of dried-up lakes. The mountain of San Andres is, in fact, very distinct. Its sides are not uniformly inclined; but they are cut up into plains, mounds, and hills, on the mountain itself. This vast whole presents a mass of domes and of crests, separated by plains and valleys; and it rises gradually by stages to the last plateau, on the level of which surges up the rounded rock which forms the highest point.

The straight path which conducts from the village of Jaripea to the place of the sulphur works, sometimes crosses the marshes of the plains, sometimes goes down into ravines, in which our steps were attended with danger every moment. The soil of the mountain is entirely composed of a bluish trachyte, crossed by an infinity of very wide lines of obsidian, so that, in many places, men and horses walk literally over glass. All the neighboring plains are of much the same character, and are besides inundated with basaltic overflowings, which have boiled up through a multitude of chinks with which the ground has been riddled during the numerous cataclysms which the incessant volcanic shocks have caused.

After several hours' march we came out suddenly on a pebbly amphitheatre, in which the most curious spectacle was presented to our eyes. At the bottom of this species of shaft is to be seen a circular pond, more than three hundred feet wide, filled with a troubled and boiling water, from which escapes a cloud of vapor loaded with mephitic gases. All the divisions of the amphitheatre are rocks completely bare of earth or vegetation, softened and whitened by the sulphurous vapors with which the atmosphere of this gulf is loaded. On these rocks are to be seen yellow and red rays, which indicate the incessant action of sulphur; and a languishing vegetation covers on all sides the edges which are perpendicularly cut. This struggle between a budding vegetation and the noxious emanations which keep it down, has something sad in it, which renders the appearance of these desolate places still more wild. The marsh of hot water which occupies the lower parts, to judge by the steepness of its edges, is of a great depth. Out of it they continually draw sulphur mixed with mud, which is used in the manufacture of powder, after it has been purified by fusion. Some earthen huts and a little building for the works have been constructed for this business, and at a distance from the lagune, at which less of the mephitical exhalations are felt; but such is still the influence of the sulphurous vapors at this distance, that it transforms the argillaceous earth of which the houses are built into different sulphates, principally into alum, so that they actually crumble away periodically. This phenomenon is one of the most curious that can be seen anywhere.

We gave the rest of the day to exploring different parts of the mountain, and, guided by two Indians, we penetrated into an elevated valley, using our hatchets to clear the way for ourselves through the thick parts of the forests, the extraordinary vegetation of which surpasses in majesty and vigor all that I had seen on the mountains of Mexico. The ground is strewed with gigantic trunks, which are heaped pell-mell under the thick foliage of living trees; and when we tried to get clear of them by stepping from one to another, they crumbled and fell into dust, drawing us in their fall down into a bed of ferns and other plants, so that we found ourselves in a manner between mountains of decayed substances.

For about an hour our attention had been attracted by a strange noise, like that of a cataract at a distance, when we perceived a great column of white smoke, whose curling flakes seemed to be thrust out over the summit of the fir-trees which cover the flanks of the valley.

On reaching the place whence the noise proceeded we were struck by the grandeur of the spectacle which it presented. Before us was a whitened slope, which appeared as if covered with porcelain.

On the top of this there was a well with an opening about six feet across, from whence escaped, with a horrible whistling noise, an immense jet of vapor, which rose into the air to a considerable height.

At the same time a flood of boiling water overflowed from this opening and ran in several streams down to the valley. This phenomenon could only be compared to that of the Geysers of Iceland ; and here, as there, the results were the same. The waters in their course deposit a quantity of silica, and form all around those white rocks whose substance I have compared to that of porcelain. All the stones which these waters moisten are in a state of growth. Their surface is soft, like a species of paste ; and when this becomes solid, it is a sort of compact opal.

San Andres has many other curiosities too. Not far from this jet of vapor, and in the same valley, there is another hot spring, in the middle of divers little basins, which look as if they had been cut by the hand of man. But this latter offers scarcely any object of interest except that of a simple mineral spring, unless it is the high temperature of its waters, which are found to be nearly 212°.

We continued our course through the woods, always guided by our Indians, and rising gradually up the sides of the valley, but without going beyond the circuit of half a league, suddenly we saw opening before us a gulf whose argillaceous and perpendicular banks threatened to give way under our feet. In the depth of this hole we saw a marsh of muddy water, agitated by a violent ebullition. Its level first fell, then rose in immense swellings, and broke out and fell on all sides in waves of foam. Some firs, which the falling of the banks had let down, were beaten up in this funnel, and agitated in the boiling waves of this grey mud, they were subjected to a regular cooking operation, and shaken about like a vegetable in a pot of boiling water. The suddenness with which we came on this spectacle rendered it still more frightful. We fell back, seized with fear at the thought that the earth might fail under our feet, and that the least imprudence would precipitate us into this gulf, where a frightful death would be inevitable.

We could not help comparing this marvellous picture to certain fairy scenes which belong to the middle ages. If, instead of being placed in the bosom of the deserts of America, the mountain which we have described had been found on the banks of the Rhine, it would have added more than one legend to the Gothic traditions of Germany. Is not the kettle of Rubezahl like this caldron of the mountain, in which the trees of the forest are cooked? And this dreadful place—if the witches of Macbeth lived in it—would it not be a perfect picture?

It is highly probable that the San Andres has many other objects worthy of attention; but the impenetrable forests which entirely cover it, prevent the traveller from exploring it at his ease. In another excursion, which I afterwards made beyond the sulphur factory, I saw a vast glade, in which the ground is occupied by a lake of bitter water, fed, no doubt, from subterranean sources. Nothing can be more *triste* than these isolated places, where an expanse of brackish water is bordered all around by the venerable trees of a silent and monotonous forest, which neither deer nor parrots ever come to enliven. It was there that, seized by a violent attack of fever, I became incapable of pushing further the exploration of the San Andres. I deplored this circumstance the more because it rendered it impossible for me to visit the peak of the mountain which the inhabitants call the Cerro Grande, the altitude of which very sensibly passes the limit of arborescent vegetation. They even assert that it is not free from perpetual snows; but the information which a traveller obtains from the natives is too vague to inspire much confidence.

Letter of M. H. DE SAUSSURE *to* M. DE LA ROQUETTE, *Bulletin de la Société de Géographie.*

XXVIII.

THE SILLA OF CARACAS.

A. DE HUMBOLDT.

I REMAINED two months at Caracas, where M. Bonpland and I lived in a large house in the most elevated part of the town. From a gallery we could survey at once the summit of the Silla, the serrated ridge of the Galipano, and the charming valley of the Guayra, the rich culture of which was pleasingly contrasted with the gloomy curtain of the surrounding mountains. It was in the dry season, and to improve the pasturage, the savannahs and the turf covering the steepest rocks were set on fire. These vast conflagrations, viewed from a distance, produce the most singular effects of light. Wherever the savannahs, following the undulating slope of the rocks, have filled up the furrows hollowed out by the water, the flame appears, on a dark night, like currents of lava, suspended over the valley. The vivid but steady light assumes a reddish tint, when the wind, descending from the Silla, accumulates streams of vapor in the low regions. At other times (and this effect is still more curious) these luminous bands, enveloped in thick clouds, appear only at intervals when it is clear; and as the clouds ascend, their edges reflect a splendid light. These various phenomena, so common in the tropics, acquire additional interest from the form of the mountains, the direction of the slopes, and the height of the savannahs covered with Alpine grasses. During the day the wind of Petare, blowing from the east, drives the smoke towards the town, and diminishes the transparency of the air.

In a country abounding in such magnificent scenery, and at a period when, notwithstanding some symptoms of popular commotion, most of the inhabitants seem only to direct their attention to physical objects, such as the fertility of the year, the long drought, or the conflicting winds of Petare, and Catia, I expected to find many individuals well acquainted with the lofty surrounding mountains. But I was disappointed; and we could not find in Caracas a single individual who had visited the summit of the Silla. Hunters do not ascend so high on the ridges of mountains, and in these countries journeys are not undertaken for such purposes as gathering Alpine plants, carrying a barometer to an elevated point, or examining the nature of rocks. Accustomed to a uniform and domestic life, the people dread fatigue and sudden changes of climate. They seem to live not to enjoy life, but only to prolong it.

Our walks led us often in the direction of two coffee-plantations, the proprietors of which, Don Andres de Ibarra and M. Blandin, were men of agree-

THE SILLA OF CARACAS.

able manners. These plantations were situated opposite the Silla de Caracas. Surveying, by a telescope, the steep declivity of the mountain, and the form of the two peaks by which it is terminated, we could form an idea of the difficulties we should have to encounter in reaching its summit. Angles of elevation, taken with the sextant at our house, had led me to believe that the summit was not so high above sea-level as the great square of Quito. This estimate was far from corresponding with the notions entertained by the inhabitants of the city. Mountains which command great towns, have acquired, from that very circumstance, an extraordinary celebrity in both continents. Long before they have been accurately measured, a conventional height is assigned to them, and to entertain the least doubt respecting that height is to wound national prejudice. The Captain-General, Señor de Guevara, directed the *teniente* of Chacao to furnish us with guides to conduct us on our ascent of the Silla. These guides were Negroes, and they knew something of the path leading over the ridge of the mountain, near the western peak of the Silla. This path is frequented by smugglers, but neither the guides nor the most experienced of the militia, accustomed to pursue the smugglers in these wild spots, had been on the eastern peak, forming the most elevated summit of the Silla.

During the whole month of December the mountain (of which the angles of elevation made me acquainted with the effects of the terrestrial refraction) had appeared only five times free of clouds.

In this season of the year two serene days seldom succeed each other, and we were therefore advised not to choose a clear day for our excursion, but rather a time when, the clouds not being elevated, we might hope, after having crossed the first layer of vapors uniformly spread, to enter into dry and transparent air. We passed the night of the 2nd of January in the Estancia de Gallegos, a plantation of coffee-trees, near which the little river of Chacaito, flowing in a luxuriantly shaded ravine, forms some fine cascades in descending the mountains. The night was pretty clear, and though on the day preceding a fatiguing journey, it might have been well to have enjoyed some repose, M. Bonpland and I passed the whole night in watching three occultations of the satellites of Jupiter. I had previously determined the instant of the observations, but we missed them all, owing to some error of calculation in the *Connaissance des Temps*. The apparent time had been mistaken for mean time.

I was much disappointed by this accident, and after having observed at the foot of the mountain the intensity of the magnetic forces before sunrise, we set out at five in the morning, accompanied by slaves carrying our instruments. Our party consisted of eighteen persons, and we all walked one behind another, in a narrow path, traced on a steep declivity covered with turf. We endeavored first to reach a hill, which towards the southeast seems to form a promontory of the Silla. It is connected with the body of the mountain by a narrow dyke, called by the shepherds the Gate, or Puerta de la Silla. We reached this dyke about seven. The morning was fine and cool, and the sky then seemed to favor our excursion. I saw that the thermometer kept a little below 57°. The barometer showed that we were already 685 fathoms above the level of the sea—that is, nearly 80 fathoms higher than at the Venta, where we enjoyed so magnificent a view of the coast. Our guides thought that it would require six hours more to reach the summit of the Silla.

We crossed a narrow dyke of rocks, covered with turf, which led us from the promontory of the Puerta to the ridge of the great mountain. Here the eye looks down on two valleys, or rather narrow defiles, filled with thick vegetation. On the right is perceived the ravine which descends between the two peaks to the farm of Muñoz; on the left we saw the defile of Chacaito, with its waters flowing out near the farm of Gallegos. The roaring of the cascades is heard, while the water is unseen, being concealed by thick groves of erythrina, clusia, and the Indian fig-tree. Nothing can be more picturesque in a climate where so many plants have broad, large, shining, and coriaceous leaves, than the aspect of trees when the spectator looks down from a great height above them, and when they are illumined by the almost perpendicular rays of the sun.

From the Puerta de la Silla the steepness of the ascent increases, and we were obliged to incline our bodies considerably forward as we advanced. The slope is often from 30° to 32°. We felt the want of cramp-irons, or sticks shod with iron. Short grass covered the rocks of gneiss, and it was equally impossible to hold by the grass, or to form steps, as we might have done in softer ground. This ascent, which was attended with more fatigue than danger, discouraged those who accompanied us from the town, and who were unaccustomed to climb mountains. We lost a great deal of time in waiting for them, and we did not resolve to proceed alone till we saw them descending the mountain instead of climbing up it. The weather was becoming cloudy; the mist already issued in the form of smoke, and in slender and perpendicular streaks, from a small, luminous wood which bordered the region of Alpine savannahs. It seemed as if a fire had burst forth at once on several points of the forest. These streaks of vapor gradually accumulated together, and rising above the ground, were carried along by the morning breeze, and glided like a light cloud over the rounded summit of the mountain. M. Bonpland and I foresaw from these infallible signs that we should soon be covered by a thick fog, and lest our guides should take advantage of this circumstance and leave us, we obliged those who carried the most necessary instruments to precede us; we continued climbing the slopes which led towards the ravine of Chacaito. . . .

The eastern peak is the most elevated of the two which form the summit of the mountain, and to this we directed our course with our instruments. The hollow between the two peaks has suggested the Spanish name of Silla (saddle), which is given to the whole mountain. . . . We were sometimes so enveloped in mist that we could with difficulty find our way. At this height there is no path, and we were obliged to climb with our hands when our feet failed us, on the steep and slippery declivity.

After proceeding for the space of four hours across the savannahs, we entered a little wood composed of shrubs and small trees, called el Pejual. We spent a long time in examining the fine resinous and fragrant plants of the Pejual. Quitting the little thicket of Alpine plants, we found ourselves again in a savannah. We climbed over a part of the western dome, in order to descend into the hollow of the Silla, a valley which separates the two summits of the mountain. We there had great difficulties to overcome, occasionally, by the force of the vegetation.

Wandering in this thick wood of musaceæ or arborescent plants, we constantly directed our course towards the eastern peak, which we perceived from time to time through an opening. On a sudden we found ourselves again enveloped in a dense mist; the compass alone could guide us, but in advancing northward we were in danger at every step of finding ourselves on the brink of that enormous wall of rocks which descends almost perpendicularly to the depth of six thousand feet towards the sea. We were obliged to halt. Surrounded by clouds sweeping the ground, we began to doubt whether we should reach the eastern peak before night. Happily, the Negroes who carried our water and provisions soon reached us, and we resolved to take some refreshment.

We were three quarters of an hour in reaching the summit of the pyramid. Having arrived there, we enjoyed for a few minutes only the serenity of the sky. We were at thirteen hundred

Bridge in the Cordilleras.

and fifty fathoms of elevation. We gazed on an extent of sea, the radius of which was thirty-six leagues.

It was half-past four when we finished our observations. Satisfied with the success of our journey, we forgot that there might be danger in descending in the dark steep declivities covered by a smooth and slippery turf. The mist concealed the valley from us, but we distinguished the double hill of La Puerta, which, like all objects lying almost perpendicularly beneath the eye, appeared extremely near. We relinquished our design of passing the night between the two summits of the Silla, and having again found the path we had cut through the thick wood of the heliconia, we soon arrived at Pejual, the region of odoriferous and resinous plants.

As there is scarcely any twilight in the tropics, we pass suddenly from bright daylight to darkness. The moon was on the horizon, but her disk was veiled from time to time by thick clouds, drifted by a cold and rough wind. Rapid slopes, covered with yellow and dry grass, now seen in shade, and now suddenly illumined, seemed like precipices, the depth of which the eye sought in vain to measure. We proceeded onwards in single file, and endeavored to support ourselves by our hands, lest we should roll down. The guides, who carried our instruments, abandoned us successively, to sleep on the mountain. Among those who remained with us was a Congo black, who evinced great address, bearing on his head a large dipping-needle: he held it constantly steady, notwithstanding the extreme declivity of the rocks. The fog had dispersed by degrees in the bottom of the valley, and the scattered lights perceived below us caused a double illusion. The steeps appeared still more dangerous than they really were; and during six hours of continued descent we seemed to be always equally near the farms at the foot of the Silla. We heard very distinctly the voices of men and the notes of guitars. Sound is generally so well propagated upwards, that in a balloon at the elevation of 18,000 feet the barking of dogs is sometimes heard.

We did not arrive till ten at night at the bottom of the valley.

A. DE HUMBOLDT, *Voyages aux régions équinoxiales du nouveau continent.*

XXIX.

CHIMBORAZO.

ASCENT BY BOUSSINGAULT.

RIOBAMBA is perhaps the most singular diorama in the world. The town presents nothing remarkable in itself; but it is placed on one of the sterile plateaux so common in the Andes, which, at this great elevation, have all of them a characteristic appearance of winter, which impresses the traveller with a feeling of sadness. In order to reach it he has to pass through very picturesque places; and this increases the depression produced by the change; for it is always with regret that one leaves the climate of the tropics for the frosts of the north.

From the house where I lived I could look over Capac-Urcu, Tunguragna, Cubille, Carguairazo, and lastly, to the north, Chimborazo; besides several other celebrated mountains of the Paramos, which, though they have not the honor of perpetual snow, are still none the less worthy of the attention of the geologist.

This vast amphitheatre, which bounds on all sides the horizon of Riobamba, is the scene of continually varied phenomena. It is curious to observe the different appearances of these glaciers at different hours of the day; and to see their apparent heights, varying from one moment to another, from the effect of atmospheric refractions; and it is with great interest that one sees produced in a space so circumscribed all the great phenomena of meteorology. Here it is one of those clouds that De Saussure has so well described as parasitical clouds, which has just attached itself to the middle part of a cone of trachyte: it sticks to it; and the wind, though blowing strongly, cannot move it. Soon the thunder bursts from this mass of vapor; hail mingled with rain inundates the lower part of the mountain, whilst its snowy summit, which the storm has not yet reached, is vividly lighted up by the sun. Further on, it is a sharp peak of ice resplendent with light; it stands out against the azure of the heavens, and all its forms may be distinguished even to the minutiæ; the atmosphere is remarkably clear, and yet this peak is covered with a cloud which seems to emanate from its own bosom, so that one might imagine it to have come out of smoke. This cloud is already become a light vapor, and soon it disappears altogether. But soon also it reproduces itself just to disappear again. This intermittent formation of the clouds is a very frequent phenomenon on the summits of mountains covered with snow. It is chiefly observable in serene weather, always some hours after the culmination of the sun. In these conditions the glaciers may be compared to condensers thrust up towards the high regions of the atmosphere, in order to dry up the water by freezing it, and to bring back in this way to the surface of the earth the water which they find in a state of vapor.

These plateaux, surrounded by glaciers, sometimes present the most lugubrious aspect, when a continued wind brings to them the humid air of the hot regions. The mountains become invisible, and the horizon is masked by a line of clouds which seem to touch the earth. The day is cold and damp,—this mass of vapor being almost impenetrable to the solar light. It is a long twilight, the only one which is known in the tropics; for in the equatorial zone the night succeeds suddenly to day, so that the sun seems to become extinguished in setting.

I could not better finish my researches on the trachytes of the Cordilleras than by a special study of Chimborazo. In order to do so, it was certainly sufficient to approach its base: but what made me go beyond the snowy boundary—what made me determine on the ascent—was the hope of obtaining the mean temperature of an extremely elevated station. And, although this hope was frustrated, my excursion, I hope, was not without its use with regard to science.

My friend, Colonel Hall, who had already accompanied me up Antisana and Cotopaxi, wished again to go with me on this expedition, in order to add to the knowledge which he already possessed of the topography of Quito, and to continue his researches on the geography of plants.

From Riobamba, Chimboraza presents two slopes of very different inclinations. The one which looks towards the Arenal is very abrupt; and there are to be seen coming out from under the ice numerous points of trachyte. The other, towards the place called Chillapullu, not far from Mocha, is, on the contrary, little inclined, but of a considerable extent. After having well examined the environs of the mountains, it was by this slope that we resolved to attack it. On the 14th of December, 1831, we went to lodge at the farm of the Chimborazo, where we found dry straw to lie on, and some sheep-skins to keep us from the cold. The farm stands on an elevation of 12,350, so that the nights are cool there; and as a resting place, it is not agreeable, because wood is scarce. We were already in the region of graminaceous plants, which has to be crossed before the region of perpetual snow is reached: there all ligneous vegetation ends.

On the 15th, at seven in the morning, we put ourselves *en route*, guided by an Indian from the farm. We followed, in ascending, a rivulet enclosed between two walls of trachyte, whose waters descend from the glacier; but very soon we quitted this crevasse, in order to direct our steps towards Mocha, going along the base of Chimborazo. We rose insensibly; and our mules walked with trouble and difficulty through the *débris* of rock which has accumulated on the foot of the mountain. The slope then became very rapid, the ground was unstable, and the mules stopped almost at every step to make a long pause; they no longer obeyed the spur. The

CHIMBORAZO.

breathing of the animals was hurried and panting. We were then precisely at the height of Mont Blanc, for the barometer indicated an elevation of 15,626 feet above the level of the sea.

After we had covered our faces with masks of light gauze, in order to preserve ourselves from accidents such as we had met with on the Antisana, we began to ascend a ridge which abutted on a very elevated point of the glacier. It was midday. We went up slowly; and, as we got further and further on to the snow, the difficulty of breathing in walking became more and more felt; but we easily regained our strength by stopping at every eight or ten steps without always sitting down. As we went on, we felt extreme fatigue from the want of consistency in a snowy soil, which continually gave way under our feet, and in which we sank sometimes up to the waist. In spite of all our efforts, we were soon convinced of the impossibility of advancing; in fact, a little farther on the shifting snow was more than four feet deep. We went to rest on a block of trachyte, which resembled an island in the midst of a sea of snow. The height noted down was 16,623 feet; so that, after much fatigue, we had only reached 997 feet higher than the place where we set out.

At six o'clock, we were back at the farm. The weather had been splendid, and Chimborazo had never appeared to us so magnificent; but, after our fruitless journey, we could not help looking at it with a feeling of spite. We were determined to attempt the ascent by the abrupt side; that is to say, by the slope which looks towards the Arenal. We knew that it was on this side that Humboldt had ascended this mountain; for they had pointed out to us at Riobamba the point to which he had reached; but it was impossible for us to obtain exact information as to the route which he had followed to get there, for the Indians who had accompanied that intrepid traveller were no longer living.

At seven o'clock the next day we took the road towards the Arenal. The sky was remarkably pure. On the east we perceived the famous volcano of Sangay, in the province of Macas, which, nearly a century before, La Condamine had seen in a state of permanent incandescence. In proportion as we advanced, the land rose sensibly. In general the trachytic plateau which supports the isolated peaks with which the Andes are, as it were, bristling, rise gradually to the base of these same peaks. The numerous and deep crevasses which furrow these plateaux seem all to start from a common centre; they become narrower as they get away from this centre. We could only compare them to the lines on the surface of a cracked glass.

We were at a height of 16,071 feet when we took to journeying on foot. The ground had become altogether impracticable for the mules; and, besides, those animals, whose instinct is extraordinary, tried to make us understand the great fatigue which they felt; their ears, usually so straight and attentive, were quite drooping, and, during the frequent halts which they made for breath, they never ceased looking towards the plain. Few riders have probably taken their steeds to such a height; and to travel on the back of mules, over a moving soil beyond the limits of the snow, requires, perhaps, several years' experience in riding in the Andes.

After having examined the locality in which we were, we saw that in order to gain a ridge which ascended towards the summit of Chimborazo, we must first climb an excessively steep ascent just in front of us. It was formed in great part of blocks of rock of all sizes, disposed in slopes. Here and there these fragments of trachyte were covered by sheets of ice more or less extensive, and in several points you could clearly see that these *débris* of rock lay over the hardened snow. They proceeded consequently from the recent falls which had taken place in the uppor part of the mountain. These falls are frequent, and in the midst of the glaciers of the Cordilleras what one has most to fear are the avalanches in which there are really more stones than snow.

At eleven o'clock we finished crossing a very extended sheet of ice on which we had been obliged to cut notches in order to make sure of our steps. This passage was not without danger, for a slide might have cost us our lives. We entered then afresh on the *débris* of trachyte, which was firm earth to us, and from that time we were able to ascend more rapidly. We marched along in a file, I first, then Col. Hall, and my Negro last. He followed my steps exactly, in order not to endanger the safety of the instruments which were intrusted to him. We kept an absolute silence during our march, experience having taught me that nothing exhausts so much as a sustained conversation at this height; and during our halts, if we exchanged a few words, it was in a low voice. It is, in a great measure, to this precaution that I attribute the state of health which I have constantly enjoyed during my ascents up volcanoes. And this precaution I imposed, so to speak, in a despotic manner on those who accompanied me, for, on the Antisana, an Indian who neglected it; and called with all the strength of his lungs to Col. Hall, who had lost his way as we were passing through a cloud, was attacked with giddiness and hemorrhage.

We had now reached the ridge at which we were aiming. It was not what we had thought it from a distance, for, in fact, there was little snow on it; but then its sides were so steep that they were very difficult to climb. We were obliged to make almost unheard-of efforts, and such gymnastics are painful in these aerial regions. At last we arrived at the foot of a perpendicular wall of trachyte which was many hundred feet in height. There was a visible feeling of discouragement in the expedition when the barometer told us that we were only at a height of 18,460 feet. This was little for us, for it was not even the height to which we had attained on Cotopaxi. Besides, Humboldt had ascended higher on Chimborazo; and we wished at least to attain the point at which that learned traveller had stopped. Explorers of mountains when they are discouraged are always very much disposed to sit down, and that is what we did on the Pena Colorada (Red Rock). It was the first rest sitting that we had allowed ourselves; and as we were all excessively thirsty our first occupation was to suck some icicles in order to quench this thirst.

It was a quarter to one P. M., and yet we felt quite cold enough, and the thermometer was down to 31°. We then found ourselves enveloped in a cloud. When this had disappeared we examined our situation. Looking towards the red rock, we had on the right a frightful abyss; on the left, towards the Arenal, we could distinguish an advanced rock, which looked like a turret. It was important to reach this in order to see if we could turn the red rock, and to ascertain at the same time if it were possible to continue our ascent. Access to this turret was difficult, but I managed it with the assistance of my two companions. I saw then that if we succeeded in climbing over a very inclined surface, covered with snow, which leant against one face of this red rock opposite to the side by which we had reached it, we should attain a very considerable elevation. And in order to get a clear idea of the topography of Chimborazo, let any one picture to himself an immense rock, sustained on all sides by such props, which from the plain seem to lean against this enormous block in order to shore it up.

Before undertaking this dangerous passage, I ordered my Negro to go and try the snow. It was of a convenient consistency. Hall and the Negro succeeded in turning the foot of the position which I occupied, and I joined them when they were sufficiently firmly planted to receive me, for in order to rejoin them it was necessary to slide down about 25 feet of ice. At the moment of setting forward, a stone detached itself from the top of the mountain, and fell quite close to Col. Hall. He tottered and fell; I thought him wounded, and was only reassured when I saw him get up and examine with his magnifying glass the sample of rock which was so roughly submitted to our investigation; the unlucky trachyte was of the same kind as that on which we were walking.

We advanced carefully; on the right we could support ourselves on the rock, on the left the declivity was frightful, and before going forward we began by familiarizing ourselves with the precipice. This is a precaution which should never be neglected in the mountains, whenever a dangerous place has to be passed. De Saussure said so long ago, but it cannot be repeated too often; and in my adventurous journeys among the peaks of the Andes I have never lost sight of this wise precept.

We began already to feel more than we had yet done the effect of the rarefaction of the air; we were obliged to stop every two or three steps, and often even to lie down for two or three seconds. Once seated we were all right again; our suffering was only during the time that we were in motion. But the snow itself soon rendered our progress as slow as it was dangerous. It was only soft for about three or four inches, and below was a very hard and slippery ice, in which we were obliged to cut notches. The Negro went before in order to make these steps, and the labor exhausted him in a moment. I went forward to relieve him, and slid; but happily for me, Hall and my Negro held me up. However, for an instant we were all in imminent danger. This incident made us hesitate a moment, but taking new courage, we resolved to go on; the snow became more favorable; we made a last effort, and in an hour and three quarters we were on the desired ridge. There, we were convinced that it was impossible to do more, being now at the foot of a prism of trachyte, of which the upper basis, covered with a cupola of snow, forms the summit of Chimborazo.

The ridge at which we had arrived was only some feet in width. On all sides we were environed with precipices, and surrounded by the strangest sights. The deep color of the rock contrasted in the most striking manner with the dazzling whiteness of the snow. Long stalagmites of ice appeared suspended over our heads, so that one might have thought that a magnificent cascade had frozen there. The weather was beautiful, some light clouds only being visible in the west; the air was quite calm, so that the view was very extensive; the situation was new, and we felt a lively satisfaction in it. We were at a height of 19,513 feet, which is, I believe, the greatest height to which men have ever climbed.

After some moments' repose, we found ourselves entirely recovered from our fatigues, and neither of us experienced those uncomfortable sensations which most persons who have ascended high mountains have done. Three quarters of an hour after our arrival my pulse, and also Col. Hall's, beat 106 in a minute; we were thirsty, and evidently under a slightly feverish influence; but it was not a painful state. My friend was very gay, and constantly saying the most piquant things, notwithstanding that he was occupied in drawing the view that lay beneath us. All sounds seemed to me, however, thinned in a remarkable manner, and the voices of my companions were so much changed that under any other circumstances it would have been impossible to recognize them. The slight noise which the blows of my hammer on the rock made also surprised us very much.

The rarefaction of the air generally produces very marked results on climbers. On the summit of Mont Blanc, De Saussure felt an uneasiness and a disposition to sickness; and his guides, who were all inhabitants of Chamounix, experienced the same sensations. This state of uneasiness increased also when he made any movement, or when he fixed his attention on any observations which he was making. The first Spaniards who went over the high mountains of America were attacked, according to the account of Acosta, by nausea and stomach complaints. Bouguer had several attacks of hemorrhage in the Cordilleras of Quito; the same thing happened on Monte Rosa to M. Zumstein; and lastly, on Chimborazo, MM. de Humboldt and Bonpland, at the time of their ascent of the 23rd of June, 1802, felt a disposition to vomit, and the blood came out of their lips and of their gums. As for ourselves, we had, certainly, found a difficulty in breathing, and extreme lassitude as we ascended; but these inconveniences ceased with the movement. Once at rest, and we believed ourselves to be in our normal state; perhaps we must attribute our insensibility to the effects of rarefied air, to our prolonged stay in the high towns of the Andes. When one has seen the activity which there is in towns like Bogota, Micuipampa, Potosi, etc., which are at from 8000 to 12,000 feet above the sea, when one has been witness of the strength and prodigious agility of the *toreadors* in a bull-fight at Quito, which is at a height of more than 9000 feet; when one has seen, lastly, young and delicate women give themselves up to dancing during entire nights in localities almost as elevated as Mont Blanc, where the celebrated De Saussure found hardly enough strength to consult his instruments, and where his vigorous mountaineers fell exhausted whilst digging a hole in the snow; if, I must add, a celebrated battle, that of Pichincha, was fought at a height differing little from that of Mont Blanc, it will be granted, I think, that man may become accustomed to breathe the rarefied air of the highest mountains.

Whilst we were occupied in making our observations on Chimborazo the weather continued fine, and the sun was so hot as slightly to incommode us. Towards three o'clock we perceived some clouds forming below in the plain; the thunder soon began to growl below our position, and though the noise was not loud, it was prolonged; we thought at first that it was a *bramido*, or subterranean rumbling.

Dark clouds then gathered round the base of the mountain, and they slowly rose towards us. So we had no time to lose, for it was essential that we should pass the bad places before we were overtaken, as otherwise we should run into the greatest dangers. A heavy fall of snow, or a frost which should render the way slippery, would suffice to hinder our return, and we had no provision for a stay on the glacier.

The descent was difficult. After we had got down from 900 to 1200 feet, we penetrated into clouds, by entering them from above: a little lower, hail began to fall, which considerably chilled the air, and at the moment at which we met the Indian who took care of our mules, the cloud broke over us in hail that was so large as to be quite painful when the hailstones struck either our heads or faces.

In proportion as we descended an icy rain was mixed with the hail. Night surprised us on the road; and it was eight o'clock when we reached the farm.

The observations which I was able to collect during this excursion tend all of them to confirm my ideas on the nature of the trachyte mountains which form the chain of the Cordilleras; for I have seen repeated on Chimborazo all the facts which I have noticed in treating of the volcanoes of the equator. It is evidently itself an extinct volcano, like Cotopaxi, Antisana, Tunguragua, and in general the mountains which stand thickly on the plateaux of the Andes. The mass of Chimborazo is formed by the accumulation of trachytic *débris*,

THE CORDILLERAS, PERU.

heaped together without any order. These fragments, of a size which is often enormous, have been thrown together in a solid state; their angles are always sharp, and nothing indicates that there has been any fusion, or even a simple state of softness. Nowhere in any of the volcanoes of the equator does one observe anything which would lead one to presume that there had been a flow of lava; nothing but muddy, elastic fluids, or incandescent blocks of trachyte, more or less solid, have come out of these craters, and these have often been thrown to considerable distances.

On the 23rd of December, in the afternoon, I quitted Riobamba, directing my course towards Guayaquil, where I was to embark in order to visit the coast of Peru. It was in sight of Chimborazo that I separated from Col. Hall. During my stay in the province of Quito I had enjoyed his confidence and his friendship; his perfect acquaintance with the localities had been of the greatest use to me, and I had found in him an excellent and indefatigable travelling companion; and lastly, both of us had served for a long time in the cause of independence. Our farewells were full of regret, and something seemed to tell us that we should never meet again. This fatal presentiment was but too well founded, for some months afterwards my unhappy friend was assassinated in a street of Quito.

BOUSSINGAULT, *Voyages aux Volcans de l'Equateur.*

XXX.

DISCOVERY OF PERUVIAN BARK.

THE whole world, and especially tropical countries where intermittent fevers prevail, have long been indebted to the mountainous forests of the Andes for that inestimable febrifuge which has now become indispensable, and the demand for which is rapidly increasing, while the supply decreases throughout all civilized countries. There is, probably, no drug which is more valuable to man than the febrifugal alkaloid which is extracted from the chinchona trees of South America; and few greater blessings could be conferred on the human race than the naturalization of these trees in India and other congenial regions, so as to render the supply more certain, cheaper, and more abundant.

It would be strange indeed, if, as is generally supposed, the Indian aborigines of South America were ignorant of the virtues of Peruvian bark, yet the absence of this sovereign remedy in the wallets of itinerant native doctors who have plied their trade from father to son since the time of the Incas, certainly gives some countenance to this idea. It seems probable, nevertheless, that the Indians were aware of the virtues of Peruvian bark in the neighborhood of Loxa, 230 miles south of Quito, where its use was first made known to Europeans, and the Indian name for the tree, '*quina quina*,' 'bark of bark, indicates that it was believed to possess some special medicinal properties. The Indians looked upon their conquerors with dislike and suspicion; it is improbable that they would be quick to impart knowledge of this nature to them; and the interval which elapsed between the discovery and settlement of the country and the first use of Peruvian bark by Europeans may thus easily be explained.

It may be added, however, that though the Indians were aware of the febrifugal qualities of this bark, they attached little importance to them —they think that the cold North alone permits the use of fever-bark, consider it very heating, and therefore an unfit remedy in complaints which they believe to arise from inflammation of the blood.....

In about 1630, Don Juan Lopez de Canizares, the Spanish Corregidor of Loxa, being ill of an intermittent fever, an Indian of Malacotas is said to have revealed to him the healing virtues of quinquina bark, and to have instructed him in the proper way to administer it, and thus his cure was effected.

In 1638, the wife of Luis Geronimo Fernandez de Cabrera Bobadilla y Mendoza, fourth Count of Chinchon, lay sick of an intermittent fever in the palace at Lima. Her famous cure induced Linnæus, long afterwards, to name the whole genus of quinine yielding trees in her honor, 'Chinchona.'

The Count of Chinchon returned to Spain in 1640, and his Countess, bringing with her a quantity of the healing bark, was the first person to introduce this invaluable medicine into Europe. ....After the cure of the Countess of Chincha, the Jesuits were the great promoters of the introduction of the bark into Europe..... In 1670, the Jesuit missionaries sent parcels of the powdered bark to Rome, whence it was distributed to members of the fraternity throughout Europe by the Cardinal de Lugo, and used for the cure of agues with great success. Hence the name of 'Jesuit's bark,' and 'Cardinal's bark;' and it was a ludicrous result of its patronage by the Jesuits that its use should have been for a long time opposed by Protestants and favored by Roman Catholics. In 1679, Louis XIV. bought the secret of preparing quinquina from Sir Robert Taylor, an English doctor, for two thousand louis-d'ors, a large pension, and a title. From that time Peruvian bark seems to have been recognized as the most efficacious remedy for intermittent fevers.....

The region of chinchona trees extends from 19° S. lat., to 10° N., following the almost semicircular curve of the Cordillera of the Andes on 1740 miles of latitude. They flourish in a cool and equable temperature on the slopes, and in the valleys and ravines of the mountains, and surrounded by the most majestic scenery, never descending below an elevation of 2500, and ascending as high as 9000 feet above the sea. Within these limits their usual companions are tree-ferns, melastomaceæ, arborescent passion-flowers, and allied genera of chinchonaceous plants. Below them are the forests, abounding in palms and bamboos; above their highest limits are a few lonely Alpine shrubs.

But within this wide zone grow many species of chinchona, and within its own narrower belts as regards elevation above the sea, some yielding the inestimable bark, and others commercially worthless. The chinchona plant has never been found in any part of the world beyond the limits already described.

When in good soil and under favorable circumstances they become large forest trees; on higher elevations, and when crowded and growing in rocky ground, they frequently run up to great heights without a branch, and at the upper limit of their zone they become mere shrubs. The leaves are of a great variety of shapes and sizes, but in most of the finest species they are lanceolate, with a shining surface of bright green, traversed by crimson veins, and petioles of the same color. The flowers are very small, but hang in clustering panicles, like lilacs, generally of a deep roseate color, paler near the stalk, dark crimson within the tube, with white, curly hairs bordering the laciniæ of the corolla. The flowers of *C. micrantha* are entirely white. They send forth a delicious fragrance which scents the air in their vicinity.....The roots, flowers and capsules of the chinchona trees have a bitter taste, with tonic properties; but the upper bark is the only part which has any commercial value.

Until the present century, Peruvian bark was used in its crude state, and numerous attempts were made at different times to discover the actual healing principle in the bark before success was finally attained. The first trial, which is worthy of attention, was made in 1779, by the chemists Buguet and Cornette, who recognized the existence of an essential salt, a resinous and an earthy matter in quinquina bark. In 1790, Fourcroy discovered the existence of a coloring matter, afterwards called *chinchona red;* and a Swedish doctor, named Westring, in 1800, believed that he had discovered the active principle in quinquina bark. Reuss, a Russian chemist, in 1815, was the first to give a tolerable analysis of it; and about the same time, Dr. Duncan, of Edinburgh, suggested that a real substance existed as a febrifugal principle. Dr. Gomez, a surgeon in the Portuguese navy, in 1816, was the first to isolate this principle, and he called it *chinchonine.*

But the final discovery of quinine is due to the French chemists Pelletier and Caventou in 1820. They considered that a vegetable alkaloid, analogous to morphine and strychnine, existed in quinquina bark; and they afterwards discovered that the febrifugal principle was seated in two alkaloids, separate or together, in the different kinds of bark, called quinine and chinchonine, with the same virtues, which, however, were much more powerful in quinine. The discovery of these alkaloids in the quinquina bark, by enabling chemists to extract the healing principle, has greatly increased the usefulness of the drug. In small doses they promote the appetite and assist digestion; and chinchonine is equal to quinine in mild cases of intermittent fever; but in severe cases the use of quinine is absolutely necessary..... India and other countries have been vainly searched for a substitute for quinine, and we may say with as much truth now as Lambert did in 1820, 'This medicine, the most precious of all those known in the art of healing, is one of the greatest conquests made by man over the vegetable kingdom. The treasures which Peru yields, and which the Spaniards sought and dug out of the bowels of the earth, are not to be compared for utility with the bark of the quinquina tree, which they for a long time ignored.....'

The species yielding 'red bark,' the richest and most important of all the chinchonæ, is found in the forests on the western slopes of Mount Chimborazo, along the banks of the rivers Chanchan, Chasuan, San Antonio, and their tributaries. . .

The collection of bark in the South American forests was conducted from the first with the most reckless extravagance: no attempt worth the name has ever been made either with a view to the conservancy or cultivation of the chinchona-trees, and both the complete abandonment of the forests to the mercy of every speculator, as in Peru, Ecuador, and New Granada, and the barbarous meddling legislation of Bolivia have led to the equally destructive results. The bark-collector enters the forest and destroys the first clump of trees he finds, without a thought of any measure to preserve the continuance of a supply of bark. Thus in Apollobamba, where the trees once grew thickly round the village, no full-grown one is now to be found within eight or ten days' journey, and so utterly improvident are the collectors that, in the forests of Cochabamba they

Rio Vinagre Cascade, in the Cordilleras.

bark the tree without felling, and thus ensure its death; or, if they cut it down, they actually neglect to take off the bark on the side touching the ground, to save themselves the trouble of turning the trunk over.

In 1839 Dr. Boyle recommended the introduction of the chinchona plants into India, pointing out the Neilgherry and Silhet hills as suitable sites for the experiment, and Lord William Bentinck took some interest in the project; . . . . . but this attempt was surrounded by difficulties, from which all other undertakings of a similar nature have been free. When tea was introduced into the Himalayan districts, it had been a cultivated plant in China for many ages, and experienced Chinese cultivators came with it. But the chinchona had never been cultivated since the discovery of its value in 1638; it had remained a wild forest tree; all information concerning it was solely derived from the observations of European travellers who had penetrated into the virgin forests, and the only guidance for cultivators in India is to be found in the report of these travellers, and in the experience slowly acquired by careful and intelligent trials. Great as these difficulties were, they were probably exceeded by the perils and risks of every description which must be encountered in collecting plants and seeds in South America, and conveying them to India.

But the vast importance of the introduction of these plants into our Indian empire, and the inestimable benefits which would thus be conferred on the millions who inhabit the fever-haunted plains and jungles, were commensurate with the difficulties of the undertaking. . . .

In 1859 my services were accepted to superintend the collection of chinchona-plants and seeds in South America, and their introduction into India;

I was authorized by Lord Stanley, then Secretary of State for India, to make such arrangements as should best ensure the complete success of an enterprise the result of which were expected to add materially to the resources of our Indian empire.

By the spring of 1861, a large supply of plants and young seedlings was established in the Neilgherry hills; and at the present moment we have thousands of chinchona-plants of all the valuable species flourishing and multiplying rapidly in Southern India and in Ceylon.

Extracts from Travels in Peru and India, by Clement R. Markham, F.S.A., F.R.G.S.

XXXI.

ANIMAL LIFE IN MOUNTAIN REGIONS.

THE CONDOR—THE EAGLE—THE JACKDAW—THE LAGOPUS—INSECTS OF THE HIGH REGIONS.

Of all the animals that inhabit the lofty, barren summits of mountains, the lammergeyer of the Alps and the condor of the Andes are the most remarkable. The latter especially, as the king of birds, by his solitary habits, and the immense heights to which he soars alone, has gained an individuality that no other bird possesses. His starting place is often from peaks, where the air is too rarified for any other animal to breathe, and soaring sublimely thence, he moves upward and upward, till he becomes a mere speck in the dark blue heavens.

Until Humboldt, in a residence of seventeen months amid the native mountains of this bird, studied his habits and peculiarities, its name was surrounded with a romance and mystery like that once attached to the ancient griffins and dragons. The exact truth, however, invests him with sufficient interest. He seems to scorn the earth, never visiting it except to gratify his hunger. The rest of the time, a mere speck in the thin ether, or else lost to sight entirely, he sails all day above the region of thunder clouds and storms, surveying with his piercing eye the earth rolled out like a map below

The Condors.

him. Enjoying existence in an atmosphere too rare for any creature but himself to breathe, and in a temperature in which neither man nor beast could exist, he is surrounded with impenetrable mystery till he descends to the earth for food. Such is his keenness of sight, that even from the lofty heights at which he soars, he can detect the lifeless carcass of an ox, or the unsuspecting lamb on the plain below. This solitary bird then becomes gregarious, and quite a flock of them will gather together around the putrefying body. But even in this filthy feast they are dainty at the commencement. First they pluck out the eyes and then the tongue as delicate morsels, when they attack the bowels and flesh, and never leave off the ravenous repast till they are so gorged that it is with difficulty they can fly at all. In this helpless condition they are sometimes attacked with clubs by the natives, and captured. The condor is not, however, always content with carrion, for he frequently comes down with his terrific swoop on sheep, deer and animals of a similar size, and there are many stories told of infants being carried off by him to the mountains.

Similar stories are told of the eagle of the Alps and of our own country. "The last known fact of this kind," says M. Pouchet in the *Univers*, "took place in the Valais in 1838. A little girl five years old, called Marie Delex, was playing with one of her companions on a mossy slope of the mountain, when all at once an eagle swooped down upon her and carried her away in spite of the cries and presence of her young friends. Some peasants, hearing the screams, hastened to the spot, but sought in vain for the child, for they found nothing but one of her shoes on the edge of the precipice. The child, however, was not carried to the eagle's nest, where only two eaglets were seen, surrounded by heaps of goat's and sheep's bones.

It was not till two months after this that a shepherd discovered the corpse of Marie Delex, frightfully mutilated, and lying on a rock, half a league from where she had been borne off.

An instance of this kind, which occurred in the autumn of 1868, is thus narrated by a teacher in County Sippah, Missouri: "A sad casualty occurred at my school a few days ago. The eagles have been very troublesome in the neighborhood for some time past, carrying off pigs, lambs, etc. No one thought that they would attempt to prey upon children; but on Thursday, at recess, the little boys were out some distance from the house, playing marbles, when the sport was interrupted by a large eagle swooping down and picking up little Jemmie Kenney, a boy of eight years, and flying away with him. The children cried out, and when I got out of the house, the eagle was so high I could just hear the child screaming. The alarm was given, and from screaming and shouting in the air, etc., the eagle was induced to drop his victim; but his talons had been buried in him so deeply, and the fall was so great, that he was killed, as either would have been fatal."

When pressed by hunger the condor will attack even larger animals. Two together will sometimes pounce on a bullock, and tear him with their talons, till exhausted with fatigue he thrusts out his tongue, when they immediately seize it and pull it out by the roots. At length the poor beast rolls bellowing on the plain, a helpless victim to his small but fierce adversaries.

The condor has a crest something like a cock's

comb. The neck is bare of feathers, except just at the juncture with the body, where it is encircled by a collar of soft, silky, white down, about two inches broad. The back, wings and tail are sometimes of a greyish black, at others of a brilliant black.

Some of these birds are of such enormous size that their extended wings reach a span of fourteen feet.

The nests of these dwellers in the mountains are very curious objects. "Fierce and solitary," says M. Pouchet in the *Univers*, "the eagles suspend their nests in the midst of the most horrible precipices without dreading either the roar of the cataract, or the crash of the avalanche. The bulk of the work and the mass of the material employed are in proportion to the strength of the architect. The eyrie of the eagle is only a heap of great branches of trees, an entangled fagot, forming a thick, rude mattress, twelve to fifteen feet in circumference. This nest serves the couples which build it for their whole lives, but its size increases with years, because the bones of all the animals brought thither by the parents and devoured by the hungry family, are heaped up round it in such a manner, that at a certain lapse of time the eyrie of one of these robbers becomes a pestilential charnel house.

The nests built by the goshawk display even less skill; it employs only little fagots, and yet its nest is four feet in circumference."

J. T. HEADLEY.

Birds naturally represent the population of the highest altitudes. In the Andes the condor; in the Alps the eagle and the vulture hover over the most gigantic peaks. Those creatures being organized for long voyages are the great sailors of the atmospheric ocean, just as the terns and the petrels are the great sailors of the Atlantic. The jackdaw, that species of very black crow, which has a yellow beak and bright red claws, does not attain to so great a height in the air; but it is, *par excellence*, the bird of high peaks,—of the regions of snows and of sterile summits. We find it on the top of Monte Rosa and of the Col du Géant, 11,373 feet above the sea. Collected in flocks in the windings and turnings of the mountain, and skimming over the steepest rocks, the jackdaw utters his noisy note. Just those places which are particularly steep and precipitous, and which make us giddy, have a particular attraction for birds; gigantic fir-trees, bell-towers, old steeples, the battlements of castles standing high above deep valleys, pinnacles of cathedrals, isolated peaks whose foundations rise out of frightful precipices, these are their chosen dwellings; it is on these heights that they build their nests. True *cenobites* of the air, condemned like those of the Thebais to the most frugal and austere diet, they delight in solitude, and appear content just in proportion to the distance which separates them from man.

There are also more graceful birds which dwell in the realms of ice and frost, and enliven the changeless and barren landscape. The greenfinch of the snow loves this cold country so much that it seldoms descends to the wooded regions. The accentor of the Alps sometimes follows it to these great heights, but prefers the stony and sterile region which separates the zone of vegetation from that of perpetual snow; others rise after them at times in pursuit of insects to the height of nearly 10,000 or 11,000 feet.

The earth has its birds as well as the air, even at these heights. Certain kinds only use their wings for a few moments at a time, and when it is impossible for them to walk. Such are the gallinaceous tribe; and of these the snowy region has its own species, as it has its own sparrows. The lagopus, or snow hen, is found in Iceland as well as in Switzerland. This bird will rise into regions of perpetual ice and remain nestled at great altitudes. In winter its plumage takes the appearance of the frost in which it lives. The snow is so necessary to it that at the approach of summer it mounts higher in order to find it. It nestles and rolls itself in it with great delight. It digs holes in order to find shelter from the wind, the only inconvenience which it fears in its icy dwelling. Any pieces of lichen or grain brought up by the wind suffice for its nourishment, together with insects which it hunts for its young ones.

Insects are, in fact, nearly the only creatures which multiply in these desolate regions; and in this respect they are like the Polar countries. In the temperate zone the coleoptera are to be seen in greater numbers and in greater variety than in the neighboring regions of the Equator. In the Arctic regions, during the short summer, the insects come out in great numbers. And in the high Alps it is the class of coleoptera which predominates; they reach to a height of more than 9000 feet on the southern side, and to about 7300 feet on the opposite side. These little creatures may be discovered in the holes, and they are almost always carnivorous, for at so great a height vegetable nourishment altogether fails. Their wings are so short that they appear to be completely destitute of them; so that they seem shielded by Nature from the great currents of air which would infallibly carry them away if their wings were not, as it were, *reefed in*. Indeed other kinds, such as the neuroptera and butterflies, are sometimes met with, but these have been carried by the wind to these heights, and they only perish in the snow. The *névés* and the ice-fields are covered with victims who have thus perished. Yet there are certain species which brave the influence of the frost and are found even at the height of 12,000 or 15,000 feet. Mr. J. D. Hooker has observed butterflies on Mount Momay, at a height of more than 16,000 feet; but, as mentioned above, they are only poor shipwrecked creatures whom the wind drives up in spite of themselves.

The arachnidæ, which in so many respects approach the class of insects, have also the privilege of being able to resist the cold of mountains. One, almost microscopic insect of the Alps, the *desoria glacialis*, inhabits exclusively the neighborhood of glaciers. But really the melancholy of their abodes seems to be reflected in the appearance of these little animals; they no longer present the variety of tints which characterizes them elsewhere; and they are nearly all of a black or sombre color, which at the first approach deceives you as to their existence in the holes which they inhabit. At these heights the habits of insects are also modified according to the localities in which they live. M. P. Lioy, who has drawn up a philosophical sketch of the laws which organic nature obeys, and of which it is the ever-changing manifestation, remarks that the nocturnal insects of the plain become diurnal in mountainous places. That is, in fact, that the elevated regions reproduce in some respects the conditions of lower places during the night; they keep, even after the rising of the sun, the freshness and the shade, which evening alone gives in the plains.

Such is a picture of animal life in those Alpine regions where the fauna gradually becomes smaller and smaller until at last it gives place to solitude and desolation. Beyond the last stage of vegetation, beyond the extreme point to which insects and mammifers attain, all becomes silent and without inhabitant; yet still the air is full of infusoria, and of microscopic animalculæ, which the wind raises likes dust, and which are found in the air to an unknown height . . . . .

So the animal kingdom does not disappear without having, so to speak, exhausted all the organizations compatible with the state of the soil as it becomes more and more chilled, and of the atmosphere which becomes more and more rarefied. Birds, like outposts of the great army of living beings, seem to defend the mountains against the invasion of death. The rapacious ones are, in some sort, the scouts; the passeres, the climbers, and some of the gallinæ, answer to the main body of the army; and they love the intermediate region between the forests and the perpetual snows. The last firs, the last bushes, are like watch-towers from which they take observations on the weather, and hold themselves ready to descend if it be threatening, or to ascend whenever there is any lessening of the cold. In this middle region the harmonious songs of the linnet and the nightingale have something doubtful about them; but the song of the mountain birds breathes joy and tells of the pleasure of living. M. de Tschudi traces in a few lines a delicious picture of the existence of birds on the mountains. I translate freely:

'Rather before the sky is colored with the first morning tints, even before a light breath of air announces the approach of day, while the stars still sparkle in the firmament, the birds give the first signal of the awakening of nature. First a light sound is heard from the fir-trees, a kind of cooing in which the notes gradually become more distinct. It gets quicker by degrees and ends by swelling into a harmonious chorus, rising and falling from branch to branch as the bow of the musician passes from the gravest chords to those which are more acute. Then a more ringing noise sounds out all at once, and voices timid at first sing each their characteristic notes, each species making itself heard, and its own song more or less distinctly. The soft and melancholy *nocturne* has ceased; and now the winged people give the sun a serenade as he comes to warm up again their cold, damp dwellings.'

. . . One would like to live a moment of this aerial existence in the intermediate belt of earth, with just sufficient vegetation to afford a shelter from the mid-day heats and from the mid-night cold, just light enough for the eye to discern the magnificent panorama of mountains, and to gaze with delight into the firmament; but man is less favored in this respect than the birds. He is not organized as they are to rise in the air and live in regions of very different atmospheric density. Happily, however, the difficulty which we feel in accomplishing a rapid and continuous ascent does not imply an absolute incompatiblity of the higher regions with human life. We may become accli-matized to great heights. . . . The town of Quito, situated at between 8000 and 9000 feet above the level of the sea, comprises a numerous popula-tion which does not appear to suffer from the ele-vation. Another town of the Andes, Potosi, is 12,300 feet high, and contains more than a hundred thousand souls. After De Saussure had remained fifteen days on the top of the Alps, his pulse re-gained its normal motion; and Boussingault, after a prolonged stay in the towns of the Andes, could easily bear the low temperature of the top of Chim-borazo. But there are precautions to be taken if we would with impunity transport ourselves into these high situations, where, once established, and in suitable circumstances, it becomes possible to live : we should begin by habituating ourselves gradually to the barometrical changes of the atmosphere.

A. MAURY, *Le Monde alpestre, Revue des Deux Mondes.*

THE END.

www.ingramcontent.com/pod-product-compliance
Lightning Source LLC
LaVergne TN
LVHW020059110826
845151LV00001B/29

* 9 7 8 1 4 2 5 5 4 5 2 2 2 *